Children's Social Competence in Context

THE CONTRIBUTIONS OF FAMILY, SCHOOL AND CULTURE

INTERNATIONAL SERIES IN EXPERIMENTAL SOCIAL PSYCHOLOGY

Series Editor: MICHAEL ARGYLE, *University of Oxford*

Other titles in the series include

HOWITT
The Mass Media and Social Problems

NOLLER
Nonverbal Communications and Marital Interaction

BROWN
Advances in the Psychology of Religion

HOLLIN and TROWER
Handbook of Social Skills Training Volume 1

HOLLIN and TROWER
Handbook of Social Skills Training Volume 2

RUTTER
Communicating by Telephone

BULL
Posture and Gesture

FURNHAM
Lay Theories: Everyday Understanding of Problems
in the Social Sciences

SCOTT and SCOTT
Adaptation of Immigrants

LIVINGSTONE
Making Sense of Television

REHM and GADENNE
Intuitive Predictions and Professional Forecasts

STRACK, ARGYLE and SCHWARZ
Subjective Well-Being

FORGAS
Emotion and Social Judgments

ALBERT
Genius and Eminence, 2nd Edition

WALKER
The Psychology of Gambling

LIEBRAND, MESSICK and WILKE
Social Dilemmas: Theoretical Issues and Research Findings

Children's Social Competence in Context

THE CONTRIBUTIONS OF FAMILY, SCHOOL AND CULTURE

BARRY H. SCHNEIDER
University of Ottawa, Canada

PERGAMON PRESS

OXFORD · NEW YORK · SEOUL · TOKYO

UK	Pergamon Press Ltd, Headington Hill Hall, Oxford OX3 0BW, England
USA	Pergamon Press Inc, 660 White Plains Road, Tarrytown, New York 10591-5153, U.S.A.
KOREA	Pergamon Press Korea, KPO Box 315, Seoul 110-603, Korea
JAPAN	Pergamon Press Japan, Tsunashima Building Annex, 3-20-12 Yushima, Bunkyo-ku, Tokyo 113, Japan

First edition 1993

British Library Cataloguing in Publication Data
A catalogue record for this book is available from the British Library.

Library of Congress Cataloging-in-Publication Data
Schneider, Barry H.
Children's social competence in context: the contributions of family, school and culture/Barry H. Schneider.
p.   cm.—(International series in experimental social psychology: v. 26)
Includes bibliographical references and indexes.
1.   Child   development.   2.   Socialization.   I.   Title.
II. Series.
HQ767.9.S38   1992
303.3′2—dc20   92-31195

ISBN 0 08 0377637 Hardcover

Front cover illustration by Penny Berry Paterson

Printed in Great Britain by BPCC Wheatons Ltd, Exeter

In loving memory of my parents,

DAVID AND SELMA

Contents

Preface

INTERPERSONAL relations have been systematically studied in North America and Europe for about 80 years (see Renshaw, 1981, for an interesting sketch of this history). Most of this research effort has been devoted to *describing* the ways people relate to each other, delineating the *consequences* of unsatisfactory or unsatisfying social relations for the individual's welfare, and finding ways of *assisting* those whose social relations are problematic. Many theorists and researchers have avoided the thorny task of charting the *origins* or *causes* of social relations and individual styles of relating.

The belief that the child's interpersonal style is moulded by the parents' discipline and the example they set is deeply ingrained in Western culture. The Book of Proverbs clearly depicts the parents' responsibilities in instructing their children, and children are admonished to pay heed. Yet, even at the time of the prophetic writings, there was some recognition that children may differ in temperament, for reasons not specified, and require different types of discipline: "Train each child in his own way, and even when he is old, he will not depart from it" (Proverbs 22:6). As will be discussed later, recent research indicates that the differences in children's "own ways" may be more important than was once thought. Many authorities now reject the idea that there is a one-to-one correspondence between the way children are raised and the persons they become, or, at least, recognize that the issue is more complex than it once seemed.

Despite this rethinking of our age-old maxims and beliefs, few would totally deny that the way we relate to others reflects to some degree the way we were brought up. Psychologists, anthropologists, epidemiologists and sociologists have accumulated evidence which, once unravelled, should enable us to understand how our backgrounds affect the ways in which we relate to others, and the extent of this impact. Yet, our "backgrounds" cannot be summarized as simply as we might imagine, and obtaining a clear grasp of this highly heterogenous research literature is no mean feat. Most of us grow up in families, but most of these families are complex systems whose individual elements (members) differ from each other. As well, the complexion of our family lives is known to change over the life cycle of the family as the family deals with internal and external change. Family members relate differently to each other; siblings do not necessarily receive the same upbringing for many reasons which will be discussed below.

The child is also sent to school in most societies. It is commonly held that schools also shape the future characteristics of their pupils to some extent. What happens when "significant others" such as mothers, fathers, teachers, and peers "teach" different lessons and display different examples? The school may inculcate values and set examples that may be consistent or inconsistent with those of the family. Furthermore, the school atmosphere may not be as consistent or congruent as some simplistic research has assumed. One might describe the atmosphere of a school as a single whole social system, but this only makes sense to the degree that the individual teachers and classroom social systems share enough characteristics to warrant a common description.

The family and the school do not operate in isolation; they are part of a larger society with values and practices which may differ from those of other societies. The teachings of home and school may represent and reinforce those of the larger society, or may be in conflict. As societies change, norms and prohibitions as to how people relate may become less circumscribed. Increasing migration may place larger numbers of children in situations where they must simultaneously learn to function in both a sub-culture and a larger society which convey different messages and demand different interpersonal behaviour.

The purpose of this book is to equip the reader to understand the dynamics by which these *contexts*—home, school and culture—may come to influence the emergence of the child's social competence. The theoretical foundations and scope of relevant research are depicted, and criticized, in a hopefully constructive way. Most of the book is devoted to a consideration of the processes by which children's social competence are linked with factors operating within families, schools and cultures, as well as a selective review of related research. The research is drawn from literatures which have been highly disconnected, obscuring the total contribution of families, schools and cultures to children's social development. The primary purpose of this book is to present a compendium of theoretical vantage points and related research strategies, not a complete encyclo-paedia of research results. Accordingly, the research reviewed is neces-sarily selective, but hopefully illustrative of the major theoretical and methodological approaches in the field. Particular attention is paid to recent work, studies which encompass larger chunks of the child's social context, and those which represent important innovations in theory or technique.

Context factors in human development cannot be understood adequa-tely without considering their interaction with dispositional factors, as discussed below. Though the question cannot be dodged in any responsible treatment of these issues, those looking for conclusive resolution of the nature/nurture conflict herein will leave disappointed. Nor will those seeking a simple causal equation to predict children's social competence find much satisfaction in the following pages.

Context has been seen as an abstraction of the multivariate actual environments in which people live (Silbereisen & Eyferth, 1986). Green and Harker (1982) define a context as a recurrent activity which occurs within a distinct boundary. Weinstein (1991) points out that ecological psychologists are more likely to use a related term, "activity segment". Activity segments are characterized by an *action structure*, which specifies the rules for social interaction, and a *physical milieu*, the defined location for the activity. Thus, the three broad domains considered in this book— home, school and culture—each contain a number of different contexts according to Green and Harker's use of the term. Taken together, the contexts which together comprise home and school life as well as social interaction among members of a culture or social culture probably represent the majority of contexts in which children function, but by no means all of them. Nevertheless, they clearly represent the contexts which have captured most of the attention of social and developmental psychologists to date. Hopefully, this book will convey to the reader a useful summary of current knowledge about context effects, though it does not and could not provide information on all of the contexts of children's behaviour.

Structure of this book

The first half of Chapter 1 traces the function of context factors within various psychological theories as they have emerged during this century. By including theories which both maximize and minimize the importance of context, it is hoped to enable the reader to better understand why, despite 80 years of research in theory-building, many important questions about the importance of context factors in development remain unanswered. The remainder of Chapter 1 tackles what is perhaps the most complex issue dealt with in this book, namely the thorny question of how social competence should be defined. A summary of the techniques used in its measurement is also included.

Chapter 2 considers the different ways in which psychologists study families. It outlines the multiple pathways by which families may influence children's development and/or by which children may influence their families. As well, the interaction of the family's influence with the many other context factors contributing to children's social development receives attention. A selective review of recent research permits the reader to appraise the empirical basis of the theoretical perspectives introduced.

Chapter 3 presents a framework for the systematic conceptualization of schools as social systems, as well as several modalities of school influence on children's peer relations.

Chapter 4 begins with a discussion of some of the ways cultures have been described by psychologists, sociologists, anthropologists and scholars of communication processes. Mention is also made of the potential benefits of cross-cultural studies to developmental theory. A selection of cross-cultural research in the area of children's peer relations is presented and criticized.

The brief concluding chapter is broader than those it follows, in that it considers the *interaction* of these context factors (home, school and culture) as well as their interplay with other influences on children's development. The book ends with some reflection upon needs for future research on the context factors that contribute to children's social competence.

1

Context Factors in Child Development Theory

The role of context in early theoretical formulations

Most sources cite the seminal work of Jacob Moreno as the initial major inspiration for research and practice in the field of peer relations. Moreno emphatically rejected the individual as the basic unit of scholarly analysis, to the point of proposing (if he is to be taken seriously) that God's perspective on the world is, or was at the time of creation, analogous to that of a social relations scholar studying interpersonal relations rather than that of a therapist understanding the intrapsychic dynamics of a patient. He introduced sociometric techniques for understanding the roles individuals play in their own social systems, elaborating in minute detail on their analysis. Describing social roles was closely tied to more applied techniques used in enabling people to better understand the roles they play in their relations with others, and, most emphatically, to make some changes in them; Moreno called these techniques psychodrama. Though most of his work is releated to roles within discrete social systems, Moreno made explicit a much broader long-term goal, to proceed from the reconstruction of single relationships to the improvement of the whole world. Moreno's sociometric schemes have been modified greatly, but descendants of his basic methods are still in use. Moreno endowed the field of social relations with its emphasis on the *description* and *modification* of social behaviour and a relative disinclination for the study of its roots or causes.

Social relations also played a prominent role in Alfred Adler's "individual" psychology. Among Adler's most fundamental departures from Freudian theory was the conceptualization of the person as a whole, to be studied in relation to other persons, as opposed to the psycho-analysts' dissection of the internal workings of a person's psyche (Ansbacher & Ansbacher, 1956). Adler hypothesized that humans were guided by basic social interest, an inherent need and desire for satisfying interpersonal relations. Unhappiness and psychopathology emanated not from conflicts within oneself, but by feeling that one was inferior to others. Adler's is a subjective psychology; relations with others play a large role, but their impact on the individual depends on how interpersonal relationships are *perceived*, not on their objective, observable nature. Presaging the contemporary "cognitive revolution" in psychology, Adler posited that an individual's interpersonal behaviour was influenced by a series of personal beliefs as to one's own worth, as to the fundamental nature of others, and as to what one *must* or *should* be. He maintained that these beliefs were essentially shaped by family experience before the age of 6 years or so, though Adler also alluded to physiological roots by including (though not elaborating on) what he called "organ inferiority" as a causal factor. However, Adler's views regarding the causes of social development are not well detailed, and are probably metamorphosed segments of Freudian theory. Adler's causal reasoning has had little enduring impact on development psychology.

While Adler believed that behaviour is directed by logic, albeit often faulty logic, Freud's psychology depicts behaviour as being governed by passion; instinctive, biological needs guide and direct. An important role of development is to transform irrational appetites and passions into socialized rational purposes which allow us to function collectively as a society (see Langer, 1969, for an articulate summary of the basic premises of psychoanalytic and other major theories of development). Parents, particularly mothers, are seen as playing a fundamental role in this transformation, providing for the infant's biological and psychological needs in a way that allows the child to develop a sense of security while adjusting to the reality of the outside world. The crucial role assigned to early mothering in psychoanalytic writings has inspired some developmental research on social competence. As will be detailed in Chapter 2, some theorists regard later interpersonal relationships as decisively contoured by the nature of the child's early attachment to her mother. As aptly put by Fonzi (1991), psychoanalysts were "forced" to discover the importance of context as they continued their exploration of the dynamics of human behaviour.

Psychoanalytically-inspired theorists who succeeded and modified Freud's theories placed greater emphasis on context factors. Ego psychologists such as Hartmann (1939; see also Langer, 1969) emphasized that the child in every generation does not have to embark independently on the task of adjusting to society, but benefits from his parents' guidance in learning how to cope with the social environment. Eric Erikson's and, more emphatically, Harry Stack Sullivan's (1953) modifications to classical psychoanalysis assigned a somewhat greater role to context factors in development. Both these theorists adapted and extended Freud's stage model. Erikson did not deny the importance of biologically-based drives or early mothering, but, in a very significant departure from Freud, postulated that important developmental tasks and crises continue well beyond early childhood. While Erikson added the wider context to traditional psychodynamic models, he did so without considering the interplay of the many contexts in which the child functions. Home, school, peer group and culture are joined in an essentially benign alliance to help the individual develop. Conflict between the individual and society, which pervaded Freud's thinking, was not accentuated. Conflict between the family and society, or between elements of society, was left to emerge as a more central element of other theories (Buss, 1979).

In a similar but more radical reinterpretation of Freud's stage model, Harry Stack Sullivan highlighted the process of "chumship", in which the ability to form a satisfactory same-sex friendship in adolescence is seen as important for the later development of intimate heterosexual relationships. Thus, childhood, and adolescent peer relations are seen as more critical to the individual's development in either Erikson's or Sullivan's model than in Freud's; the cultural context, including the family, is portrayed as having some ongoing impact. Buss (1979) saw this post-Freudian era as an optimistic one, reflecting a belief in the possibilty of progress, accommodating historical change and cultural differences.

Though Darwin can be seen as having influenced in one way or another many subsequent theorists and researchers (Dixon & Lerner, 1988), their use of the evolutionary approach depends heavily on their interpretation of it and on which aspect of the theory captured their attention. Researchers of divergent theoretical leanings sought to confirm that the various stages of development mirror the stages in the progressive evolution of species. Arnold Gesell developed a very influential methodology for the study of normal children's development. He was persuaded that nature was the major driving force (Dixon & Lerner, 1988). Since he believed that maturational changes unfold independent of learning or context, he understood the need for a careful cataloguing of children's development at various stages. In doing so, he was refining a more informal method characteristic of Darwinian-inspired scientists, who would often chart the growth of their own children (or other children they knew) by compiling "baby biographies", including Darwin's biography of his own son (see Butterworth, Rutkowska & Scaife, 1985). Partly as a result of Gesell's influence, the field of of developmental psychology from about 1930 to 1960 devoted most of its attention to collecting precise data to be used in comparing children of various ages (Bronfenbrenner, 1963; Dixon & Lerner, 1988).

Gesell's almost exclusive emphasis on maturational unfolding did not receive unanimous endorsement. Many well-known contemporaries, including Miller, Dollard and Watson, set out to prove that learning could have at least some enduring impact on the child (Dixon & Lerner, 1988). In principle, no theory could attribute a more central role to context factors in development than stimulus–response theory. Langer (1969) used the metaphor of a mechanical mirror to describe behavioural approaches to development. This image accurately captures the classic behaviourists's view that all psychological activity is determined by stimulation from the environment. Behaviour is shaped both by concurrent stimuli and previous stimuli by means of association processes. Everything is learned, and, in theory, everything can be unlearned or relearned, though the basic apparatus that makes this happen may be innate. The predominant role of behavioural approaches in psychology throughout much of this century has no doubt inspired many of the studies to be described in Chapter 2 on the effects of parent's child-rearing practice.

Social learning theorists have elaborated extensively on pure stimulus–response theory, and retreated considerably from a pure "mechanical mirror" model. Bandura (1978) proposed a model of reciprocal determinism, which features the mutual influences of the person (imbued with abilities, personality and a belief system), the environment and the person's behaviour. While the child is generally reinforced for becoming like the parent, specific extrinsic reinforcement of the imitation of individual responses is not seen as necessary (Bandura & Walters, 1963a; Sears, 1957; Langer, 1969). In social learning theory, as in classic stimulus–response theory, the context of development moves to the forefront. The home, the school, the community and mass media continually provide salient models of social competence to children.

Feinman and Lewis (1991) chronicled the extent to which theorists during the middle of this century engaged in heated debate about the virtues of the two predominant schools of thought at the time, i.e. behavioural and psychoanalytic. Some scholars have also invested considerable effort in attempts to integrate them. With so much attention to the contrasts between the two theories, their similar attributes were largely overlooked. As noted by Feinman and Lewis, both approaches are didactic, in that the parent possesses the "right" answers and must teach them to the child, though there are differences: behaviourists see children as *un*guided, while psychoanalysts see them as *mis*guided. Neither approach provided for individual child differences; neither recognized any inherent child propensity as an important factor in the socialization process.

The social context in cognitive-developmental theory

While the processes of development play virtually no role in behavioural approaches, they are the very cornerstone of Piaget's theory. Piaget, as no other theorist, sensitized us to the very profound transformations in children's thinking that occur as the child develops. He also emphasized and demonstrated the impact of the child's cognition on interpersonal relations. For example, the child's basic understanding of reciprocity and causality has much to do with the emergence of a sense of fairness, of the awareness that others may see a social situation in a way that differs from one's own, and of their understanding that rules of a game, for instance, may be developed by those who play it (i.e. they are not rigid and inherently imposed from outside). In recent years, many of the details of Piaget's thory have been re-examined. Young children have been found far more intellectually capable and far more socially competent than Piaget believed (Siegler, 1991). Though the link between cognitive and social development is hardly being denied, few contemporary portraits depict children's peer relations as mirroring cognitive structures as directly as Piaget's.

Development according to Piaget is a process of continuous interplay between the individual and the environment, but the origin of the processes that govern this interchange are intrinsic within the organism, and do not depend on socializing agents in the environment for their activation. Of course, an excessively impoverished environment, or one which restricted the child's exploration, would be seen as impeding the processes of development, just as a house plant will not flourish without water, light and room to grow. This suggests a principle that may well be worth remembering, namely that context factors may be of greater value in explaining development in extreme cases as opposed to those in the centre of the spectrum. This idea is by no means new to psychology. Sir Francis Galton worked in the late nineteenth century, and was firmly committed to the view that nature—heredity—is the prime mover in human development and the genesis of individual differences. However, he speculated that the predominant role of heredity factors is operational only within a relatively restricted range of environments. As one examines more extreme fluctuations of environment, the role of the environment is seen as much more substantial (Bronfenbrenner & Crouter, 1983). Despite this recognition, few Piagetian-inspired researchers or behaviour geneticists would invest much energy studying the effects of parents, schools and cultural settings on social development.

The heyday of socialization research

Studies on parents' socialization of their children burgeoned during the 1950s and 1960s. (Maccoby and Martin, 1983, present a thorough review of family socialization studies.) A comprehensive vocabulary for describing the rearing of children was developed (e.g. Schaefer, 1965). In most studies, the outcome variable was children's honesty, resistance to temptation, or altruism, though there was some attention to sociability and successful peer relations. While the studies were invariably correlational, there was little doubt at the time that the parents' behaviours were the cause of the child's outcome. In most cases, the correlations were also relatively small (Maccoby & Martin, 1983). Not surprisingly, the scientific community's acceptance of the findings and beliefs of this era was somewhat ephemeral. However, some of the pioneers, especially Baumrind (1967), continued their work, adding an important longitudinal perspective. Baumrind's longitudinal data provide better evidence than the earlier one-shot correlational studies that certain types of parenting, especially the harsh, authoritarian kind, have deleterious effects over an extended time period, while an active, "authoritative" approach appears to have long-term benefits. These dimensions of parenting are discussed in Chapter 2.

Temperament research: the emergence of individual child differences

While Piaget revolutionized developmental psychology by changing the conception of the child from one of passive recipient of socialization to one of active participant, individual differences in maturational or constitutional factors play very little role in his theory, which mostly sought to describe developmental changes thought to be species wide. Another upheaval brought recognition of largely unlearned inherent differences among children. Individual differences were not prominent features of any of the major theories influencing developmental research during its infancy, whether behavioural, psychoanalytic or cognitive-developmental (Feinman & Lewis, 1991). While character types have been discussed since ancient times, researchers earlier in this century developed elaborate typologies of "character" (Fromm, 1955, 1964). Concepts of temperament, which have come to the forefront in recent developmental theory, are somewhat analogous to typologies of character in adult personality. Kagan (1989) provided an interesting critical review of the history of the concept of temperament. The exact nature of temperament is a subject of continuing controversy (see Goldsmith et al., 1987, for a comparison of approaches to its definition). However, most theorists would concur that temperament refers to the child's stable, largely inherited way of responding to social stimuli. There is little consensus regarding the structure of this construct either. Children can be described as being of either "easy" or "difficult" temperament, but most approaches contain many more dimensions. The extensive longitudinal work of Chess and Thomas in New York (Thomas & Chess, 1977) demonstrated that children's general social "response tendencies" in social situations do tend to be somewhat stable.

The recognition of stable dispositional patterns in children's social responses engenders a profoundly different understanding of the genesis of children's development (Feinman & Lewis, 1991). In a meaningful attempt to evaluate the effects of context variables, one must consider how these variables interact with characteristics which appear to be inherent to the child. In my view, this imposes important challenges to socialization theorists and researchers, but does not spell the end of socialization research as some have claimed.

Overlooked socialization agents: peers and siblings

Youniss (1980) invoked Piagetian theory, as well as the personality theories of Harry Stack Sullivan (mentioned above), in criticizing the traditional emphasis on parenting as the chief determinant of children's social development. Youniss's interpretation of Piaget differs substantially from many other interpretations in insisting that "if socialization theories have overemphasized the child's passivity, cognitive theories have drifted too far in the opposite direction' (p. 10). His departure from other interpretations of Piaget represents a difference in emphasis rather than a difference in basic structure. He accentuates much more than others the child's interchanges with peers from which the child develops a fuller understanding of interpersonal relations and their possible forms. Though the role of peer exchange is emphasized throughout Youniss's work, the contribution of parents is also acknowledged, though grudgingly. Parent and peer interaction are seen as serving somewhat different purposes. Parents transmit the precepts of society, imposing limits on social interaction. While these functions are seen as more or less indispensable, true understanding of mutuality in interpersonal exchange is attainable only within the realm of peer relations (Youniss, 1980).

Greater attention is also being paid to the role played by siblings in introducing their brothers and sisters to the social world of peers (Abramovich, Pepler & Corter, 1982; Cicerelli, 1983; Stewart, 1983). This leads to other issues which have not yet been widely explored. For example, what happens when there is lttle continuity between what is "taught" by parents and siblings? A vocabulary for describing relationships with siblings is just emerging. For instance, Stewart (1983) suggested that attachment theory be extended to encompass attachment relations between siblings.

Vygotsky's genetic theory: the contributions of nature and nurture differentiated

Generations of scholars have been embroiled in heated debates about the relative contributions of genetic and environmental factors in human development. Whle these polemics continue to this day with unabated fury, there have been some important voices raised against reductionist models in the social sciences which attempt to apportion the relative influences of "nature" and "nurture" in a manner not unlike that of someone slicing a pie. As carefully documented by his biographer James

Wertsch (1985), the Soviet psychologist Lev Vygotsky developed a genetic theory that emphatically rejected the "naive" positions of both organismic and mechanistic theorists. Working at the beginning of this century, Vygotsky's approach was perhaps the first to suggest that while both sociocultural and genetic determinants shaped part of the course of human development, the relative weight of each influence depended on the aspect and stage of development one considers. As one considers progressively higher stages of development, the explanatory framework must be expanded in order to accommodate new influences and their interactions with factors previously considered.

Vygotsky (1978; see also Wertsch, 1985) introduced a number of important distinctions between "simple" and "higher" mental functions. In higher mental functions, mediating processes which entail mental manipulating of signs and symbols are used more extensively. The individual is seen as endowed with some leverage, rather than as a passive recipient of the impinging forces, be they biological or environmental. Vygotsky emphasized the social origins of higher mental processes. While he acknowledged the role of biological influences especially on elementary mental functions, he seems to have devoted little energy to tracking this causal path.

Vygotsky's notion that the causes of development are different depending on developmental stage is echoed by recent life-span developmentalits (see, e.g., Baltes, Reese & Lipsett, 1980). These theorists sensitized psychologists on the ongoing developmental changes experienced by people of all ages, not only children and adolescents. In their extension of developmental psychology, they have found it useful to differentiate among three modes of causal influence. First of all, there are biological and environmental influences common to all individuals of a given age; these are seen as crucial determinants of development during childhood. The second mode consists of collective experiences common to individuals living at a particular era within a culture, which are seen as shaping most extensively the development of adolescents. Finally, individual experiences and personal life events are seen as more powerful determinants of development, particularly during the adult years.

Invoking the wider social context

"Systems" approaches may be known for their insistence on studying the child as one element of a dynamic family system. In portraying the family as a system, it is implicit that the system is seen as something of a discrete entity, closed to some degree to the outside world (Stryker & Serpe, 1983). However, the family functions actively as part of a larger network of social systems. The family's influence on the child is in turn heavily influenced by the impact of surrounding social and economic conditions on the parents (Bronfenbrenner, 1979). Bronfenbrenner's formulations emphasize the simultaneous contributions of many social systems, some close to the child (e.g. family, school), some more remote (e.g. cultural mores, national autonomy). The interplay of these systems (for example, the family's relations with the school) is seen as affecting child behaviour in turn. While Bronfenbrenner assigned a primordial role to context factors, the context is seen as working in conjunction with characteristics of the person and with the developmental process—a "person–process–context" model (Bronfenbrenner, 1986a, 1986b). Chapter 2 contains descriptions of some recent studies which have considered the broader social environment in formulating research on parents' socialization of their children's social development.

New challenges: psychology rethinks its concepts of causation

The cinema psychotherapist reveals to the client the hidden cause of his suffering and all is cured. Such simplistic thinking about causation has in the past plagued not only the field of psychotherapy, but also some areas of human development research. Until very recently, most researchers have formulated rather narrow models of causation, attempting to isolate a single cause, and using correlation methods to validate their models. This is no longer acceptable in rigorous developmental psychology research. The facile search for the "cause" of behaviour may prove less than fully fruitful, and the debate between those who wish to implicate a given "causal" factor and their colleagues who are more interested in other "causes" may not be very productive. There is a growing recognition that most behavioural phenomena have more than one "cause". This reasoning has become more prevalent with greater appreciation in the West of the viewpoints of Vygotsky and other Soviet psychologists. Vygotsky argued that behaviour at any particular stage must be studied as a function of the multiple forces impinging on the organism at that stage, and of the interrelationships of these forces. The relationships among these forces is not stable, and, therefore, the relative value of any explanatory principle or set of explanatory principles will change over the course of development (Wertsch, 1985).

The assumption that "causes" may act in more than an additive fashion is implicit in such multivariate models. If a child of a given temperament type A is subjected to home environment B and school environment C, the resulting outcome X will not be the simple sum $A + B + C$. Outcome X may be heavily coloured by the interaction of A, B and C, the way children of temperament type A react and function in environments B and C. In research on temperament, this concept is known as "goodness of fit" (Thomas & Chess, 1977). Both research design and statistical analysis have changed to reflect this more complex understanding of causation. Multivariate statistics—constructed to simultaneously analyse the effects of a series of variables—have come to the fore.

Students of psychology have long been made aware that correlations between variables do not indicate a causal link between them. If a punitive atmosphere in schools is correlated with higher levels of aggressive behaviour, this may be because the punitive atmosphere leads to an aggressive reaction, *or* it may be because the school staff become more punitive in response to the high levels of aggression which characterized their charges to begin with. While this has long been expounded in statistics textbooks, early theorists did not take seriously the possibility of bidirectional causation. With few exceptions, they gratuitously assumed that it was the environment that caused the child outcome, not vice versa.

Recent statistical advances have permitted a more sophisticated look at causation in the social sciences, though it is still clear that only true experimental methods can permit unqualified causal inferences. Techniques such as cross-lagged correlation (Kenny, 1975) enable the researcher to examine changes in the relations between variables over time. Analysis of these changes are useful in assessing the *likelihood* of a causal relation between variables. Other technical advances such as structural equations modelling (Jöreskog & Sorbom, 1986) are useful in testing complex, multidimensional causal models. To pursue the example introduced above, suppose an experimenter contemplates a causal model in which the child's difficult temperament and *a priori* aggressive behavioural style causes harsh discipline in homes and schools. Under certain very precise conditions, structural equations modelling techniques can assist this experimenter in estimating the likelihood that this model corresponds with the data obtained, in comparison, for example, with an alternate model which posits that the harsh discipline causes the child's aggression. However, these useful new techniques can be abused. The basic dictates of the scientific method have not been abrogated. The experimenter must start with a sound, well-conceived theoretical model against which the data can be tested. The LISREL computer program cannot do our thinking for us (Rogosa, 1988). These and other methodological refinements greatly diminish the value of most older studies on the "socialization" of childhood social competence. Quite a few new, more sophisticated, studies on the contribution of context factors are underway.

Reinterpretation of the importance of a "small" effect

As we have seen, belief that context factors make large contributions to children's social competence has been seriously questioned. Heredity may play more of a role than many were previously prepared to accept. Simple supposed causes of behaviour must be seen in wider, multivariate perspectives; the child's environment is being construed in a more complex manner to reflect the many interlinked systems in which an individual functions. Therefore, it is not realistic to expect, in theory or in practice, that a single given environmental variable will by itself have an enormous impact on childhood social competence. Very large correlations in this field have always been elusive. However, recent theoretical and methodological advances have led to a reappraisal of what a small correlation might mean in real life. As is the case for the methodological advances discussed in the previous few paragraphs, these new methods have been the subject of considerable controversy.

Summarizing the collective findings of a series of studies on a given topic in the social sciences is a subjective, often frustrating, process. Many studies are conducted with small samples; their results often appear contradictory. It has been recognized of late that if a number of studies are conducted to establish a particular correlation—for example, between harsh school discipline and pupils' aggression—and each study involves a relatively small sample, not all of these studies should be expected to have statistically significant findings. New techniques, known as meta-analysis, have been developed which permit the statistical aggregation of the findings from different original studies. It is then possible to test the statistical significance of the combined findings. If a hundred hypothetical studies were conducted of the effects of school discipline on aggression, let us suppose, for purposes of illustration, that forty studies would determine that there was a significant correlation between the two, at varying levels of significance. In twenty others, the results might approach significance, while the remaining forty might have non-significant findings. A reviewer using traditional subjective methods might determine that this body of research is inconclusive at best. However, meta-analysis would probably reveal that the original findings depict a significant, though small, correlation. If there really is no "true" correlation between school discipline and child aggression, far fewer than forty of the studies would have reported significant findings. That the combined effect size of this set of studies might be significant but small should no longer come as a surprise given the many other factors that are known to impinge on aggression during childhood (see Light & Pillemer, 1984, for a fuller discussion of the process of reviewing research, or Schneider, 1991, for applications to interpersonal relations).

Along with the emergence of statistical procedures for meta-analysis has come a reappraisal of the importance of small effects, including the small effects one often encounters in psychological research. Supposing a colleague wanted to extend the study of school discipline and aggression by developing an intervention component. She decides to conduct teacher workshops on positive classroom management techniques. Given the small (but, remember, potentially important) relationship between the variables, and the fact that the success of teacher workshops is not limitless, the outcome data for the intervention component of the study might again be small but significant.

Where are we now?

Contemporary theorists vary in the importance they assign to context factors in human development almost as much as the historical figures whose positions have been described in this chapter. Feinman and Lewis (1991) contend that as psychology's understanding of socialization processes becomes more complex, and increasingly encompasses inherent biological factors which assign a more active role to the child, scholars' interests in the study of socialization tend to wane. However, a glance at the current contents of pertinent journals and the programmes of recent international conferences and publications does not confirm any such decline in enthusiasm. Indeed, sweeping, unidirectional causal explanations seem well on their way to becoming less respectable, if not totally extinct. However, the task of capturing more of the many forces impinging on social development may be seen as something of a challenge that has stimulated renewed investment of energy.

While the theoretical positions outlined above have fluctuated in their appeal, it is interesting to note that few have totally disappeared. Nevertheless, the contemporary scholar approaches the examination of context factors in human social development with understandings far different from those of the pioneers in this area of research. This field can be seen as highly pluralistic at this point. It has been bolstered with methodological innovations which will hopefully bring the design of research closer to the more comprehensive scope of current theory and the available reservoir of background knowledge. This implies a degree of modesty in recognition of the multiple origins of social competence implicit in the approaches discussed here. Because of these changes, the studies reviewed in the next three chapters must be seen as pieces of a puzzle that is still being assembled, though we have been working on the puzzle for some time now.

The Construct of Social Competence and Its Measurement

Scholars of many backgrounds have converged on a common interest in children's social development. It is not surprising that their conceptions of social competence are often highly dissimilar, which may confuse the reader at times. Therefore, it may be helpful at this point to reflect upon the ways conceptualizations of social competence vary, and upon the reasons for this diversity. In order to demonstrate the diversity among prevailing definitions of social competence, a series of dimensions useful in classifying many existing definitions and concepts of social competence and social skill is presented next, in question form.[1]

HOW EXTENSIVE IS THE DOMAIN OF SOCIAL COMPETENCE?

One must be competent in many ways in order to get along with others. One approach in defining social competence or social skills has been to include all behaviours and traits that are associated with peer acceptance or effective behaviour in social situations. The range of these behaviours and traits can be quite broad. This has at times been referred to as the "bag of virtues" approach (Anderson & Messick, 1974; Greenspan, 1981; Zigler & Trickett, 1978). Stephens (1976) included an extensive array of classroom survival behaviours in his repertoire of social skills, extending as far as bringing appropriate school supplies, disposing rubbish in its proper container and standing appropriately in line before dismissal from school. In an implicit call to keep the "social" in social skills, Hops (1983, p. 3) criticized this approach for "threatening to encompass all of a child's waking activities". However, in attempting to restrict the domain to the "social", one runs the risk of being overly specific (Greenspan, 1981), perhaps eliminating many subtle but important features of a social exchange and important variables which bear upon effectiveness in social situations.

IS THERE PROVISION FOR SITUATION SPECIFICITY?

Definitions vary in their recognition of the variations in environmental press experienced by children. In most contemporary Western societies, children function in a variety of settings. Therefore, in order to interact effectively with others, they must learn the rules which govern social interaction in various settings. Since these rules are rarely explicit (Weade & Green, 1985; Weinstein, 1991), understanding them requires heightened sensitivity to subtle verbal expressions and non-verbal behaviour (Argyle, 1988; Erickson & Schultz, 1981). Some define social competence as the ability to behave in socially appropriate ways in different contexts (Mehan, 1980; Weinstein, 1991), in contrast with "trait" approaches which assume that a socially competent person will be competent in all social situations.

Greenspan (1981) noted that the difficulty of the golf course is among the determinants of success in a golf game. Furthermore, the anxiety

---

[1] Appreciation is extended to Roger Weissberg for sharing his personal collection of definitions of social competence and encouraging me to articulate mine.

experienced in a situation may inhibit appropriate social behaviour more than the lack of knowing what to do. Many children who are shy and isolated at school seem to have a surprisingly sound network of interpersonal relationships at home (Daniels-Beirness & Leshono, 1988). Surprisingly few prevailing definitions of social competence provide for this degree of situation specificity. Hargie's (1986) definition of social skill as a "set of goal-directed, situationally-appropriate social behaviours" (p. 12) is a recent exception.

IS SOCIAL COMPETENCE NESTED WITHIN A BROADER CONCEPT OF GENERAL COMPETENCE?

Many theorists explicitly recognize the importance of such factors as physical ability, motor coordination, abstract reasoning to self-acceptance, adjustment to society, and acceptance by peers, but decline to include these dimensions within the domain of social competence. This can be accomplished by making explit the relation of social competence to general (or personal) competence. These concepts are critically deliberated by Greenspan (1981) and Oppenheimer (1989). The importance of the social and non-social aspects of competence in achieving psychological well-being is particularly emphasized by scholars studying competence as a protective factor in overcoming the effects of stress (e.g. Garmezy, 1989; Rutter, 1979).

HOW ACTIVE IS THE INDIVIDUAL?

A number of theorists have emphasized personal needs and goals in their conceptualizations of social competence. Accordingly, a person would be socially competent if he/she is able to satisfy his/her needs for affiliation or social support. An example of the fullest incorporation of personal goals in a model of social competence is that proposed by Parks (1985), in which competence is defined as "the degree to which individuals have satisfied their goals in a given social situation without jeopardizing their . . . opportunity to pursue other subjectively more important goals" (p. 175), or in Ford's (1982) definition of social competence as "the attainment of relevant social goals in specified social contexts, using appropriate means and resulting in positive developmental outcomes". It is worth noting that Parks's definition contains no constraint that the goals be "appropriate", only the means for achieving them.

IS SOCIAL COMPETENCE ATTRIBUTED BY OTHERS?

In sharp contrast with definitions which emphasize the individual's needs and goals, many theorists base their concepts of social competence on the opinions or reactions of peers. As detailed below, McFall (1982) considers social competence as essentially an evaluative term. Libet and Lewinsohn (1973) defined social skills as the ability to emit behaviours that are reinforced by others and to refrain from emitting behaviours that are punished by the group. Bellack and Hersen (1979) defined social skills as "interpersonal behaviours which are normative and/or socially sanctioned" (p. 169). This approach has the advantage of permitting a clear determination of what is socially competent and what is not. However, it cannot accommodate the increasing emphasis within the field on individual differences in children's social goals (Parkhurst & Asher, 1987). Furthermore, it can be seen as empowering deviant sub-groups to define behaviours or persons as socially competent that the majority would consider antisocial.

Defining social competence in terms of endorsement by the peer group or society at large automatically assigns a premium to social behaviours directed at group acceptance or popularity. However, there has been a recent shift of attention toward "socially competent" behaviour that leads to the formation of a single close friendship or small network of intimate friendships (Asher & Parker, 1989; Furman & Robbins, 1985; Schneider & Murphy, 1990). Some theorists have also focused on attributions of children's social competence made by adults, especially teachers (see Chapter 3).

ARE INDIVIDUALS OR BEHAVIOURS CONSIDERED SOCIALLY COMPETENT?

Greenspan (1981) offered another useful sports analogy helpful in illustrating this distinction. If one wanted to define competence as a golfer, one approach would be to look at certain behavioural elements of a golf game—the putting stroke, swing, alignment, etc. Parallel behavioural elements in children's social competence might include such actions as appropriately approaching a group of peers at play. One might also look at a golfer's ability to concentrate on the task of golf, to understand the game and to cope with the stress of an intense golf game. These are essentially parallel to such constructs as temperament, character and knowledge of social situations as factors in social competence. Such "constitutional" determinants as size, strength and coordination also have much to do with success in golf, just as physical attractiveness, intelligence and freedom from anxiety contribute to effectiveness in social situations.

McFall (1982) distinguished between trait models in which social skills are seen as a response predisposition which underlies behaviour and is stable across situations, on the one hand, and molecular models which view social skills as discrete, observable behavioural units. Neither approach is without its limitations. Trait models are seen as poorly defined and somewhat incongruous with research results that indicate that human behaviour varies enormously from situation to situation. Molecular models suffer from their failure to provide assistance to the theorist or researcher in determining which discrete units of behaviour and which situations to observe when one wants to study social competence.

IS SOCIAL COMPETENCE INFERRED FROM ITS OUTCOME?

In many prevailing models, social competence is inferred from a *post hoc* indicator such as acceptance by peers. Borrowing Greenspan's (1981) golf analogy one more time, this would be directly parallel to inferring golf competence from the golfer's final score. According to Greenspan, this might have substantial heuristic value; it would be of little use in diagnosing the difficulties of an aspiring golfer in need of corrective coaching. Similarly, measuring social competence as an end product contributes little to the design of home or school environments to maximize co-operative interaction, or to social skills training for children without friends, though it might contribute to the measurement of the success of these interventions.

WHAT PORTION OF SOCIAL COMPETENCE IS VISIBLE?

While some theorists limit their concepts of social competence to observable behaviour, many imply that these overt behaviours are but the tip of a large iceberg. "Motoric" social behaviour is often seen as driven and guided by crucial perceptual and cognitive processes, as in Trower, Bryant and Argyle's (1978) model of social competence. Meichenbaum, Butler and Gruson (1981) include cognitive "structures" which are motivational or affective, and seen as underlying both overt behaviours and cognitive processes. In Strayer's (1989) ethologically-inspired view, social competence "must be viewed as a dynamic system of knowledge and value that both emerges from and structures the child's perceptions, representations and actions in the social world".

DOES SOCIAL COMPETENCE REPRESENT WHAT ONE IS CAPABLE OF DOING OR WHAT ONE ACTUALLY DOES?

Theorists have taken liberties with the usual meanings of "competence", "competency", "skill" and "skills" in attempting to accommodate this distinction. This is compounded by the fact that standard usage of language is not particularly helpful in resolving the confusion. In the *Shorter Oxford English Dictionary* (1973), "competence" is defined as "sufficiency, adequacy or capacity". "Skill" can mean "practical knowledge in combination with ability, cleverness, expertness" or "to know how to do something". Thus, the distinctions between the two are quite subtle.

One solution is to propose that social competence or social skill refer to one's abstract ability in social relationships or in handling social situations adequately, whether or not one actually uses these abilities. In most cases, this distinction is probably not very important, since those capable of forming social relationships would probably proceed to do so. Yet there is an increasing awareness in the field of the need to distinguish between individuals who are capable of initiating social contact but choose not to do so and those who experience distress because of their social isolation and inability to remedy it. The former individual is not well served by trait approaches, which would lead to the conclusion that he is socially incompetent. Gresham (1986) introduced a useful distinction between social skills defects and social performance deficits. The latter describes children who possess the necessary social skills (abilities) but do not perform them at adequate levels. There are a number of reasons why individuals might not perform social behaviours of which they are capable, ranging from excessive anxiety to excessive impulsivity.

ARE THERE HIERARCHICAL LEVELS OF COMPETENCE?

The dictionary definitions of "competence" and "competency" are essentially identical, and many theorists use them interchangeably. However, Walters and Sroufe (1983) proposed that competence refers to "a general ability to generate and coordinate flexible adaptive responses to demands and to generate and capitalize on opportunities", whereas competency would refer to "specific skills". Many theorists consider social competence as larger than and encompassing social skills (Gresham, 1986). In McFall's (1982) model, social skills refers to specific behaviours performed well, whereas social competence is an evaluative term based on judgements by others of the adequacy of task performance. Gresham and Reschly (1987) proposed a model of social behaviour which consists of two components: adaptive behaviour—referring to self-care skills, physical development, academic achievement, etc.—and social skills. In doing so, they accommodate the fact that peer or adult judgements of acceptability are influenced by behaviours which some may have difficulty seeing as social.

Nonetheless, one needs only to examine several prevailing notions of social skill to discover that many users of the term resist its being limited to overt behaviour. Spitzberg and Cupach (1989) delineate three prevalent uses of the term "social skill": (1) overt molecular behaviours, (2) mid-range ability constructs, and (3) abstract (higher-order) processes, and justifiably conclude that the distinction between social competence and social skill is often fuzzy.

DOES SOCIAL COMPETENCE DEPEND ON THE INDIVIDUAL'S
DEVELOPMENTAL LEVEL OR STAGE?

Judgements of the social adequacy of any given behaviour are best tempered by the perspective of normal development at the person's age level and developmental stage. Waters and Sroufe (1983) noted that this developmental perspective makes it difficult to accept a notion of competence that is composed of specific skills, few of which would be relevant across developmental levels. They note that individual differences which can be considered assets at certain levels of development can be liabilities at other stages. As an extreme example, consider direct, rote imitation of peers' play behaviour. Nadel and Fontaine's (1989) work indicates that, in very young children, this skill may be an important means of achieving interpersonal contact, which could not be achieved using language by children at this level of development. The same "skill" would hardly be an asset, and would possibly be a liability, in achieving social relations at later stages. Going over and joining in a game is very competent among very young children, and enhances the type of interpersonal relationships they form (Howes, 1989). This skill probably applies to individuals of all ages. Skilled use of social language, such as understanding subtle messages communicated by sarcasm, may be less relevant to the delineation of social competence in young children. The developmental perspective in defining social competence is considered in greater depth by Attili (1989).

Implications of This Diversity in Basic Definition

By this point, most readers would probably concur with Phillips's observation, cited by Spitzberg and Cupach (1989), that defining competence resembles "trying to climb a greased pole". It is extremely confusing for scientists to claim to be studying the same phenomenon when they actually are looking at a number of different albeit related things. These divergencies in the basic definition of social competence have led to widespread frustration. For instance, Zigler and Trickett (1978) asserted that social competence theorists find themselves "adrift on a sea of words" because social competence "is definable only in terms of other constructs whose own definitions are vague" (p. 793). They remarked that social competence has not been widely adopted as a variable in studying psychological adjustment because of the lack of consensus on its definition.

Similar discrepancies in basic definition do plague scholarly activity regarding a number of other fundamental psychological constructs, such as anxiety and intelligence. Even so, social competence research is not furthered in any way by the observation that problems of definition are not unique to this area. Consensus on a definition of social competence would surely have helped the field, and still would. Nonetheless, we might speculate that no single definition could satisfy the broad range of needs and biases of those interested in this area. It is no accident that we are unable to agree on a common definition of social competence. The apparent chaos regarding the basic conceptualization of social competence reflects the richness of the many influences on the field.

Accordingly, the following attempt at bringing order to this chaotic state of affairs must be recognized as a personal one, which reflects my own biases and experience. I propose that *social competence* be defined as:

> *the ability to implement developmentally-appropriate social behaviours that enhance one's interpersonal relationships without causing harm to anyone.*

Within this framework, a social skill is defined as one of the more specific, discrete abilities which together comprise social competence. Each element of the proposed definition requires a bit of further elaboration.

The ability to implement

This phrase implies, first of all, that competence is not limited to abstract mental maps of how behaviours might be performed, but requires that the individual be able to actually display the behaviour (see also Trower, 1982). This does not mean, on the other hand, that competence is exactly equivalent to behaviour. For example, if an individual is capable of forming friendships with others, but for some reason elects not to, he is still competent because he has the ability to implement the behaviours at will. However, a person who has a mental map of how friendships are formed, but is unable to translate this knowledge into practice, possibly because of anxiety, could not be considered socially competent.

Defining social competence in terms of the ability to implement certain behaviours dictates the nature of the sub-components which I call social skills. These social skills must logically include knowledge of *what* to do in a social situation, social-perceptual and social-cognitive skills which enable the individual to determine *when* the particular behaviours should be implemented and to select among them, as well as the *self-control* skills which enable him/her to coordinate behaviour with the desired mental map or play of what should be done. Thus, while social skills are defined as more discrete, specific abilities than their aggregate, social competence, it is not contemplated that each social skill represents an ability which necessarily should or could be translated into overt behaviour.

Appropriateness to the individual's stage of development

Following Waters and Sroufe (1983) and Attili (1989), this concept is included in order to clarify that what is socially competent at one stage may not be socially competent at another.

Social behaviours

The term "social" is included in an effort to restrict the domain of social competence to behaviours which pertain most directly with individuals relating to one another. Examples of such behaviours include conversational skills with acquaintances, skills of persuasion, negotiation and compromise, planning and evaluating one's relationships and appropriate self-disclosure to intimate friends. Other "non-social" skills which do indeed enhance interpersonal relationships are excluded. It is not easy to distinguish which of the behaviours that might enhance a relationship should be considered social. For example, competence in the game of tennis may well lead to many satisfying interpersonal relationships; having a common pastime has been found to be a very important feature in friendship (Argyle, 1983; Argyle & Furnham, 1982). Let us consider the case of a lonely individual who recognized the need for a venue in which to meet others. The self-evaluation inherent in realizing that he could not initiate relationships in the absence of a place to meet people might well be considered a social skill. Nevertheless, it would not be very productive to classifying one's prowess on the tennis court as a social skill. Being a good cook might lead to more and better interpersonal relationships in some circles, but baking ability is not a useful component of a concept of social competence. Similarly, children who do well in school are likely to win the esteem of their peers, but it would not be useful to conceptualize mathematics and reading skills or remembering one's school supplies as parts of social competence. Ford (1982) presented additional considerations relevant to the distinction between social and general competence, and argued as well that it is possible to distinguish the two to some extent.

Enhancement of interpersonal relationships

This element implies that social competence is determined to a degree by its outcome, and to a large extent by the approval of peers or significant others. While the word "relationships" might imply that a certain premium is assigned to closer, more intimate relationships, this is not necessarily the case. One has interpersonal relationships at various levels, including relationships with classmates at school, colleagues at work and neighbours at home. Children also have important interpersonal relationships with their parents and teachers. Nevertheless, this element of the definition might serve as a useful corrective in a field that has so extensively concentrated on popularity in large groups as opposed to relationships within dyads. The very evocation of the term "relationships" will hopefully serve as a reminder that various levels of relationship are important. "Enhancement" refers to the initiation, maintenance and repair of a relationship. Thus, a person who is truly socially competent must be skilled not only at making them, but at keeping them.

Without harming anyone

This element excludes certain social behaviours which might build interpersonal relationships with some individuals at the expense of others. In children's groups, taunting a "sissy' might increase one's esteem in the eyes of certain other group members. In some circles, excluding members of racial or ethnic minorities might make one more popular with a sub-group or even with the majority. A psychopath who is a good conversationalist, but uses this talent to deceive and defruad, cannot be considered socially competent, since whatever relationship enhancement ensues occurs at the expense of the victim (note that this psychopath does, nonetheless, possess certain *social skills* in the area of conducting conversations in a skilful way). While it would not be acceptable to consider such behaviours as socially competent, this does not mean that social competence is the same as moral judgement and moral behaviour (this issue was raised by Duck, 1989). In certain situations of conflicting claim, what is morally imperative may be socially unacceptable to the peer group and may cause many of one's interpersonal relationships to deteriorate. Doing what is morally correct would not be described as socially competent in these, presumably rare, circumstances under the definition proposed above. Said otherwise, social competence is not a synonym for what is good in all situations.

Assessment of Social Competence in Developmental Research

When one refers to "a measure of social competence", most likely one means a measure of one or more social skills (perceptual, cognitive or motoric), their manifestation in overt behaviour, or their outcome in terms of enhanced interpersonal relationships, casual or intimate. For example, the ability to understand the social messages sent by others is an important social skill whose presence we might consider a necessary but not sufficient indicator by itself that an individual is socially competent. Strictly speaking, a test of this ability should be referred to as a measure of a social skill. Similarly, a role-play measure of the ability to engage in appropriate conversation is a measure of social skill according to the definitions proposed in this chapter.

Suppose a researcher decides to observe the extent to which children are involved in play interactions with other children, rather than playing by themselves, or to ask a group of individuals who their best friends are. These measures of outcome will identify individuals having achieved a degree of peer contact or satisfying interpersonal relations. However, they could not establish how this social success was achieved—was it because of the individual's social skills, or because of athletic or academic ability or physical attractiveness? It would be best to refer to these techniques when used in isolation as measures of "social behaviour" or "social interaction" and "peer relations" or "peer acceptance", respectively, rather than "measures of social competence". Along similar lines, Trower (1982) has argued that assessments of social competence should encompass both an individual's social knowledge and the ability to act upon it. In practice, it would be rare that the social competence of any individual could be adequately measured against this yardstick. Nevertheless, the literature contains so many references to "measures of social competence" and "subjects identified as socially competent" that this has become part of the vernacular. Since it is important for the reader to know the basis for designating subjects as socially competent, the study descriptions in Chapters 2–4 include information about which indicators of social competence were used to the extent possible.

Dimensions of Social Competence

Early studies often classified children as either socially competent or incompetent, popular or unpopular, etc. The positive pole, competence, is, of course, still of interest. However, more recent research has indicated that it is deceptive to consider a single dimension of *in*competence, given the many important differences among children regarded as lacking in competence and popularity. Therefore, the incompetent pole is now largely replaced by two dimensions. One of these subsumes problems of excess, such as aggressive behaviour, which often leads to active dislike or *rejection* by peers (Coie, 1985). The other dimension relates to *deficit* behaviours, such as lack of social interaction, or social withdrawal, which may lead the individual to be overlooked or *neglected* by peers rather than actively disliked.

These dimensions have not been explored in relation to school, family and cultural contexts. Understandably, predictors of aggression have been studied in detail. In many studies on context effects, particularly those of schools and cultures, *co-operative behaviour* among children has been selected as the outcome measure. As the next chapters will reveal, the effects of these contexts on withdrawal has received much less attention. As in most research on children's peer relations, children's competence in large group situations has received the lion's share of research energy. We know relatively little about whether and how contexts affect children's ability to develop more intimate friendships at the dyadic level. This is most unfortunate, because this network of satisfying intimate friendships may be most crucial to individuals at times of stress, and, therefore, more closely linked to psychological adjustment over the life-span than popularity in large groups.

Measures of Children's Social Competence

Information from children's peers

As introduced in Chapter 1, Moreno's sociometric methods were the major measurement tool in the earliest years of social competence research. Peers were seen as having the best-informed vantage point on children's peer relations. To a considerable extent, this impression has not changed (Asher, 1985). Though sociometric techniques have been in use for over 70 years, efforts to enhance their validity are still underway. Many of the important issues currently debated about sociometric measurement were quite alive during Moreno's career. For example, Moreno discussed the distinction between what he called the sociometric *test* and sociometric *questions* (1978, p. lxxi). He was well aware that merely asking individuals who they would choose as play partners would be of only limited use. Therefore, in his original study of the sociometric structure of an elementary school, he supplemented the structured choice measures with open-ended questions about the reasons for their preferences, and discussed developmental differences in these reasons (Moreno, 1978, pp. 175–206).

The sociometric test (now called a measure of sociometric *choice*) asked the individual to *choose* the peers with whom they wanted to associate, while sociometric questions (now called *nominations*) used peers as informants, asking, for example, who the most popular children in the class were. These techniques help identify which children are popular or rejected. More recent research has featured finer distinctions among children who are disliked, differentiating among those who are actively rejected, those who are neglected (i.e. not mentioned as actively disliked but not chosen as a play or work partner) and those who are controversial (i.e. liked by some and disliked by others) (Coie & Kupersmidt, 1983). *Sociometric rating scales* (see Asher, 1985) have been featured in more recent research. Rating scale techniques involve children's judgements of various attributes of their peers. For example, all members of a class might be rated on a five-point scale for friendliness, shyness, aggressiveness, etc., in comparison with a nomination technique in which all would be asked to indicate which peers were the most friendly, most shy, etc. Therefore, rating scale techniques are more useful than the original nomination techniques in obtaining information on all subjects in the group, and in portraying changes in social behaviour over time when repeated measures are obtained from the same subjects.

While sociometrics do measure an individual's position within a social group, they do not involve the group reaching consensus regarding an individual (Northway, 1952). Instead, the sociometric method must be understood as an aggregate measure of the "attractions and repulsions" (Moreno, 1978, p. 93) of each member of a social system to each other member. Moreno recognized that "the introduction of sociometric procedure, even to a very small community, is an extremely delicate psychological problem" (1978, p. 94). Descriptive sociometry was to be accompanied by "remedial sociometry" or "sociatry" (p. 119), designed to increase the participation of isolated individuals with as much precision as the descriptive work. This clear position foreshadowed more recent research linking sociometric measurement with social skills training (Asher, 1985). However, the postwar years saw a rapid proliferation of sociometric testing in schools. For instance, it was recommended for use by regular classroom teachers in the United Kingdom, which many saw as a positive step (Northway, 1952). It is not clear that this large-scale sociometric testing was always linked with improvements to the classroom community, and sociometric techniques are no longer administered routinely other than for research purposes. Despite misgivings in some quarters, the limited research available does not indicate that children are harmed in any way by these methods. For example, Bell-Dolan, Foster and Sikora (1989) administered a mood questionnaire to primary school youngsters before and after they completed a sociometric test; there was no appreciable change in mood or consistent change in peer interaction. Similar results were obtained with younger children by Hayvren and Hymel (1984). Therefore, sociometrics—administered with the care advocated by Moreno and for their original purpose of at least eventually helping improve the relationships assessed—seem likely to remain prominent instruments in the measurement of children's social competence. They are most useful as measures of *outcome*—for determining which children have extensive or restricted networks of acceptance and rejection within their groups. Sociometrics convey no information regarding the *processes* which resulted in the configuration of relationships that is discovered.

Direct observation

The use of direct observation in assessing children's social competence has a history as long as that of sociometrics. Moreno was disenchanted with observational techniques. In his observations, he attempted to establish which children formed sub-groups or cliques, but concluded, understandably, that sociometrics and interviews with group members would provide more meaningful data on the structure of groups (1978, pp. 100–101). On the other hand, observation offers a myriad of possibilities for understanding the dynamics of children's social play. Nurtured extensively at the university-based laboratory schools which opened during the 1920s, observational methods have benefited the most from their central position in behaviourly-inspired research. Observations can be conducted either in natural settings such as playgrounds, schools or homes. Observing in natural settings has the obvious appeal of authenticity, but there are many practical challenges. For instance, once they are in primary school, children spend much of their time in formal lessons; observation of the interspersed social interaction may be uneconomical. Observations may also be conducted in structured laboratory situations constructed for the study underway. These have the disadvantage of being contrived, but do permit greater control of the environment and greater efficiency. The reader is referred to Mash and Terdal's (1988) comprehensive treatment of methodological considerations in behavioural observation. If used competently and creatively, observations can help describe the quality of children's play—aggressive, co-operative, exploratory, etc. They can also be used to establish the sequence of events in a social exchange (see Bakeman & Gottman, 1986) and the links between play and its physical setting (see Chapter 5). Some researchers have made inferences about children's play based on the rate of interaction with peers. This captures the quantity, not the quality, of interaction, and may result in highly misleading conclusions about the subjects' social competence (Asher, Markell & Hymel, 1981). Unfortunately, this "rate of interaction" approach has been used extensively in research on social interaction in schools and across cultures.

Information obtained directly from the child

Neither observations nor sociometrics can convey an individual's perceptions of his/her own interpersonal relationships, or one's feelings of adequacy in relating to others (Cairns & Cairns, 1984). In addition, both the major methods discussed above have severe limitations in providing information about closer, more intimate relationships as opposed to peer acceptance in large groups (Furman & Robbins, 1985; Schneider & Murphy, 1990). Psychologists have traditionally been wary of self-report measures. It is indeed very difficult to be objective in providing information about oneself. However, the subject himself is the best person to provide data on his feelings about a relationship and his personal sense of competence. Self-report measures have been widely developed for use with adults (Spitzberg & Cupach, 1989), and are beginning to see wider use with children (Hymel & Franke, 1985).

The child is obviously the best source of information about such dimensions as empathy, perception of important social cues, understanding of social situations, social problem solving, social goals, interfering social anxiety and evaluation of one's own social behaviour. These are among the elements of a complex process of social information processing described by several theorists (Argyle, 1983; Dodge, 1985). Unfortunately, the measures used currently to assess children's social perception and social problem solving have often been highly reductionistic (Schneider, 1989), probably capturing only tiny fragments of the social information processing described by theorists.

Role-play measures of social competence are predominant in research with adults. These techniques permit researchers to carefully manipulate the stimuli presented, which enables them to study situations that occur too infrequently to be captured by direct observation, or private events not accessible to observers. However, role-play methods are not used widely with children, because children's performance on them is known to be completely unlike both their behaviour in naturalistic settings and their peers' impressions of their behaviour (Gresham, 1986). However, it seems likely further study of the non-verbal aspects of children's social communication will require continued use of role-play methods.

Researchers have also developed a number of structured interaction tasks in order to study children's behaviour under relatively standard conditions. This is particularly useful in cross-cultural research, as illustrated in Chapter 4. As detailed in that chapter, these are most judiciously used in conjunction with information obtained by teachers in the natural setting.

Ratings by teachers and parents

Parents and teachers get to know children very well. Teachers also get to know many youngsters of the same age, enabling some degree of normative reference. Some researchers have found it useful to tap these potentially useful sources of information. There is some evidence that teacher ratings can discriminate among aggressive, withdrawn and popular children (Ollendick, Oswald & Francis, 1989) and accurately identify children who are known to display exceptionalities of behaviour and learning (Gresham, Elliott & Black, 1987). However, teacher ratings have been found less accurate with regard to children's skills in relating positively to other children than in portraying behaviours which are more salient in the classroom, such as aggressiveness (Byrne & Schneider, 1986). There have been a number of recent improvements in teacher rating scales.

The recent increased interest in them should lead to clarification of their validity.

Which measure to use?

Each of the available tools can be of use in conveying information about some aspect of a child's social competence, though none is without its limitations. It is well established that different sources of information tend to convey conflicting information (Ledingham & Younger, 1985). Many authorities have insisted on the use of multiple measures of social competence, which seems to be the best strategy. In interpreting the research discussed in the next three chapters, it is important to bear in mind that the conclusions derived in each study depend heavily on the researcher's selection of measures.

2

Family Life and Children's Peer Relations: Towards an Integrated Research Strategy

Ethologists often draw useful parallels between the development of human children and the offspring of other species. In most of the animal world, a single dyadic relationship between mother and child is of primary, and often virtually exclusive, importance in equipping the young for survival (Lewis, 1984). The truism that the child's personality and social behaviour are forged within the family has been more or less unchallenged throughout most of history. The scientific method in psychology has had a much shorter life than philosophical and religious prescriptions for bringing up children, but most psychologists have accepted this contention as readily as their lay counterparts.

The tendency to attribute family origin to children's individual characteristics has come under serious attack in the past few years. Scholars of children's peer relations are being increasingly admonished that "the sociometric status of peer researchers in the scientific community may itself increase in proportion to [their] insightful borrowing of the methods of behaviour genetics" (Rowe, 1989, p. 296). Some are worried that such "insightful borrowing" may go too far. For instance, Dunn and Plomin (1990), who are well-established scholars in the area of behaviour genetics, expressed a concern that "the lurching from antipathy toward acceptance of genetic influence was in danger of swinging the pendulum of fashion too far—from environmentalism to biological determinism" (Dunn & Plomin, 1990, pp. xii–xiii).

There is also some sentiment that the influence of the family may actually be declining as society changes. This phenomenon is discussed at length by Saal (1982), who sees this decline as a burden to children. Most adults now work at jobs which remove them from the child's immediate visual and auditory field, diminishing their ability to play roles as socializing agents. At the same time, recent social and economic changes bring the child into increased contact with individuals who are more diverse, and who may have values and norms different from those of his or her family. Even if children receive a clear, consistent message from their immediate families regarding social rules and norms, they will be well aware that neighbouring families may not see things the same way. This was less typical of previous generations.

The structural-functionalist framework predominant in family sociology also recognizes that families play a somewhat diminished role in our lives today when compared to the role of the family a century or more ago. Parsons and Bales (1955) visualize the contemporary family as stripped of many of the basic economic functions which it exercised throughout much of history. However, several important functions remain uncurtailed, including socialization of the young and stabilizing adult personality, even though the family is not institutionalized in society the way it once was. This functionalist position in sociology sees contemporary families as transmitting the values and norms of society in a more or less passive way, compared to the interactionist perspective, which portrays the family as a more dynamic, active and independent unit with extensive influence of its own (Stryker & Serpe, 1983).

This chapter is a selective review of ways in which the family may influence children's social competence. The aim is neither to attack nor defend "environmentalistic" theory-building and research in this area, but to summarize the basic assumptions and current scope of current research on the family's contribution. The following review of studies is, necessarily, selective, and, wherever possible, features recent research that incorporated pivotal social competence outcomes rather than more peripheral variables. Space considerations preclude consideration of the many interesting studies on the family's contribution to the emergence of children's empathy and emotional expressiveness, for instance. In the selection of studies, special attention has been paid to explorations of the interplay of several dimensions of family life, or of family life and external variables. Where the database is very sizeable, the reader is referred to competent reviews of the literature.

Multiple Modes of Family Influence

Family functioning can be conceptualized in a myriad of ways. Figure 2.1 is a graphic depiction of the major modalities of direct family influence on children's social competence discussed in the developmental literature; each will be explained further below. Consistent with contemporary views on the bidirectionality of influence between parents and children, these mechanisms of family influence are depicted in interaction with child temperament.

As introduced in Chapter 1, it would be grossly incomplete to conceive of these family influences as operating independently of the family's interaction with the outside world. Figure 2.2 sketches some of the ways by which the extrafamilial context is thought to affect the most frequently

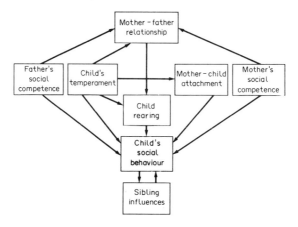

FIG. 2.1. Major modalities of family influence discussed in the socialization literature.

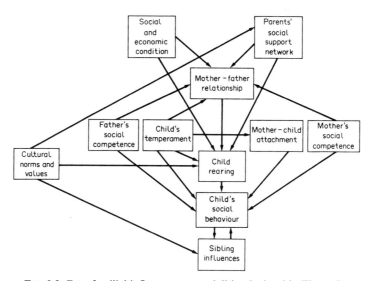

FIG. 2.2. Extrafamilial influences on modalities depicted in Figure 2.1.

discussed family influences on children's social development. Webster-Stratton's (1990) model attempts to delineate the processes by which family processes are regulated by events in the surrounding community and culture. The concept of stress is used as an umbrella for a variety of factors which may affect parent–child relations. These include, first of all, stressors emanating from the family's social environment, such as poverty or unemployment. Major stressful life events—for example, the death of a close relative—may increase the stress level of a home. Some parents may also perceive more minor but chronic daily "hassles" as very stressful (Lazarus & Launier, 1978). The second major category of stressor within the family environment is interparental conflict, which may lead to the child witnessing the parents' quarrels or having to cope with their separation. Stress may also emanate from the child. Having a child with a difficult temperament may strain relations and make managing a home a most trying experience. Individuals react differently to these challenges. Where a psychologically well-adjusted parent might seek solutions to problems, a depressed parent might magnify them and allow them to dominate the scene. A troubled personality might amplify the effects of stressful life events (see Elder, Caspi & Nguyen, in press) and alienate individuals who might potentially serve as sources of support.

Being integrated into a satisfying network of community contacts and friendships is seen as a buffer, reducing the repercussions of the collective "pile-up" of stressors. In the absence of counterbalancing buffering influences, these stressors affect the child's development *because they disrupt* the warmth, nurturance and discipline that parents provide their children. The various stressors which "pile-up" may also have direct effects on the child as well as this important indirect effect through disruption of child rearing.

The absence of each of the stressors of Webster-Stratton's model does not necessarily explain the family's effects on normal as opposed to atypical development. For example, if marital disharmony leads indirectly or directly to social behaviour problems, that does not necessarily mean that marital *harmony* leads to social competence. While effective disciplinary practice may lead indeed to social competence just as ineffective discipline leads to deviant social behaviour, such converse paths of influence should not be assumed. It is quite conceivable that family stress has a negative impact on social development, but that individual differences in social competence among children from unstressed homes depend on a completely different set of influences.

Moving from Theory to Research

These rich, complex theoretical formulations pose a substantial challenge to researchers. Some use of shorthand is inevitable when a theory is translated into standard measures and workable research designs. Many of the processes involved are more or less private ones not easily accessed by researchers. In the vast majority of studies, the aim is to demonstrate that a given family variable is *correlated* with a given child variable. Relatively few have captured the intervening mechanisms which may have generated the correlation in question. Researchers typically acknowledge the complexity of the family system, but such "confessions" only occasionally result in more comprehensive strategies for studying its workings.

Mash and Terdal (1988) distinguish between traditional and behavioural approaches to assessing families. Broadly speaking, the "traditional" approach refers to a wide range of assessment techniques which are mostly based on the assumption that an individual's personality consists essentially of stable traits which can be measured by tests, questionnaires, projective techniques, etc. In contrast, the "behavioural" approach, as its name implies, is based on the observation and description of the actual behaviour of individuals or families rather than inferences about personality features. While the dichotomy between the traditional and behavioural approaches is quite frequently mentioned, Mash and Terdal express some reservations about it. Each of the two rubrics subsumes a highly heterogeneous set of techniques. As new measures proliferate and assumptions evolve, the distinction between behavioural and non-behavioural tends increasingly to become blurred. Nonetheless, in looking at the results of any given study, one very fundamental question well worth asking is whether the family process under study was actually observed or whether the results are based on tests, questionnaires or other methods which may be affected by the impression (positive or negative) family members wish to make on the researcher, among other considerations. On the other hand, results based on direct observation are inevitably affected to some degree by the presence of the observer.

Another measurement issue is *specificity* of technique. Interviews with families continue to be the most frequent tool (Matarazzo, 1983). As outlined by Mash and Terdal, interviews with families vary enormously in terms of specificity and structure, often resulting in lack of uniformity. Therefore, it is imperative that the issues of reliability and validity receive attention whenever family interview results are reported. Interviews also vary in scope, with some focusing on the entire process of child rearing or family interaction, while others are more specific.

Checklist techniques have been developed in an effort to obtain more objective information about family life. Using standard response formats, these instruments require the respondents to indicate the extent to which descriptions of behaviour apply to their own situation, or whether they agree with a specific opinion statement. These have been used very extensively in the measurement of parents' attitudes toward child rearing and marital satisfaction. Checklist data may be more uniform than interview data, though they do restrict the respondents' latitude of expression. Reliability and validity data are necessary in evaluating each checklist.

Self-monitoring techniques have also been developed to enhance the uniformity and specificity of family responses. For example, Ladd and Golter (1988; see description below) asked families to maintain a log of children's afterschool contacts with friends, the extent to which the parents were involved in arranging each activity and the degree of the parents' supervision of the activity.

Observing family interaction. Observational methods have undeniable face validity, though not all important aspects of family life are readily accessible to the observer. It has been argued that observational techniques are imperative when the researcher is interested in a dimension of family life which family members have not fully conceptualized and remembered; this would be needed for any meaningful use of rating scale or interview methods (Patterson, 1986). The most important difference among observation techniques is the situations in which the observations take place. In some studies, families are observed in their homes (Baskett, 1985), which has enormous intuitive appeal. Nevertheless, their behaviour in the presence of the observer may be atypical. Furthermore, such techniques are very time-consuming. Another shortcoming of *in vivo* observation techniques is that the specific aspect of family functioning one wishes to study may not be evident during a home visit. For example, if one wanted to study the parents' directiveness with regard to their adolescent children's choice of friends, it is quite conceivable that no instance of relevant behaviour might occur even if observers were present in the home for many hours. Observational methods may be most useful for families with younger children, where frequent interaction is needed to regulate the children's behaviour.

In many of the studies reviewed below, family interaction was observed during artificial laboratory situations contrived by the experiments. This permits the experimenter to set the task or topic of discussion. However, the contrived nature of the situation may well influence the behaviour of the family being observed. Also, the fact that a family member displays a particular behaviour in the laboratory may only mean that he or she is capable of displaying that behaviour, not that it is a behaviour typical of that family member in regular home life. It is also important to consider whether the task set up is truly representative of the theory the investigator wishes to validate. Finally, it may require more commitment on the family's part to travel to the laboratory than to be observed at home. This may result in even greater sampling bias.

Sampling. Only certain families will consent to be studied. Their motivation in volunteering to participate is often unclear. The sample of families who volunteer to participate in most studies is probably not fully representative of the community at large. While this is more or less inevitable, the research report should include comparisons of the sample and the population for key demographic variables.

The Parents' Genetic Contribution

It is an undeniable fact that a portion of the parents' impact on children's social competence occurs by means of genetic transmission. There are several strategies for establishing this. One of these is studying resemblances among family members in a given characteristic. If children raised in the same home tend to differ, it is unlikely that the *shared* family environment has had much impact on the attribute, though some aspect of family life which differs from child to child may well account for part of the difference (Dunn & Plomin, 1990; Scarr *et al.*, 1981). Another strategy involves comparing the biological parents of children who have been adopted when very young with their adoptive parents. Twin studies have also been used (and misused) extensively in establishing the degree of genetic transmission. These techniques have unquestionably established that there is a genetic influence in many key aspects of social competence (Rowe, 1989). However, many of the most balanced readings of this literature conclude that the genetic contribution is not so strong that it precludes the possibility of very important environmental influence (e.g. Ahern *et al.*, 1982; Pedersen *et al.*, 1988; Rutter, 1985).

While much of this has been known since the nineteenth century, emphasis on hereditary influences has waxed and waned with each successive generation of psychologists. These fluctuations in the acceptability of heredity as a causal explanation may have occurred because of the many misinterpretations and abuses that have been made of the work of behaviour geneticists. As chronicled by Gould (1981), data about real and falsified heredity influences on behaviour has been used to justify excluding immigrant populations and as a pretext for the most virulent forms of racial prejudice. Given the implications of such data and the potential for their misuse, one might argue that whenever the results of this type of research are in any way equivocal, the assumption of genetic transmission must be made only with the greatest hesitation. In addition to the blatant abuses documented by Gould, such inferences can serve to mistakenly diminish the support accorded those who strive to improve home, school and family environment. This is most unfortunate, since the fact that a certain trait has a large hereditary component does not preclude its being amenable to change by a facilitative environment.

On the other hand, there can also be unfortunate implications and misconstruals of the opposite position, i.e. that the child's behaviour is exclusively determined by the parents. Caplan and Hall-McCorquodale (1985) criticized the widespread phenomenon of blaming mothers for all shortcomings of their children, and catalogued the incidence of such gratuitous attributions of blame in journals of the helping professions. At the very least, such mother blaming may lead to needless feelings of guilt and helplessness.

Within the genetic perspective, the study of socialization within the family is not necessarily a worthless enterprise, though it must be understood in a totally novel way. The parental socialization behaviour is in essence an integral part of the total unfolding of the natural processes of development, rather than the cause of development.

Studies of genetic influence

Most of the evidence available regarding parents' genetic contribution to children's social competence derives from studies in which parents' and children's responses to personality questionnaires were compared (Rowe, 1989). Though somewhat peripheral, the information on such dimensions as extraversion/introversion, sociability and other dimensions is useful. The Texas Adoption Study (Loehlin, Willerman & Horn, 1987) is a good example of research of this type. The subjects were 300 Texas families who had adopted children through a home for unwed mothers. Personality and IQ measures of the biological mothers were available from the files of that home. Of the original 300 families, 181 were available for follow-up assessment 20 years after the original study, when the children were 17 years old. Tests performed on all available data suggested that these 181 were reasonably representative of the original sample. At follow-up time, about 40% of the adoptive parents had natural children of their own as well. On such variables as warmheartedness, dominance, enthusiasm, self-sufficiency, sensitivity, there were some significant though small correlations between natural parents and their biological offspring, with a median correlation of +0.26, compared to a median of +0.01 for parents and their adoptive offspring. According to the authors, these data suggest that about one-fourth of the variance in outcome measures appears attributable to heredity. These results are similar to those of most other major adoption studies, which may be difficult to interpret if adoption agencies try actively to place children in new homes similar to their original ones. While this estimate leaves substantial room for a contribution by environmental factors, no substantial amount of variance can be accounted for by *shared* family environment. Family influence may still be important if parents provide substantially different environments to different children, or treat natural and adopted children differently. There is substantial reason to doubt that siblings within the same family receive the same environment, which was once assumed somewhat naively (Dunn & Plomin, 1990; Plomin & Daniels, 1987).

According to Loehlin, Willerman and Horn, twin studies typically indicate somewhat higher heritability estimates than adoption studies. For example, a study of almost 13,000 twin pairs in Sweden (Floderus-Myred, Pedersen & Rasmusen, 1980) revealed that the correlations of extraversion scores between identical twins was 0.51, compared to 0.21 for fraternal twins, which would indicate considerable heritability. Loehlin, Willerman and Horn interpret the twin findings as still leaving room for considerable environmental influence, while Plomin's interpretation (1990, p. 93) is that the trait of extraversion shows substantial heritability, though less than the hereditability of IQ.

Rowe (1989) analysed data from a large, multisite American study of children's sociometric status; data on siblings, including twins, were available. These data are particularly interesting because, as discussed in Chapter 1, sociometric status is far more pivotal an index of social competence than scales of personality questionnaires. The correlation in sociometric status for identical twins was 0.70, compared with 0.52 for fraternal twins. This would yield a hereditability estimate of 36%, suggesting that 34% of the variance was attributable to shared environmental factors. There are many problems in interpreting these data. For one thing, classmates may tend to confuse twins or perceive them as similar psychologically as well as physically; this may have affected the sociometric ratings. Rowe noted that this estimate of environmental influence is quite high for a twin study.

Given the inherent difficulties in using sociometric data on twins, observational data would be of great value. Plomin (1990, pp. 98–99) reviewed the very limited literature on genetic influences in children's observed social behaviour. Most of these few studies appear to have been conducted by Plomin and his colleagues. One of these involved observing infants' social response to a stranger in their homes, and suggested a degree of genetic influence in the infants' shyness. In another study, schoolchildren's imitation of an aggressive model who hit an inflated clownlike plastic figure indicated no evidence of hereditability. Clearly, research on hereditability of social competence would benefit from greater use of observational measures.

While the evidence for the genetic basis of children's social competence is far from complete, it does provide some corroboration of the existence of an important genetic component, enough to warrant acceptance of Rowe's (1989) suggestion that, in order to study the influence of the family environment on children's social behaviour, one must first partial out genetic influence. Unfortunately, this has rarely been done until now. Dunn and Plomin (1990) have estimated that 40% of the variance in personality is due to genetic factors, 35% to environmental factors *not shared by siblings* and 5% to shared family environment (allowing 20% for error of measurement). In their view, this justifies renewed investment in the study of environmental effects. Eaves, Eysenck and Martin (1989) concur essentially with these estimates, but do not express similar enthusiasm for a new look at the socialization processes. Scarr's (1987) position is that while non-shared environments may well account for a considerable degree of the variance, such individual differences in environment arise in response to the genotypes.

Family Constellation and Birth Order

Adler (Ansbacher & Ansbacher, 1956) emphasized the consequences of basic family composition and birth order for child development, recognizing many years ago that it is "common fallacy to imagine that children of the same family are formed in the same environment" (Ansbacher & Ansbacher, 1956, p. 376). The first-born child is seen as reacting for life to the experience of first being pampered and spoiled, then "dethroned" when the next sibling is born. The first-born enjoys experiences of authority and may tend to dominate peers in later life. The second child, while more accustomed to sharing, may be prone to resist and rebel against such domination. The youngest child is never dethroned, and is usually the most pampered. An only child is one who never shares, and expects to be the centre of attention all the time (Ansbacher & Ansbacher, 1956). While Adler emphasized that there is considerable variation in the ways children interpret and utilize the family environment, the family constellation itself is seen as determining to a large part the ways in which both parents and siblings react to a particular child. To the degree that his speculations are confirmed in actual studies of families, the family constellation can be seen as shaping the ways one interacts with peers and expects peers to behave.

Baskett (1984) observed parents interacting at home with their first-born and last-born 4–8-year-old children. There were some important differences. First-born children directed their behaviours at parents far more than younger siblings, and were more likely to be on the receiving end of negative responses from both parents and siblings. If older-born siblings are indeed more involved in the adult world, and less oriented toward peers, their relations with other children may well be affected. This was confirmed by Miller and Maruyama (1976) in a study conducted with 1,750 California primary school pupils; later-born children received significantly higher sociometric ratings of popularity than first-borns.

Brody, Stoneman and MacKinnon (1982) observed 8–10-year-olds playing a board game with their younger same-sex siblings and best friends (on different days). Their coding system differentiated the social roles assumed in the game: teacher, learner, manager, managed and playmate. Older siblings assumed dominant roles in playing with their younger siblings, but shifted to greater reciprocity when playing with their best friends—or indeed in playing with their younger siblings when their best friends were present. The results of this study indicate that children may be more capable of shifting roles from one context to another than Adler assumed.

A similar conclusion could be drawn from Berndt and Bulleit's (1985) study of the social interactions of 3–5-year-olds at home and at school. They found that older siblings were more dominant while playing at home than children who did not have younger siblings. Conversely, younger children were more often on the receiving end of aggressive play at home. However, these patterns in terms of birth order had little to do with patterns of play at school.

The only child grows up in a home without play companions close in age. One might suspect that this would be mirrored in the children's peer relations. There has been much research on the psychosocial adjustment of only children. Falbo (1987) compiled a meta-analytic review of 115 studies published between 1925 and 1984. The majority of these studies focused on such issues as leadership, autonomy and maturity, and together demonstrate that only children display more characteristics of self-reliance than children with siblings. This conclusion is based on ten studies that included measures of the children's peer acceptance and twenty-four focused on introversion or need for affiliation. The meta-analysis indicated no significant differences between only children and children with siblings in social competence.

However, some recent studies have provided a more in-depth perspective on the social world of the only child. In Bermann and Hartup's (1991) study of preschoolers, only children had fewer disputes with playmates than children raised with siblings, but were found to resolve these disputes more often by fighting. This pattern would seem to reflect lack of experience in resolving conflicts with other children. As well, only children—as well as older siblings—were less likely than others to report having another child they could call a "best friend".

Studying a relatively small sample of forty-two families, Hops and Finch (1985) found a positive correlation between children's social competence (measured by parent, peer and teacher ratings) and the number of siblings, despite the fact that number of siblings was a negative correlate of the amount of attention a child receives from his parents.

Thus, research has provided some support for Adler's contention that family constellation is a major determinant of children's social behaviour. It may be fruitful in the future to study the associations between birth order and such specific relational variables as intimacy and conflict management.

Sibling influences

Readers of the early socialization literature would surely conclude that the influence of the family on a child's social development depended exclusively on the parents, if not only on the mother. However, other members of the nuclear family may play distinct roles in shaping the child's understanding of interpersonal relations. Siblings as "peers at home" may play a particularly important role in shaping peer relations.

Older siblings may provide information and guidance to their younger brothers and sisters about the peer culture. Twenty-six first-born children participated in a study by Volling, Youngblade and Belsky (1991), which explored their peer relations at age 4 years, relationship with a close friend at age 5 years and relations with a younger sibling at age 6 years. The participants' social behaviour with a friend of their choice was observed during a 2-hour laboratory visit. They were observed playing with their siblings during two 1-hour home visits. Subjects who engaged in more conflict with friends were involved in significantly more conflicts with their younger siblings; there were similar findings for co-operative play.

Relations between older and younger siblings involve an inherent asymmetry because of the age difference. Therefore, Furman and White (1991) studied the parallels between twins' relationships with each other and with their friends. Seventy sets of twins were sampled from upper primary schools. There were a number of significant parallels between the twin–twin and twin–friend settings in terms of perceived warmth and exclusivity in the relationships. Thus, both these studies demonstrated some degree of transfer of relational characteristics from sibling to peer relations, though neither described any mediating process which might explain the parallels. Interestingly, while both studies document similarities between the ways siblings relate to friends and to each other, in both cases the sibling relations were less positive and more conflictual than relations with friends, consistent with the findings of previous studies (e.g. Abramovitch *et al.*, 1986). Besides their contribution to knowledge about siblings' influences on children's social competence, both studies are of interest because of their focus on more intimate friendships as opposed to peer acceptance in larger groups. Volling, Youngblade and Belsky incorporated measures of both peer relations and closer friendships. While these data were collected a year apart and from different sources, they confirmed that, when children are with their close friends, their interactions may be very different from their general style of social exchange with peers at school.

Grandparents

Children in most Western societies today see less of their grandparents than their counterparts in other parts of the world, or children prior to the Industrial Revolution. Nevertheless, in a very careful review of literature on the subject, Tinsley and Parke (1984) summarily refuted the contention that grandparents have little influence on the social development of their grandchildren, though the nature of their contribution has no doubt changed considerably. They reminded us that the increased life expectancy in Western countries means that more grandchildren will know their grandparents for extended periods of their development. While this is counterbalanced somewhat by the recent trend for couples to postpone having children until they are well established in their professional careers, there is also a marked increase of children born to teenage mothers, many of whom are unwed, and many of whom urgently require the type of emotional support many grandparents can best provide.

Tinsley and Parke noted that developmental psychology has rediscovered the virtues of grandparenting as part of its quest to extend the range of its theories and research to encompass developmental changes throughout the life-span. They outline both direct and indirect ways by which grandparents influence their children.

Though this is not an important function in most middle-class families, the grandparent can serve as direct caregiver, filling in for parents who find themselves in certain types of special circumstances, such as financial difficulty, illness, wartime separation, etc. Interestingly, grandparents also spend considerable time *playing* with their grandchildren, thus serving as role models of social interaction. They also communicate cultural history, including precepts and taboos relevant to interaction with others. As well, grandparents can serve an important buffering role as mediators or negotiators between parents and their children (and perhaps between the two parents), thus potentially mitigating the effects of parental discord or parent–child disharmony. While Tinsley and Parke described most of these influences in a positive light, they did note that any of these roles can be misplayed, resulting in negative effects on the child.

Many grandparents are invaluable in providing guidance and emotional support to the child's parents, enabling them to better influence their own children in the ways outlined earlier in the chapter. They often duplicate the parents' roles in guiding children's social behaviour, possibly adding additional credence to the parents' advice. Tinsley and Parke contended that the media image of the meddling, overindulging grandparent, though not uncommon, is overstated. They also pointed out that grandparents often provide financial support as well, perhaps sparing the child some of the effects of family financial stress, which may disrupt family life and authoritative child rearing.

Furman and Buhrmester (1985) explored qualities of the relationships between 199 11–12-year-olds and their parents, siblings, grandparents, friends and teachers. Their study was based on Weiss's theory that individuals seek different types of social support from different members of their social networks, which was partially confirmed. Parents were seen as sources of affection and reliable comfort and aid. Grandparents were the second most important source of affection and enhancement of worth. Friends were the greatest source of aid, whereas teachers were a source of instrumental assistance in specific situations. While members of the social network, including grandparents, thus seem to have differential impact on the child's social support, the children nonetheless considered their relationships with their parents as the most important.

Mother–Infant Attachment as Harbinger of Future Peer Relations

Lamb and Nash (1989) delineated a number of different approaches to the conceptualization of early attachment relationships as precursors of later peer relations. Perhaps the most radical version holds that there is a *causal* relationship between the early infant–mother attachment history and subsequent social competence with peers. The skills learned in early interactions with the mother, and the security accrued from a satisfying early mother–child relationship, are applied to later contacts with peers and intimate interpersonal relationships. Many proponents of this model assume that the infant is biologically preprogrammed to interact with the mother in order to achieve satisfaction of primary needs, whereas other social relationships reflect the quality of that first primary relationship. The quality of the mothering provided to the infant determines the quality of the attachment relationship. Very obviously, such weighty contentions have very serious implications for parents and policy-makers, for example, in assessing the possible impact of institutionalized day care environments. Aside from its insistence on the long-term sequelae of early "trauma", the basic properties of this theory, as outlined by Sroufe and Fleeson (1986), are similar to those of systems theory in several respects: (1) relationships are wholes; therefore, relationships, not wholes, should serve as the unit of analysis (see also Hinde, 1989); (2) relationships exhibit coherence and continuity across time; (3) individuals internalize, or form internal representations of relationships; and (4) represented relationships are carried forward and applied to new relationships. Obviously, the unique interpretation of this fourth principle is the major differentiating feature of the attachment precursor theory.

Lamb and Nash described several other implicit models considered by theorists interested in the sequelae of early attachment relationships. Many of the alternate models of attachment are less sweeping in attributing a global causal role to early attachment bonds. For example, Vandell (1985, cited by Lamb & Nash) underscored the bidirectional influences between peer relations and mother–child relations; a sociable infant (i.e. one who is presumed to be sociable by temperament) would be sociable both with peers and with his mother. Similarly, a child of difficult temperament might have troubled peer relations because of his/her difficult temperament, which might also have disturbed early relations with his/her mother.

Bowlby's original writings are not very specific as to the origins of attachment patterns. There has been greater attention in recent years to the mother's social network and life stress as context factors contributing to strained attachment bonds. This is fully consistent with Sroufe's (1985) position that attachment is a relationship construct, heavily dependent on the mother's sensitivity, which is, in turn, heavily influenced by stress in the mother's life. Hiester and Sapp (1991), in their study of 132 mothers and their first-born children, determined that the *combination* of stressful life events (such as loss of a family member, impending separation of partner) *and* the lack of a suitable social support network was associated with patterns of anxious-resistant attachment.

Mother–child attachment patterns are not necessarily stable over time. Bowlby (1988) himself recognized that there are important changes in many families. However, the usefulness of attachment theory does depend on their being a reasonable degree of stability in usual circumstances. Sroufe (1985) maintained that there is adequate evidence of such stability, and that changes in attachment patterns can be reliably traced to changes in the mother's life circumstances. He acknowledged that there is greater change in attachment patterns of infant–mother dyads in economically deprived homes, but that this instability probably relates to the heightened and unpredictable stress experienced by these families.

Some theorists use the term attachment in describing secure, trusting parent–child relationships throughout childhood and into adolescence (e.g. Greenberg, Siegal & Leitch's [1983] work with adolescents). Ainsworth (1991), a pioneer in classic attachment theory, has indicated that attachment relationships continuing throughout development can be seen as a continuation of the early attachment bond and part of the same process. However, she feels that the consequences of a troubled early attachment relationship can be mitigated by positive life experiences, or, hopefully, by successful psychotherapy. Albersheim and Carter (1991) developed a therapeutic intervention for mothers, and have demonstrated the effectiveness of this approach in improving the quality of mother–child attachment.

Z. Rubin and Sloman (1984) referred to a secure "home base" in parent–child attachment as a base the parents can use from which to provide guidance, direction and positive peer play experiences in optimizing *their* children's social development. Implicit in their model is the contention that early attachment by itself—and, indeed, ongoing attachment—may not be the sole determinant of later interaction, but rather a partial cause. Its effects may interact with other aspects of family life in shaping the child's peer relations, possibly constituting a necessary but not sufficient condition for the emergence of satisfying interpersonal relationships later on.

Research on the attachment precursor hypothesis

Measurement of attachment. The literature describes two major means of assessing attachment. The Strange Situation task, developed by Ainsworth and her colleagues (Ainsworth, 1971), is an observational method in which the child's reaction to introduction of an unfamiliar adult and brief separation from the mother are directly observed. Infants are classified according to this method as secure if they attempt to establish contact with the newcomer, but seek to re-engage the mother upon her return. Insecure-avoidant types avoid the parent at the time of reunion, whereas insecure-resistant types display either anger or helplessness. Bowlby's (1969) theory implies that the infant constructs an internal model of the caregiver's availability and his/her own worthiness in relation to situations of this type. In many studies (e.g. Pastor, 1980) inferences are based on such observations of two or more periods of the child's infancy, e.g. at 12 and 18 months. This method has the clear advantage of preventing sweeping conclusions based on reactions to transitional situations of stress. Grusec and Lytton (1988) have pointed out that there are only very limited validity data demonstrating that infants' behaviour in these tasks corresponds to their behaviour at home.

Research findings. The working hypothesis is that securely attached infants will display higher levels of social competence in later years. Lamb and Nash (1989) reviewed the most widely cited studies offered in evidence of the attachment precursor hypothesis. The best known of these is a series of studies conducted by Sroufe and his colleagues (LaFreniere & Sroufe, 1985; Sroufe, 1983), who followed several cohorts of youngsters from infancy to age 5. A variety of assessment techniques were used in follow-up measurements of the youngsters' social competence: direct observation, teacher ratings and sociometrics. The securely attached infants became more socially competent preschoolers according to peer and teacher informants as well as several of the observational indices. Though these results have been widely publicized, other studies conducted in different settings with very similar methodologies have not consistently replicated them. For example, Jacobson et al. (1983) found that insecure-resistant infants actually engaged in more positive peer interaction than securely attached subjects. Fagot and Kavanagh (1990) followed eighty-one youngsters who were classified as either insecure/avoidant or securely attached at age 18 months. In direct observations during playgroups at the same age and at age 27 months, the social behaviours of the two groups were indistinguishable, though teachers rated the insecure-avoidant girls, but not boys, as more difficult to deal with and prone to problems with peers. Pierrehumbert et al. (1986) found that securely attached infants tended (the results were a non-significant trend in the predicted direction) to be more responsive and interactive with both peers and mothers when observed at ages 2 and 5 years.

Elicker's (1991) 10-year longitudinal study is useful not only because of the length of the follow-up period, but also because it explored the effects of early attachment history on a variety of interpersonal competence dimensions. He conducted interviews with forty-six 11-year-olds whose mother–child attachment patterns had been measured at age 1. At the time of these interviews, the children were participating in summer day camps. The interviews focused on the children's understanding of social situations presented to them on film. The transcripts of the children's interview responses were coded for interpersonal sensitivity, positive or negative bias in rating their own peer group, level of interpersonal understanding (see Selman, 1980) and social-cognitive skill (generation of possible outcomes for an unfamiliar social situation). The camp counsellors also rated the children's competence in relating to peers. Participants who had anxious-avoidant attachment histories displayed lower levels of interpersonal sensitivity, and were more negative in their evaluations of their own peer group. Attachment history was unrelated to depth of interpersonal attachment or social-cognitive skill. However, youngsters with a history of secure mother–child attachment were rated by their camp counsellors as more competent with peers. Elicker's study suggests, first of all, that the continuity between early attachment history and later peer relations is not explainable in terms of difference in sociocognitive bias or ability. These findings also indicate that, in attempting to study the sequelae of early attachment relationships, it may be necessary to differentiate the aspects of social competence which may be differentially affected by early attachment.

Lamb and Nash (1989) discussed several important problems with these studies. One problem is their correlational design. Only a few of the studies have involved cross-lagged panel correlations, which permit cautious conclusions about the direction of causality. These cross-lagged panel results yield only partial support for the hypotheses, with some studies suggesting that the *infants's* earlier behaviour in the attachment situation is more predictive of later peer relations than the mother's (see, e.g., Vandell & Wilson, 1987).

Sampling has been another problem. Sroufe's study in particular, and perhaps others, may have maximized the volunteer effect by selected families who were likely to be available for, and willing to participate in, follow-up studies several years later. The studies conducted to test the attachment precursor hypotheses have almost without exception been conducted with very small samples. In the LaFreniere and Sroufe (1985) study, for example, the number of correlations reported far exceeds the number of subjects. These studies are particularly prone to problems of small sample (and selective sampling, as discussed above) because of the intensive and expensive nature of the procedures. Also, many parents are reluctant to involve their infants in studies, visit laboratories or welcome researchers to their homes.

Lamb and Nash's overall conclusion was that available evidence for the contention that mother–infant attachment history is predictive of later child peer relations is equivocal, and that the limited data available have been widely overinterpreted. Lewis and Feiring (1989) reached a similar conclusion, and pointed out that there have been very few studies of these phenomena, in contrast to the widespread attention this theory has received. While their objections are not without foundation, there is a danger in *prematurely rejecting* a hypothesis because of insufficient evidence. Sroufe (1985) argued convincingly that the design of the studies is very sound in a number of respects, especially reliability of measurement and separate assessment of attachment status and social competence outcome. Therefore, it is perhaps safest to leave open the question as to whether research supports the attachment precursor hypothesis until further studies are conducted. Also, secondary analyses (see discussion of meta-analytic methods in Chapter 1) could be very useful, and quite feasible given the availability of data from a dozen or so respectable laboratories in North America and Europe.

Attempts at cross-cultural replication of attachment research have yielded mixed findings. Turner (1991) studied the links between child–mother attachment and social behaviour observed at preschool in a sample of forty English 4-year-olds. Individual differences in the children's social behaviour were related to security of attachment. However, this study investigated links between social competence and *concurrent* attachment patterns, and is therefore not an adequate test of the attachment precursor hypothesis. Grossman *et al.* (1989) reported marked continuity between mother–infant attachment patterns and the social-behaviour styles of German 5- and 6-year-olds. Similar continuity from infancy to age 3 has also been found in Dutch families (van IJzendoorn, van der Veer & van Vliet-Visser, 1987). The predicted effects were not found on Israeli kibbutzim, where attachment to the community caregiver, but not the mother or father, predicts later social competence (Oppenheim, Sagi & Lamb, 1988; social competence of kibbutz children is discussed in Chapter 4). Other attachment data from several countries differ from American findings in several respects. For example, the highly-publicized American findings that maternal employment is associated with insecure attachment patterns has not been replicated in the Netherlands (van Dam & van IJzendoorn, 1991). The distributions of attachment data have been found to be markedly different in Germany, Japan and the United States (Grossman *et al.*, 1981; Sroufe, 1985). Therefore, additional evidence is needed in support of the cross-cultural validity of the attachment precursor hypothesis.

Few studies have been comprehensive enough to establish whether the early attachment history is consistent with other indices of family functioning. Are the mothers of the securely attached infants more empathic than others? What types of discipline do they use as their children are growing? Are their marriages characterized by clear communication and efficient resolution of problems? Are they themselves socially competent in their own friendships, and do the children have access to such competent models? The intriguing theory that has inspired these studies may also have served as a blinder which precludes evaluation of the possibility that attachment is a *partial* predictor of later relationships, or a *necessary but not sufficient* condition.

Attachment patterns caused by temperament

Some research suggests that disturbances in early attachment relationships may be symptomatic of wider difficulties. For example, mothers who themselves lack opportunities for social support *and* are under personal or financial stress *and* have babies with more difficult temperaments *and* provide adverse caretaking may also be those whose infants form insecure attachments. This is one of the scenarios sketched by K. Rubin, LeMare and Lollis (1990) as leading to peer rejection. Much more data about attachment relationships in their broad context are needed in order to determine how typical this scenario is in child development, and which if any of the precipitating factors is the most salient (Grusec & Lytton, 1988).

Posada's (1990) study is of some value in assessing the relative contributions of attachment and temperament, as well as family discord, which will be discussed later in this chapter. His initial sample consisted of 161 3-year-old sons of intact families and their mothers. The mothers completed questionnaires regarding marital adjustment, parental disagreements about child rearing and the extent of the child's exposure to the parents' discord. Rating scales of child temperament were also administered. Ratings of child social behaviour were obtained a year later, when the children were 4 years old.

Both attachment and temperament data contributed uniquely to problematic child behaviour. The interaction of temperament and attachment was also a significant predictor. The three marital variables predicted a significant proportion ($p < 0.001$) of the variance in problematic child social behaviour; this is consistent with previous correlational studies (see below). Interestingly, of the three marital variables, it was the child's *exposure* to the marital discord that made the largest unique contribution to problematic child behaviour. When ratings of attachment security and child temperament were considered together with the parental discord variables, there was a significant improvement in the prediction. The deleterious effects of anxious attachment were greater in the presence of marital discord, as were the effects of difficult temperament.

There are problems in using multiple regression equations like this to establish the relative importance of the predictors when the underlying theory does not dictate clearly the relative importance of predictors. While Posada's study does not implicate any of the variables considered as the direct cause of children's atypical social development, the results do suggest that attachment history, child's temperament and family discord may each contribute uniquely to the causation. More importantly, Posada's findings suggest the possibility of interesting indirect effects and interactive effects among the marital, attachment and temperament variables, which are worthy of further study. It is unfortunate that Posada relied exclusively on rating scale methods, as the mothers' ratings of the child variables may have been affected by their own stress. It is also important to remember that the study was limited to problematic social behaviours and did not include positive interpersonal relationships.

In response to theorists who propose temperament as the origin of attachment patterns, Sroufe (1985) cited data which indicate that an individual infants' attachment to her father is often very different from her attachment to her mother. Obviously, this would be unlikely if temperament was the salient cause. However, a recent meta-analysis suggested that the security of attachments to one parent is in fact somewhat dependent on the security of attachment to another (Fox, Kimmerly & Schafer, 1991).

Parents' Involvement in Their Children's Social Behaviour

There is considerable variation among parents in their involvement in their sons' and daughters' social behaviour (Z. Rubin & Sloman, 1984). Studies on the effects of parental involvement have been conducted with children from preschool age to adolescence, with the most attention devoted to younger children. Different modalities of involvement have been targeted, ranging from participation in the children's physical play to directing their play with peers to emotional involvement and support.

The parents' role as "gatekeeper"

As mentioned in Chapter 1, parents are by no means the only salient models for developing children. Peers are thought to contribute extensively to the youngster's social-cognitive repertoire. Nadel and her colleagues (Nadel & Fontaine, 1989) believe that imitation of peers by very young children is a transitory mechanism on the way to more mature forms of social and communicative competence. Children establish contact and communicate with each other by means of imitating each other's play behaviour at this early stage of development, when they are unable to use language to form relationships. Later on, peers are thought to enhance the child's social-cognitive repertoire and, more specifically, their understanding of interpersonal relationships (Youniss, 1980).

Nonetheless, parents play a vial role in regulating children's access to peers. In Z. Rubin and Sloman's (1984) model, such parental manipulation of peer contact is referred to as "setting the stage" for the emergence of peer relations. Parents may maximize children's opportunities for play with other children in a number of ways. For example, they may take into account the availability of age-compatible playmates when selecting a home and neighbourhood. While their children are young, they may arrange for them to visit other children's homes and invite other children to theirs. They may arrange social contacts for themselves with other couples or parents who have children the same age as theirs. Parents may permit extensive peer contact by the youngster, allow such contact with appropriate guidance and support, or excessively restrict it.

Becoming involved in children's play

Due to increased urbanization, parents' work commitments may remove them from direct involvement with their children for larger portions of the day. While the expenditure of time with children does not ensure the formation of positive bonds, it is difficult to see how a close, supportive relationship can emerge if parents and children do not spend time together (Zigler, 1983). Hops and Finch (1985) found that the total parental attention received by preschoolers was positively correlated with their social competence.

MacDonald and Parke (1984) explored the effects of the parents' direct involvement in playing with their 3- and 4-year-old children. Mothers and fathers were observed interacting with their youngsters at home. Information on the children's social competence was obtained from teacher ratings. Boys rated as popular by their teachers had fathers who were involved but not directive, while their mothers were directive, positive and verbally stimulating. Both parents of popular girls were more involved in their daughters' social play. Fathers' directiveness was a strong negative correlate of daughters' popularity, whereas mothers' directiveness was a strong positive correlate. Thus, in all cases, the parents' readiness to become involved in their children's play was associated with positive peer relations, whereas parental directiveness seems to have more complex effects. It could also be argued that a more friendly, outgoing child engages the parent in physical play and is also held in high esteem by peers. Thus, both the parents' involvement and the children's social competence might be related to temperament.

Parents as facilitators of children's social play

Bhavnagri and Parke (1991) set up a paradigm designed to determine whether parents functioned as facilitators of their toddlers' social play. In one condition, 2-year-olds played with an unfamiliar peer without any adult intervention; the mothers were present but instructed not to become involved. In the contrasting condition, one mother was instructed to help the children play together; the other mother was given the same role later. These conditions were alternated in order to obtain multiple measures on the same group of children. The children's social play was rated as significantly higher in quality during the periods of maternal supervision. Mothers' ability to initiate and sustain interaction, their responsiveness, synchrony and level of positive affect were all positive correlates of the quality of the children's play.

Howe (1992) conducted an interesting study on mothers' influence on early sibling relations. The siblings ($n = 26$ pairs, mean ages $= 3.5$ and 6.2 years) interacted with their mothers during a structured task (tower building) as well as an unstructed "farm play" game. Maternal control and maternal positive behaviour were both stable across sessions. There was a negative correlation between control by mothers and children's negative behaviour. However, the siblings' play was more positive in the absence of their mothers. This last finding is inconsistent with Bhavnagri and Parke's results, which pertain to play among unfamiliar peers. It is quite possible that Howe's study tapped a dimension of maternal influence that is specific to sibling relations.

Russell and Finnie (1990) devised a situation in which the mothers of popular, neglected and rejected preschoolers were given a 5-minute preparatory period before the children were to join a new playgroup. The mothers were told to provide any suggestions, ideas or comments which they felt would be helpful to their children. After the preparation period, the parents were present as their sons and daughters began interacting with two previously unfamiliar youngsters. Once the children had begun playing, the mothers were instructed to intervene to help their children only when they considered it necessary. There was only a slight, non-significant trend for the mothers of rejected children to intervene more extensively than other mothers. However, there were some important differences in the style of intervention. Mothers of popular children, particularly, gave suggestions which reflected awareness of the ongoing group process and group activity. Therefore, the results of this study suggest that the type of advice given is quite important, that parental intervention may only be helpful when it is competent.

Ladd and Golter (1988) asked parents to complete logs at home of their initiation of social contacts for their children and monitoring of their children's behaviour. A total of fifty-three preschoolers and their parents participated in this study. The parents were initiated into this procedure during a telephone interview. The children's social play was observed in their preschool classrooms and was rated by their teachers. Sociometric rating scale and nomination data were also obtained. Parents were found to vary considerably in their management of the children's peer relations. Those who initiated more social contacts for their children tended to have children with more extensive networks of social contacts. "Indirect" monitoring of the children's peer relations, i.e. being generally aware of the child's social behaviour, was positively associated with measures of child social competence, whereas a more direct, domineering style of parent monitoring was a negative correlate. These findings provide further indication that parental direction can have a facilitative effect if executed competently and supportively. Ladd and Golter offer an alternative explanation for the data, speculating that children who are by temperament difficult and aggressive may incur the rejection of peers and lead their parents to more directive forms of monitoring.

Denham, Renwick and Holt (1991) compared the mother–child interactions of forty-eight preschoolers aged 33–56 months with teachers' ratings of the youngsters' peer-related social behaviours. The mother–child dyads were observed in the laboratory while completing several challenging play/learning activities. Mothers who positively structured the play situation for their child had children whose social play was portrayed by teachers as happier than the interaction of children of mothers who failed to provide positive structure. Such positive structuring by mothers was also linked significantly with girls', but not boys', positive social behaviour. On the other hand, mothers' allowance of autonomy was linked with children's assertiveness in general, and with positive social behaviours of daughters but not sons. Denham, Renwick and Holt emphasized the combined effects of these parenting dimensions. The combination of low level of support and high provision of autonomy may be seen as a manifestation of maternal rejection, to which girls may be particularly vulnerable. Austin and Lindauer (1990) videotaped the conversations of four more-popular and four less-popular 5-year-old boys while playing with their own mothers and fathers, the mother and father of a popular boy, and the mother and father of an unpopular boy. The toys were provided by the examiner, but the parents and boys were told they could make anything they wish with them. Parents of popular children initiated more interactions while playing with the children, but these interactions were supportive and encouraging. In contrast, the parents of the rejected children were more directive and controlling. Thus, the results of these interesting small-sample studies provide further indication that the nature of parent involvement must be considered together with its extent. This is consistent with Engfer and Godde's (1991) observation, based on a study of the social networks of thirty-nine German 6-year-olds, that mothers often encourage social contacts if they perceive their children as being shy, but that such prodding is unsuccessful because, in this situation, the mothers goad their children on without empathy or sensitivity to the children's needs and anxieties.

Land and DiLorenzo (1990) used an interview method to assess mothers' and fathers' involvement in the social worlds of their 5-year-olds. The mothers and fathers of 219 children were interviewed regarding the degree to which they initiated social activities for the offspring and monitored their children's social play. As might be expected, mothers were found to be more involved than fathers in their children's play. However, there were no significant links between these parental facilitation behaviours and the children's membership in popular, controversial, neglected, rejected or average sociometric groups. Given the conflicting results of other studies with youngsters of the same age, as reviewed above, one might speculate that significant findings might have emerged had Land and DiLorenzo used a more fine-grained measure of children's social behaviour to supplement the more global sociometrics, or dealt with the full range of social acceptance rather than grouped data.

As with many other aspects of socialization, recent studies attempt to consider the possibility of bidirectional influence. Lollis and Ross (1992) studied mothers' interventions in ongoing positive and negative interactions of very young children ($n = 32$ pairs, aged 20 and 30 months). The mothers were told to react naturally, but not to initiate any of the children's interaction. They found that the mothers' interventions were very closely keyed to the tone of the children's play, suggesting that parental strategies for managing children's peer relations may be related to children's interactive styles.

Parent involvement during middle childhood and adolescence

Van Aken, Riksen-Walraven and van Lieshout (1991) observed parents interacting with their 12-year-olds during an instruction task, and compared the parent–child interaction with sociometric data obtained from the children's peer group and with teachers' ratings of the children's peer-related behaviour. The correlations between the parent–child and peer data were in general quite small, but children who were least liked by their peers and rated as antisocial by their teachers tended to have parents who were rated lowest in supportive presence and lowest in respect for the children's autonomy. These results mirror, albeit weakly, Austin and Lindauer's conclusions based on parent–child conversations of 5-year-olds, as discussed above.

Christopoulos (1991) studied the associations between parent involvement and peer rejection in early adolescence. Participants in the study were interviewed regarding the intimacy of their relationships with their parents and the level of their involvement. There were two age cohorts, approximately 12 years and 14 years. The rejected adolescents were found to be more involved with their parents. There are several possible explanations of these data, but Christopoulos speculated that, by this age, youngsters who do not achieve success with peers seek refuge in relationships at home, whilst their parents, recognizing the children's social difficulties, attempt to compensate for the peer rejection. It must be remembered that Christopoulos's study focused on self-ratings of global involvement, while van Aken and his colleagues rated the quality of parent involvement during structured activities in the laboratory.

Parental overprotection

Oh and her colleagues (Oh *et al.*, 1989) conducted a study on parental overprotection with forty-three upper primary schoolchildren in Vermont and their parents. Based on a review of theoretical writings, they defined overprotection as a combination of infantilization, encouragement of dependency and prevention of independence. Three measures of overprotection were included: direct observation of parent–child interaction (coded for excessive precautions, overly restrictive limits, "moralizing" and correcting), parent self-report questionnaire and child questionnaire. The results were somewhat inconsistent. The observational data showed that overprotective parents had children with lower social self-concepts and lower peer ratings of popularity (though the report contains little details of these analyses). In contrast, parental overprotectiveness as measured both by self-report and child report was marginally associated with positive peer relations. One possible explanation of the latter counterintuitive findings is that overprotective parents and their children may have a poor sense of age norms in child rearing, which would bias their ratings.

In summary, a simple linear relationship between parent involvement and children's social competence is not evident in research to date. There is evidence that certain types of parental involvement can facilitate social development, particularly in studies involving multidimensional measurement of social behaviour and assessment of the quality of the parents' involvement. However, even these data are somewhat incomplete and inconsistent, and require further replication, with particular attention to age and sex differences as well as qualitative distinctions among modalities of parental intervention. On the other hand, available data do not bear out those interpretations of Piaget which call for children to be left on their own in order to develop socially.

Involvement of fathers

While many of the studies just discussed involved mothers only, there has been some attention to the child's need for the father's involvement. Modern Western societies probably permit greater variations in father involvement than most traditional societies in previous eras. Radin and Russell (1983) outlined the direct and indirect paths by which fathers might exert influence. Direct roles include the father as a direct role model or as a disciplinary agent. Fathers may overtly or covertly establish rules and expectations for the child's behaviour, and may provide direct, explicit training to the child on the formation and maintenance of peer relations. Indirect father influences include, first of all, his possible intervention into the mother's behaviour with the child. Fathers often serve the role of gatekeeper—including the child in his own network of social relationships and helping arrange social activities for the child that typically involve fathers (e.g. sport, scouts).

Several of the studies already discussed contain findings useful in evaluating the importance of fathers' involvement, especially those by Zigler (1983) and MacDonald and Parke (1984) in the section on general parental involvement. The MacDonald and Parke study, which demonstrated that fathers' involvement in children's physical play was associated with beneficial outcome, is of particular importance because it provides some insight into possible mechanisms of influence, such as modelling. While father involvement may be important, direct comparisons have sometimes revealed that the mother has more influence on the child's social competence than the father (e.g. Hops & Finch, 1985).

The Parents' Belief System

Parents' belief and attitudes as to how children should be raised have been studied extensively for many years. Palacios (1991) delineated four dimensions of theory building and research regarding parents' beliefs: (1) determining the nature and content of the beliefs; (2) tracing the sources of the beliefs; (3) determining the relation between parents' beliefs and their behaviours with children; and (4) identifying the consequences for children of their parents' ideas. Psychologists and philosophers have debated the connection between thought and behaviour since time immemorial. While many theorists value behaviour that is the product of sound reasoning, they had been compelled to recognize that much of the behaviour of parents—and others—is spontaneous and not related to conscious forethought (Schneider, 1977).

Palacios (1991) proposed a typology for parents' belief orientations, which emerged from his interviews with parents in Southern Spain. *Traditional* parents, often living in rural areas and with little formal education, hold innate beliefs about the origins of their children's behaviours, and believe that they as parents can do little to influence the course of child development. *Modern* parents, in comparison, attribute children's behaviour to the interaction of genetic and environmental factors, and are optimistic about the benefits of a facilitative environment. Finally, *paradoxical* parents hold very optimistic beliefs about the effects of the environment. Belsky (1984) and Janssens (1990) refer to this dimension as internal locus of control with regard to parenting. This is a specific application of locus of control theory (Rotter, 1966), which holds that an internal locus of control orientation—the belief that one's own efforts help determine one's outcomes in life—facilitates psychological well-being (see review by Gilmore, 1978). In the experience of Palacios and his colleagues, the expectations of paradoxical parents regarding the role of the environment are often unrealistic. As a result, these parents do not feel that they can influence their children's development to an optimal degree, and frequently attribute their failures to the shortcomings of other environmental agents.

There is considerable reason to believe that these attitudes are transmitted from generation to generation by a variety of direct and indirect processes (Caspi & Elder, 1988). Thus, the parents' thinking about how their children should be disciplined is affected by many aspects of their own backgrounds, not the least of which is how they were raised by their own parents. As well, parents' beliefs may be the result, not the cause, of a child's behaviour. If parents must contend with a child who is hard to manage by disposition, it might be more difficult for them to maintain an internal locus of control regarding their role as parents.

Mills and K. Rubin studied the beliefs and reactions of parents of Canadian 4-year-olds regarding children's adaptive and maladaptive social behaviours (Mills & Rubin, 1990; Rubin & Mills, 1990; Rubin, Mills & Rose-Krasnor, 1989). Their sample was quite large, consisting of 122 mothers and 67 fathers, who were either interviewed at home or sent a questionnaire by post. Most parents expressed concern about both aggression and social withdrawal, and puzzlement about social withdrawal. They typically attributed both children's aggression and withdrawal to transient states, such as mood, fatigue or frustration, rather than to more stable dispositions. On the whole, the parents indicated that greater directiveness was needed in dealing with children's aggression than with children's withdrawal. A somewhat different picture emerged when the specific responses of the parents of the ten most withdrawn and ten most aggressive youngsters were examined. The mothers whose children were withdrawn during the behavioural observations advocated directive teaching of social skills, though they felt that maladaptive social behaviour was likely attributable to stable child traits. The mothers of withdrawn subjects indicated that they would feel very embarrassed by the children's social behaviour, and feel compelled to intervene actively. The mothers of the aggressive group similarly advocated active teaching of social skills, but indicated that they would not intervene very extensively. The authors wisely note that their data were correlational. Therefore, it would be somewhat premature to conclude that the children's aggressiveness was caused by a lack of parental intervention. It is also plausible that the parents' lack of involvement results from the aggressive children's behaviour, which may have proven refractory to parents' efforts to change it.

Regardless of the causal path, it is interesting to note that some similar findings were reported by Janssens (1990), who worked with the parents of 120 older primary school youngsters in the Netherlands, evenly divided by sex. Janssens' study involved three variables—locus of control regarding parenting (see Chapter 3), children's temperament and child-rearing style. All data on these variables was obtained from questionnaires administered to the parents. Parents who displayed an external locus of control as parents (i.e. who believed that their child's development was largely outside their control) tended to be more authoritarian and less authoritative in their self-reported parenting behaviours. This was particularly true of parents who rated their children as socially maladaptive. As in the Rubin and Mills studies, parents who perceived their children's social behaviour as externalized (characterized by poor impulse control) reported more external locus of control in regard to their parental role. Hopefully, parental beliefs will be incorporated as a variable in longitudinal research that takes into account children's temperament; this clarifies the importance of parents' beliefs very adequately.

Parents' belief orientations may be partly determined by the cultural context. Heath (1983) studied two American communities which are very close to each other, and where most of the adults work at the same textile mill. The population of one of the communities was mostly black, the other mostly white, at the time of the study. In the black community, parents' language contained frequent references to children "comin' up", whereas parents in the white community spoke of "bringin' up" their children. Perhaps the more external locus of control displayed by the black parents reflects the fewer opportunities traditionally offered them, and their relative lack of influence on their own outcomes in life throughout much of recent history.

Child Rearing

Dreikurs and Soltz (1964) remarked that, of all species, the human parent is the only one that does not instinctively know how to raise its young. Advice for parents as to how to raise children is sold at bookstores everywhere, in newspapers, on radio and television. Several generations of researchers studied the "effects" of parents' disciplinary style with little self-doubt, until it was proposed that the parents' discipline might be the *result* rather than the *cause* of the child's behavioural style (see, e.g., Bell, 1968).

One of the major achievements of the spurt of socialization studies in the 1960s was the development of a vocabulary to describe parents' disciplinary styles. For example, Schaefer's (1965) well-known classification of parental behaviour consists of the two dimensions of Love/Hostility (called Acceptance/Rejection by others, e.g. Goldin, 1969) and Control/Autonomy. Goldin (1969), in a review of sixty-four factor-analytic studies, suggested a differentiation between the control styles of Demand-ingness, Psychological Control and Punishment. The use of induction or reasoning in child discipline has been emphasized by scholars interested in empathy and moral development (e.g. Hoffman, 1976). Baumrind's (1968, 1975, 1989) studies featured longitudinal follow-up and multiple measures of social competence. They illustrated quite conclusively that an *authoritative* style of discipline, consisting of clear limits and high expectations within a context of mutual respect and positive communi-cation, was associated with several indicators of social assertiveness and social responsibility, while an *authoritarian* style, characterized by harsh control and lack of mutual respect, was associated with negative social interaction. Some more recent research on these issues is discussed next.

East (1991) studied parents' and children's perceptions of their relationships with each other in connection with the children's sociometric status. A large sample ($n = 290$) of American 12-year-olds and their parents rated their relationships in terms of warmth/closeness (including com-panionship, intimacy and reliable alliance), support and reliable alliance. In general, withdrawn and aggressive youngsters were found to have less supportive relationships with their parents. Interestingly, youngsters with problematic social behaviour tended to provide depictions of the parent–child relationship which were more discrepant from their parents' opinions. Rothbaum (1988) found that maternal acceptance, as assessed by direct observation and interview, was correlated with teacher-reported social competence among 6–8-year-olds even after child intellectual functioning, maternal education and family socioeconomic status were partialled out.

Putallaz and Heflin (1986) observed the interactions of mothers and their 6-year-olds in the laboratory. The children of mothers who were agreeable, positive, emotionally expressive and attentative to their children's conversation received higher ratings of social competence from their classmates. In contrast, unpopular children had mothers who were negative, disagreeable and demanding.

Parental control strategies

Patterson's (1982) model of coercive family process has been subjected to considerable empirical confirmation. This model addresses itself to the origins of deviant, antisocial behaviour. Maladaptive parent–child interaction patterns, including "nattering" (nagging), ineffective limit setting and lack of supervision of the child's behaviour, result in an unintended process whereby the child is reinforced progressively for negative and antisocial behaviour. Such negative behaviour occurs in a variety of settings: with parents at home, with siblings and with peers. If ineffective parental control persists, antisocial behaviours escalate. When they reach extreme dimensions, the child begins to display antisocial behaviour at school. This leads to academic failure and rejection by the peer group. In a final consolidation of the proclivity toward antisocial behaviour, the youngster gravitates to virtually the only available source of positive reinforcement, an antisocial peer group. The research supporting this model constitutes the best evidence available in documenting the direct and indirect impact of parenting practice on children's long-term social adjustment in schools, homes and in the community. Patterson's research programme involves a series of complementary studies designed to validate the model in a systematic way; samples of at least a hundred children have been used in most of the studies. According to Patterson's outline (Patterson, 1986), the first step in the programme was field observation and clinical experience, which were conducted over a number of years at the Oregon Social Learning Center before the model was formally articulated. The next step entailed developing multiple measures of the elements of the model: parents' inept discipline, children's "coercive" behaviour at home (tantrums, whining, etc.), antisocial behaviour, academic failure and peer rejection. Patterson's measures include direct observation, teacher, peer and parent reports, telephone interviews and others. Some of the correlations reported in the first few studies are among the largest of any study reviewed in this chapter. For example, the correlation between inept discipline and antisocial behaviour was 0.63 and 0.64 for two different cohorts (Patterson, 1986). Once the model had been articulated and measures refined, structural equations modelling was applied to test the goodness of fit; data from several cohorts were used (Patterson, 1986). The data were judged to be very consistent with the model—which does not mean that they cannot be consistent with other models, as Patterson hastened to remind us. The research plans include further replication of the findings and additional longitudinal study of their stability. The final step involves experimental manipulation to determine the causal status of the variables. Hopefully, these intervention studies will include long-term follow-up.

Dishion *et al.* (1991) explored the effects of parenting practice on the antisocial behaviours of boys aged 10 at the start of the study; the boys were reinvolved in the study at age 12. Ineffective discipline and poor parenting at age 10 were very significantly associated with gravitation toward an antisocial peer group at age 12 as measured by parent, teacher and self-report. However, several other intervening variables also exerted an important influence, especially academic failure and rejection by peers between age 10 and age 12. Thus, this study provides some support for Patterson's multistage developmental model of antisocial behaviour and illustrates the need for a simultaneous focus on family, peer group and school contexts. The importance of studying these multiple contexts in predicting negative social behaviour and gravitation towards an antisocial peer group by older adolescents was demonstrated in a study by Snyder, Dishion and Patterson (1986).

Olweus's (1980) analysis of the determinants of aggressive behaviour in Swedish adolescent boys aged 13 and 16 years included measures of temperament as well as child rearing. Aggression was measured by peer rating, whilst information on early temperament as well as early rearing conditions were obtained from retrospective interviews with all the mothers and most of the fathers. The results for both age groups were similar, but stronger for the younger cohort. They indicated that several factors contributed additively to the prediction of aggression: power-assertive discipline by both parents, mothers' permissiveness for aggression, mothers' negativism and sons' temperament. There were very high correlations between mothers' general negativism and use of power-assertive disciplinary techniques. Thus, Olweus's path analyses demonstrated the value of considering child-rearing dimensions together with child dispositional variables. In addition, these data are valuable because they suggest that the familial and temperamental determinants of aggression in Swedish adolescent boys are similar to those reported in North American research such as Patterson's. Like many other studies, only males participated.

While parental control strategies appear to be associated with the development of aggressive behaviour, their link with positive indices of social competence and with social withdrawal is less clear. Armentrout (1972) collected sociometric ratings of ninety-six upper primary school-children, as well as the children's perceptions of their parents' child rearing. Popular children reported significantly more parental acceptance than their non-popular peers, whereas measures of parental control technique were unrelated to sociometric status. Hops and Finch (1985) found that neither parental reinforcement of positive behaviour nor punishment of aversive behaviour was associated with peer, teacher and parent ratings of the social competence of forty-two preschoolers.

Pettit and Bates (1989) conducted a longitudinal study with twenty-nine very young children (seventeen boys and twelve girls) in order to explore family correlates of both aggression and social withdrawal. At ages 6, 13 and 24 months, mother–child interaction was observed at home; when the children were 4 years old, observers visited the families near the evening mealtime on three occasions within the same week at each data collection point. Three kinds of events having psychological significance were coded. The results revealed considerable continuity in problematic social behaviour; the correlation between total behaviour problems as rated at age 2 and social withdrawal at age 4 was 0.38, compared with 0.64 for aggressiveness at age 4. Not surprisingly, difficult temperament at age 2 predicted aggressiveness at age 4. While the predictors of aggressiveness and withdrawal were somewhat different, as might be expected, low rates of positive behaviour by the mothers at age 2 were associated with both types of problematic social behaviour at age 4. In addition, mothers' negativity towards her 2-year-old was associated with children's social withdrawal at age 4, and high rates of mother–child conflict at age 2 predicted aggressiveness at age 4. There were no significant correlations between mothers' control events at age 4 and either form of problematic social behaviour at that age, which was unexpected given Patterson's (1982) observation that aggressive children are subjected to constant but ineffective parental control attempts. However, lower rates of social contact events at age 4 were strongly correlated with both aggressiveness and withdrawal. Pettit and Bates concluded that, while ineffective control attempts by parents appear to have some connection with problematic social behaviour, increased attention needs to be paid to the *absence* of positive, supportive behaviours by parents, which emerged as a more salient predictor in their study.

Olweus's work in Norway has focused on victims as well as bullies. Retrospective interviews with the parents of seventy-six 13-year-old boys and fifty-one 16-year-old boys indicated that maternal overprotectiveness was associated with a pattern of victimization by bullies, in combination with paternal negativism and poor identification with the father. The path-analysis results also indicate that temperament played a role: victims were characterized by a somewhat placid and passive response style (Olweus, in press).

Social cognition as a mediator. Pettit, Dodge and Brown (1988) collected data from mothers on the several aspects of their socialization of forty-six 4- and 5-year-olds from distressed socioeconomic backgrounds: exposure to aggressive models, harsh discipline, physical punishment, use of reason during disciplinary encounters and provision of early peer experience. Multiple correlation analysis revealed very significant correspondence ($R = 0.59$; $p < 0.01$) between these family variables and children's social skill as rated by peers and teachers. There was a similar strong correlation between the family variables and children's social problem solving. However, in a multiple regression analysis, these family variables generated no incremental prediction of social skill after measures of the children's social problem solving were entered. This suggests that social-cognitive ability may function as a mediator between parenting and children's social competence.

There have also been other studies of the relation between child-rearing style and children's social-cognitive skills. Brown (1989) assessed the child-rearing practices of the parents of 310 5-year-olds by asking them to indicate how they would respond to hypothetical situations in which their children responded aggressively to a peer. The children were also presented with a series of hypothetical situations in which they were provoked by a peer or wished to join a group of children at play. They were asked to analyse the situations in terms of what their alternatives were in each, and to indicate how they would respond to each situation. The children whose mothers indicated that they would use reasoning rather than power assertion in their discipline displayed significantly more competent response generation and indicated more competent solutions. The effects for fathers' child rearing were less clear.

Clark and Jones (1990) studied the concordance between parents' inductive discipline and children's social communication. The participants were eighteen early primary school pupils and eighteen early adolescents and their mothers. The mothers were asked to respond to hypothetical situations in which their children were hurt by others or had hurt some one. The responses were coded for encouragement of reflection by the children. Children were asked to indicate how they would act in several situations involving peers; the responses were coded for recognition of other children's needs and goals. Mothers' use of reflection-enhancing strategies was a significant correlate of children's person-centred communication for both age cohorts. Significant links were also found for the older cohort only between mothers' reflection enhancement and children's teacher-rated social competence, and between children's person-centred communications and their social competence.

Roth (1991) explored some of the same issues with a small sample of 13- and 14-year-old adolescents, fifteen males and sixteen females. The participants completed questionnaires about their parents' decision making and communication with them. They were also asked to indicate how they would respond to hypothetical and real dilemmas regarding relations with peers. Children who perceived their parents' communi- cation style as authoritative displayed more mature interpersonal negotiation strategies in their responses to both the hypothetical dilemma presented to them and a personal dilemma related to getting along with others.

Burleson, Delia and Applegate (1989) studied mothers' disciplinary and comforting strategies. They focused specifically on the mothers' ability to produce reflection-enhancing disciplinary and comforting measures, and hypothesized that this facilitative style would be associated with peers' acceptance of their children. The mothers were presented with seven hypothetical situations in which children engaged in misdemeanours, and asked to state what they would do in each situation. Sociometric ratings of the subjects, who were fifty-one pupils in their early primary school years, were obtained twice at 1-year intervals. As hypothesized, there were significant though not large correlations between the reflection-enhancing, supportive parenting style and peers' acceptance of the children at both measurement times. There was inconsistent support for a hypothesized pathway of influence whereby mothers' communication style determines the children's communication style, which in turn influences the children's reputations among their peers.

Child behaviour outcomes of intervention with parents. As introduced above, one powerful way of confirming the importance of a hypothesized causal path is to attempt to change the predictor variable and examine the effects on the criterion measure (Patterson, 1986; Schneider, 1989). Johnston (1992) randomly assigned parents of hyperactive schoolchildren to either an experimental condition, during which they received systematic training in parenting, or a wait-list control condition. According to daily telephone reports and parent ratings, there was a marked reduction in problematic aggression by the children in the experimental group. Johnston expects that the observational data, currently being analysed, will confirm these improvements. Similar gains were reported by Pisterman *et al.*, (1989) on both observational and rating-scale measures. These researchers worked with a preschool hyperactive population.

Conclusions: child-rearing effects. The data linking parents' child rearing to children's aggression are quite convincing if not unanimous. While it is not possible to determine conclusively the direction of influence, structural-modelling techniques have corroborated the causal path from parental discipline to children's antisocial behaviour in several major studies. Nevertheless, even these sophisticated techniques cannot overcome completely the obstacles imposed by the correlational nature of the data. Inept discipline could still be either the cause or the result of the child's aggression. These issues should become clearer as interventions to improve child rearing are incorporated into longitudinal studies. It is logical to expect that parents' control techniques contribute more heavily to antisocial behaviour than to children's social success or social withdrawal, since, if left uncorrected, a child's aggressive behaviour is one of the most likely causes of peer rejection (Coie, 1985). This is borne out to some degree by the relative magnitude and consistency of available results. Some preliminary data also suggest an association between parents' disciplinary style and social withdrawal and social competence, but additional work is needed to confirm these links and establish how important they are.

Is child rearing consistent and stable?

If disciplinary style is so important, it becomes equally important to establish how stable it is. The reader of early socialization studies would be left with the impression that parenting practices were invariable across time, age of child, child temperament and child sex. This assumption has been subjected to serious question only in the past few years. The implications of this issue are far more profound than it might at first seem. Researchers and practitioners alike typically assume that the child's home and school environments must be consistent and stable if development is to be optimized. However, as pointed out by Peters and Kontos (1987), this conjecture has never been verified by systematic research. Furthermore, there has been little effort at defining exactly what is meant by continuity, stability and congruity in this regard.

It has been observed that "human behaviour is about as predictable as the weather; . . . long-range forecasting . . . is a risky business" (Cairns, cited by Hood & McHale, 1987). Palkovitz (1987) presented a framework useful for cataloguing dimensions of continuity within the family environment. The first element in his framework concerns the consistency and compatibility of the internal beliefs, assumptions and values of each parent. The second element of the framework is the compatibility of such beliefs, values and attitudes between marital partners. The next dimension is the consistency between the parents' beliefs and their actual behaviour with children; this mirrors psychology's classic deliberations about the dichotomy between thought and action, and is disussed in greater detail below. One must then examine whether there is consistency and congruity between the parenting behaviours of the two partners.

While many traditional perspectives on development assign a clear premium to environmental consistency and stability, the more recent dialectical models (Datan & Reese, 1977; Riegel, 1976) have portrayed developmental change as emerging when a changing individual encounters a changing world. From these vantage points, conflict and inconsistency are thus seen as positive if not necessary forces leading to both the growth of the individual and to societal change. These theorists have been heavily influenced by Marx and became the cornerstone of much twentieth-century Soviet psychology (Dixon & Lerner, 1988). Whether or not one fully subscribes to such dialectical models of development, they do dictate that the virtues of consistency should not be assumed outright. It is possible that a child raised in an "airtight" home, wherein all behaviours and opinions are in close alignment, may be ill equipped to relate to others whose behaviours and convictions are not as predictable or stray from the familiar mould. This does not mean that conflict *per se* is beneficial. According to Hartup (1991), the presence of conflict itself does not seem to predict beneficial developmental outcome, whereas learning to *manage* conflict does.

Palkovitz (1987) presented a useful review of studies on several aspects of consistency and continuity within the family system. Only a handful of studies have examined consistency of attitudes between the two parents of a given child. These studies indicate a generally high degree of correlation between mothers and fathers. There are several possible explanations for this high concordance. First of all, it is quite possible that individuals tend to marry others who share similar opinions and values. Another possibility, perhaps specific to American society, is that mothers tend to teach fathers how to parent, thereby influencing the attitudes of both. Data on the consistency of an individual parents' beliefs are similarly sparse, but do tend to indicate that one's beliefs about children are usually compatible with one's beliefs in other domains. Palkovitz noted several shortcomings in these studies, aside from their limited number. First of all, the simplistic correlational designs cannot help elucidate how the consistency between parents' attitudes, or between the spectrum of an individual's beliefs about various personal issues, comes about. As well, the research instruments tend to measure one's attitudes about children *in general*, not about one's own child, which is not by any means a trivial distinction. While the literature is replete with suggestions that parents' attitudes change as both their children and they themselves develop, the somewhat limited available evidence suggests that parents' child-rearing attitudes remain relatively stable. The best evidence for this is probably a 9-year longitudinal study conducted by Roberts, Block and Block (1984).

The studies on attitudinal consistency reviewed by Palkovitz were aimed at establishing norms of consistency and stability, not at exploring individual differences among families. In a typical study, the correlation between a father's and a mother's scores on a questionnaire of basic parenting beliefs might be 0.50 or 0.60, meaning that there would still be many children growing up in homes where the parents' beliefs are quite incompatible, despite the general trend toward consistency. It would be very interesting to explore the effects of this very incompatibility on the family and child.

The reader familiar with discrepancies between individuals' thought and behaviour in other areas of psychology will have surely predicted by this point that parents' behaviour will often be incongruent with their beliefs and attitudes. Is there any reason to expect greater consistency between thought and behaviour with regard to parenting than as relates to political, social or moral issues? (see Liska, 1975; Schneider, 1977). Results of original studies and of research reviews in this area are themselves conflicting (Palkovitz, 1987), with no apparent pattern to explain why some researchers find that parents' behaviours are congruent with their attitudes, while others are not. While there has been some suggestion that middle-class parents are better able to adjust their behaviours in light of their beliefs, the limited data here are not consistent (Palkovitz, 1987; Tulkin & Cohler, 1973). Palkovitz suggested that empirical findings of inconsistency between parents' behaviours and beliefs are confounded by the fact that these aspects of family life are measured by sharply dissimilar research tools (typically interviews for measuring attitudes vs. behavioural observations). The incongruent results may be attributable to differences in method rather than true gaps between beliefs and behaviour. In any case, it is inappropriate to assume that parents actually engage in child rearing according to the attitudes they endorse in questionnaires.

Dunn, Plomin and Daniels (1986) studied mothers' treatment of pairs of natural and adopted children. Their children were studied at both ages 12 and 24 months, using conceptually similar but unidentical measures, as necessitated by the children's development changes. A combination of direct observation and interview techniques were utilized during home visits. For a portion of the observation, standard play materials (e.g. doll's house, toy xylophone) were introduced in order to permit comparisons of mother–child play under standard conditions. For the remainder of the observations, the parents and children were allowed to play as they would "mutually enjoy". This combination of techniques greatly enhances the value of the study, whose results are likely to be specific to the measurement method employed.

Dunn, Plomin and Daniels found that, *at a given measurement time*, mothers were consistent toward their two children in affection and verbal responsiveness, but quite different in terms of maternal control of the children's behaviour. Furthermore, there was little consistency between the behaviour of mothers toward the same child at ages 1 and 2 years. These issues are important in meaningfully estimating the hereditability of social competence, which requires an assessment of the extent to which siblings receive the same family environment.

Cummings, Zahn-Waxler and Radke-Yarrow (1984) added an additional dimension of interest: the possibility that children of different ages might react differently to the same types of parental behaviour. They focused on children's reactions to anger and affection in the home, following eleven boys and thirteen girls from ages 10 months to 7 years. Individual differences in responding to aggression and affection remained essentially consistent over age. However, at about the time they reached school age, children began to exhibit a marked increase in emotional self-control and in strategies for attempting to change others' expressions of anger. At about the same time, boys became less likely than girls to react emotionally to aggression, a finding often confirmed informally by parents. Children who displayed more marked or emotional reactions to anger were not necessarily those who reacted more intensively to affection.

There are several important implications of these results, which underscore the limits of earlier socialization studies. First of all, the influence of a specific child-rearing style may depend on the child's individual level of emotionality, which itself appears to be quite stable. Thus, not all parenting styles appear to be of equal salience to all children. Furthermore, the impact of a particular style may vary according to the age and sex of the children.

Thus, considerable research effort has been undertaken to determine whether the parents typically provide their children with experiences that are internally consistent and stable over time. Presumably, there are important individual differences among families in these respects. However, the benefits to children of consistency and stability, argued heavily in some theoretical writings, remain largely unconfirmed by empirical data.

Parents' Marital Satisfaction and Children's Social Competence

A systems-oriented approach to the study of family dynamics would affirm that the parent–child relationship contributes to the emergence of childhood social competence, but that the parent–child relationship is affected in a cartesian fashion by the functioning of the marital dyad. There has been considerable attention devoted to these links. Adherents of classic systems theory point out that the child may become actively involved in the parents' squabbles, prematurely forced into an adult role and denied the child's prerogative of innocent neutrality (Christensen & Margolin, 1988; Haley, 1967). Siding with one parent means alienating the other, and the entire process absorbs enormous emotional energy, perhaps at the expense of energy which might otherwise be invested in peer relations.

There are a number of possible alternative causal paths that implicate other child and parent variables. For example, a child who is difficult by temperament may place considerable strain on the parents' marriage. The child's tenacious behaviour may lead to disagreement as to how the children should be managed (see, e.g., Belsky, 1984). Also, the time and energy expended on managing a difficult child may leave the parents little time to enjoy their lives as a couple. There is also a conceivable genetic explanation for the "influence" of marital discord, which would hold that both the parents' litigious behaviour with their spouses and the child's hard-to-manage behaviour are manifestations of an inherited difficult temperament. Modelling is another possible explanation for the effects of parents' marital discord on children's social competence. It is difficult for parents to avoid squabbling in their children's presence, which may indeed lead to the child's imitating the parents' quarrelsome behaviour when engaging in relations with other children.

It has been proposed that preschool children are more intensely affected by marital conflict than their older counterparts for several reasons (Jouriles, Pfiffner & O'Leary, 1988). First of all, preschoolers often have more frequent and more extensive contacts with their parents, resulting in more intensive exposure to their parents' quarrels. They have fewer cognitive resources to help them in coping, and fewer opportunities outside the home to locate alternate adult models and other sources of support. There are also some indications that boys are more susceptible than girls to the effects of marital discord. Several explanations are possible, but perhaps the most plausible is that boys react to conflict at home by aggressive behaviours which are more salient to resarchers and more likely to lead to clinic referral (Emery, 1982).

Older children may be less vulnerable to family conflict. Amato and Ochiltree (1986) conducted a study with over 2,500 Australian schoolchildren. Information on family cohesion and family conflict, among other issues, was obtained by parental interview. The family process variables accounted for 10% of the variance in social competence ratings for a cohort of 8–9-year-olds, but only 4.4% of the variance for a group of 15–16-year-olds. The family cohesion data yielded no significant findings for either cohort.

Family discord: Cause or caused?

The possibility of bidirectionality of influence must be considered in evaluating the role of discordant family atmosphere in impeding children's social development. Having a difficult child may lead to marital discord. However, Easterbrooks and Emde (1988) argue that this causal pathway is not a likely one, citing behavioural intervention studies which show that parents' satisfaction with their marriages did not accompany the improvements in child behaviour that the interventions brought about. Longitudinal studies have also shown that in families where marital discord is associated with maladaptive child behaviour, the marital discord was very evident even before the birth of the child.

Jouriles, Pfiffner and O'Leary (1988) incorporated a variety of measurement techniques in their study of the relationship between marital discord and problematic toddler social behaviour. These included direct observation of mothers' interventions in children's play as well as questionnaires about the children's social play in other situations. The mothers who reported higher levels of marital conflict had children with the most problematic behaviour. This applied to girls and boys alike, in contrast with earlier studies which suggested that this association applied to boys only. Mothers who reported higher levels of maternal conflict tended to interact *less* negatively with their daughters when they misbehaved, but *more* negatively with their sons. These results suggest a complex interconnection between marital discord, disciplinary practices and child's sex. It should be noted that Jouriles, Pfiffner and O'Leary used a sample of normal children, in contrast with several other studies, whch are limited because they involved only children referred for psychological care.

Another interesting pathway by which marital discord might affect children's social behaviour was suggested in a longitudinal study by

Howes and Markham (1989). A relatively large sample of couples had completed ratings of their relationship just before marriage. Of these, thirty-nine parents, of twenty children, had young children at follow-up and were willing to participate in a new study. They rated their marital satisfaction again and completed ratings of their children's behaviour on an attachment inventory. Relationship satisfaction both before and after marriage was found to predict child sociability. Secondly, marital satisfaction before and after marriage predicted children's secure attachment according to parent ratings. While Howes and Markman's sample was not adequate for path analysis, it is possible that the quality of the parent's relationship affected children's social development through parent–child attachment. While this study is limited both by its small sample and reliance on a single source of data (parent ratings), it does offer an interesting hypothesis for future corroboration.

Pettit and Sinclair (1991) studied the associations among family harmony, children's social perception and children's social competence, using a large sample ($n = 165$ families) of parents with 4- and 5-year-old youngsters. Families were observed at home on two occasions for a total of 4 hours. The children's social competence was rated by their teachers 6 months later. As a measure of social perception skill, the children were asked to recall the important points of twenty-four videotaped vignettes depicting a negative social event such as a rebuff by another child. The authors hypothesized a path model whereby family harmony affects children's social perception, which in turn affects their social behaviour. There was some support for this model, though many of the correlations were quite small. Teacher ratings of social competence were predicted by children's competence in social perception, which was in turn predicted by low levels of family *dis*harmony. The opposite emerged for predictions of social withdrawal. Ratings of withdrawal were associated with lower levels of social perception, which was linked with higher levels of family *dis*harmony. Withdrawal was also directly linked to lower levels of family harmony. Children's aggression was directly correlated with family *dis*harmony, and did not appear associated with social perception skill.

Gottman and Katz (1989) proposed a very interesting path model, whereby marital discord affects children's peer interaction by causing physiological changes in both parents and children and disturbing the children's regulation of emotion. A relatively small sample of fifty-six Illinois families with 5-year-old children were subjects. This sample size is not surprising when one considers the intensity of the measures, which included direct observation of parent–child interaction as well as children's social play, cardiac interbeat interval, pulse transmission to the finger, skin conductance and general somatic activity. Unfortunately, the sample was positively skewed, with a disproportion of couples with happy marriages. Nevertheless, there were some interesting results. First of all, the results fit the model quite well. In addition, children's levels of play were significantly correlated ($r = 0.45$, $p < 0.01$) with marital satisfaction, which was also correlated with the children's level of dopamine ($r = -0.39$, $p < 0.001$).

Marital discord and child rearing

Strain in the parents' relationship may lead to disruptions in their disciplinary practice, which in turn affects the child's social behaviour and peer relations. There are a number of studies which provide evidence of this pathway. For example, Snyder *et al.* (1988) conducted a more detailed exploration of the links between self-reported marital distress and parents' ratings of their children's behaviour on several variables including social skills. A total of 110 couples participated, about one-half sampled from the general population, one-fourth identified on the basis of their children's known psychiatric problems and the remainder sampled from couples engaged in marital therapy. Their children represented both sexes and a wide age range. Global measures of marital dysfunction were found to be unrelated to ratings of children's social skills as well as most personality traits. However, conflict over child rearing and dissatisfaction with children were significant correlates of lower ratings of children's social skill, expecially at younger ages. The authors interpret these findings as offering little support for the family systems model of behaviour problems. These data provide further evidence that disciplinary procedures may be a mediating variable between family stress and problematic social behaviour in children. Therefore, in designing new studies, such factors as marital discord and child rearing might be considered together and in combination with other potential influences such as the nature of the child's social behaviour with which the parents must contend.

Divorce and children's peer relations

There has been considerable research on the social relations of children from single-parent families. Emery (1982) observed that there are three major shortcomings in research on the effects of divorce: biased sampling, usually from a clinic population; non-independent data, e.g. having the mother rate both the divorce experience and the child's social behaviour; and poor reliability and validity of measures. As most of the studies discussed below will illustrate, there has been excessive reliance on ratings by individuals in the child's environment who are well aware of the divorce, which may colour their ratings. McCord (1990) discussed several other methodological challenges. Most importantly, it is difficult to separate problems which might have been caused by divorce from problems associated with poverty, disorganization or urban clutter, since a disproportion of single-parent families must contend with such conditions. Nevertheless, there are certain obstacles associated with being a single parent, especially having less help in rearing children and diminished ability to become involved in their lives.

While many assume that the single-parent situation has deleterious effects on children's social adjustment, this is not necessarily the case. Deutsch (1983) conducted an observational study of thirty-five first-born and only children aged 3–5 years. The children hailed from one- and two-parent families of lower socioeconomic status. Both boys and girls from one-parent families displayed *greater* social participation and more advanced levels of play. This study is limited by its small sample, though the use of observational methods is a positive feature.

Results from several other studies are in the opposite direction. Weinraub and Ansul (1985) conducted an observational study which illustrated that young children from single-parent homes were more fearful of strangers than children from two-parent homes. Both divorce and socioeconomic status were included in a study of 115 American kindergarteners conducted by Guidubaldi and Perry (1984). The youngsters' peer relations were rated by their teachers using two well-validated rating scales. Single-parent status predicted ratings of lower social competence on all measures, even after socioeconomic level was considered.

Steinberg (1987) compared adolescents from single-parent, stepparent and intact family backgrounds in terms of their susceptibility to peer pressure to join in antisocial behaviour. The adolescents were asked to indicate what they would do in a series of hypothetical situations. Steinberg found that youth from both stepparent and single-parent families were more likely to succumb to their peers' exhortations to deviant behaviour.

Recent research efforts have recognized that a separation may or may not be a positive situation, depending upon how it is handled by family members. Heath and MacKinnon (1988) explored the social adjustment of the 8–11-year-old children of eighty mothers who had sole custody of them for at least a year. Social competence was measured by means of a child self-report checklist. Children also rated their parents' disciplinary practices. On the whole, the single mothers were lax with their sons, though not with their daughters. Higher levels of firm control by mothers was a very significant predictor of higher levels of social competence for boys (not a single male subject above the mean in social competence had a mother perceived as lax), but lower levels of social competence for girls. These results, like those of Hetherington and her colleagues discussed below, illustrate the importance of considering sex differences.

The effects of divorce may also depend on the support network available to the child or family. Taylor, Hurley and Riley (1986) studied the social experience of 129 preschoolers from single-parent Texas families of Hispanic origin. In families who were most assimilated into the English-speaking community, the children displayed restricted social experience and more limited understanding of social situations. Those raised in more traditional Spanish-speaking backgrounds displayed more adequate social adjustment. The authors attributed their findings to the availability of supportive individuals in the extended family network characteristic of Mexican–American culture. In another study conducted in Texas, but with youngsters of varied cultural backgrounds, Phelps and Huntley (1985) examined the behavioural adjustment of ninety-four 6–10-year-old oldest children who were living with their divorced mothers. The *quality* of the family's social support network was found to be strongly associated with children's behavioural adjustment as rated by the mother.

According to Emery's (1982) review, it is the divorcing parents' conflict, rather than the fact that they are separated, which appears responsible for children's problems. In a study of forty-four early adolescents whose parents had recently divorced, McCombs, Forehand and Brody (1987) found that when the divorced couple continued to interact regarding issues other than parenting, such stressful interactions were associated with lower levels of social competence at school as rated by teachers.

By far the best data available on the long-term effects of divorce are from a longitudinal study by Hetherington, Cox and Cox (1985). This study is of considerable value because of its longitudinal design and use of multiple outcome measures for both dependent and independent variables. Unfortunately, the sample consisted almost exclusively of middle-class parents, precluding generalization of the findings to other socioeconomic strata. Nevertheless, there are many appealing features. In contrast with comparisons of children of divorced and non-divorced homes at a single point in time, Hetherington and her colleagues studied the sequence of family changes which may occur following divorce. Measures were obtained at 2 months after divorce, 1 year, 2 and 6 years from the seventy-two families undergoing divorce and a matched non-divorcing control group. Furthermore, multiple measures were used: peer nominations, teacher ratings, child self-ratings, home observations of family interaction and observations of social behaviour at school.

By 6 years after divorce, daughters in the care of their mothers who had not remarried reached the same level of adjustment as daughters of intact marriages. In contrast, sons in the same circumstances were showing more externalizing behaviour than controls, and, according to some measures, greater social withdrawal and lower social competence. Things were very different if the mother had remarried. For the first 2 years after remarriage, both sons and daughters displayed higher rates of externalizing behaviour than controls. However, after 2 years, the son's behaviour settled down, while the daughters displayed many social relations problems.

Hetherington's results demonstrate the limited value of earlier studies with narrower scopes. An interesting study by Heath and Lynch (1988) confirmed that time since divorce by itself is not a correlate of children's peer acceptance, but the combination of time since divorce together with mothers' control strategies and use of social support explained a significant portion of the variance. In any event, it appears appropriate that contemporary researchers have become more interested in finding out *when* and *how* divorce affects children's peer relations, rather than just *whether* it does.

Peer relations as a protective factor. Kunze and Brandt (1991) determined that positive peer relations may be a strong asset to children undergoing the experience of parental divorce. Questionnaires were administered to ninety-two children ranging from 5 to 17 years old about their attitudes towards divorce and towards peers. Children who indicated more positive attitudes toward divorce and who reported greater use of friends for support received higher ratings of social adjustment from teachers. Similarly, Roseby and Deutsch (1985) found that group social skills training was more beneficial to primary schoolchildren whose parents had recently divorced than either a discussion group which focused on issues related to divorce or no treatment. This improvement was limited to a measure of acceptance of the parental separation, possibly a result of having included empathy training in the intervention; none of the experimental conditions engendered reduction in depression or psychopathology.

Conflict Between Parents and Children

Disputes between parents and children are often seen as normal aspects of family life. Larson's (1983) analysis of adolescents' daily experiences indicated that they regard family experience as somewhat restrictive and negative relative to their experiences with friends, though time spent with families was associated with several indices of positive psychological adjustment. While learning to cope with disagreement and conflict has been seen as facilitative of children's adjustment, Hartup (1991) noted that conflict has been discussed far more than it has been studied. Putallaz (1991) analysed videotapes of mothers interacting with their 6-year-old children in a laboratory situation. Each of the 835 disputes were coded for instigation and resolution. It was clear that children who are more popular with their friends are involved in fewer disputes with their parents, suggesting continuity between family and peer systems. Noack (1991) asked ninety-two German adolescents to complete a questionnaire assessing harmony in parent–child and in friendship relations. Contrary to popular conceptions of adolescence as a stormy period in development, most of the ratings of family and friendship indicated considerable harmony. However, perceptions of family life as harmonious were significantly correlated with perceptions of harmony in relationships with friends, confirming the hypothesized continuity.

Modelling

Social learning theorists contend that much of the child's acquisition of social competence occurs by means of imitation of adult and peer models (see Chapter 1). However, this does not necessarily mean that children are expected to be carbon copies of their parents. Many variables are thought to mediate the processes of modelling (see Grusec & Lytton, 1988). Modelling may depend, first of all, on characteristics of the model. As laboratory studies have demonstrated, children may not be equally inclined to imitate all adults and all parents. They may somehow select the models with whom they feel a particularly close bond or perceive as nurturant. They may also more extensively imitate models who are themselves socially successful and influential (Grusec, 1972; Yando, Seitz & Zigler, 1978). Modelling may also depend on a number of situational factors. Adult role models (father, mother, teacher, scoutleader, clergyman) may display behaviours that are highly consistent with each other and with the behaviours modelled by peers. However, these adults may well model conflicting behaviours. Nor is it necessarily true that each adult model will display the same type of behaviour each time he or she is placed in a similar situation. Social learning theorists have said little about the rules governing imitation when models are incongruent with each other. Obviously, the probability of the child's imitating a parental behaviour may be greater if the child has frequent opportunity to observe it. Imitation processes cannot be invoked to explain the correspondence between parent and child social behaviours if the parents' modelling occurs in social situations that do not include the child. Finally, imitation may depend on the particular behaviour to be modelled. Behaviours differ in their salience to the child. Some emotionally-laden behaviours, such as angry or aggressive ones, capture the rapt attention of every one in their proximity; they are unlikely to be overlooked by a child who is learning how to interact with others. Obviously, if parents and children resemble each other in terms of social competence, it does not necessarily mean that modelling processes are responsible for the similarities. Common genetic make-up, cultural experience or child rearing could explain their resemblances as well. However, if children are found to be dissimilar to their parents, it is reasonable to dismiss modelling as a method of influence.

A host of early studies attempted to illustrate that parents and children were similar in terms of such traits as sociability, extroversion/introversion and aggressiveness. Typically, the researchers administered a questionnaire to both parents and their adolescent sons and daughters. These studies are well summarized by Maccoby and Martin (1983). They correctly summarize the overall picture portrayed by these studies as disappointing. Most authors report only marginally significant findings. However, these studies are limited for several reasons. For one thing, adolescence is a period in which there is a decline in adult influence according to some (but not all) authorities. Secondly, the dyadic relationships within the family are usually considered in isolation, i.e. the similarity between fathers and sons is considered without reference to the ratings of the mother. Most importantly, the many mechanisms which may mediate the influence of models are not contemplated in this literature.

Some recent efforts have employed more comprehensive research designs and more sophisticated analysis strategies. Strassberg and Dodge (1990), for instance, studied the link between parental conflict resolution strategies (with both child and spouse) and children's aggression and peer acceptance with a large sample ($n = 219$) of two-parent families whose 5-year-old children were not diagnosed as disordered in any way. Conflicts within four relationships were studied: mother–child, father–child, mother–father and father–mother. Consistent with the results of the studies summarized by Maccoby and Martin, they found a marginal significance between parents' aggressive conflict strategies and children's level of aggressiveness. However, parental aggressiveness was a very significant predictor ($p < 0.001$) of the children's social acceptance. Thus, parents' aggressive behaviours may have deleterious effects on the child's peer status for reasons above and beyond the child's aggression. One possible implication is that agonistic behaviour in the home may lead to other problem behaviours in addition to aggression, or to feeling states or self-presentation styles which are deleterious to peer acceptance. Strassberg and Dodge also speculate that families characterized by more belligerent styles of conflict resolution may become known and stigmatized in the community, leading to rejection of the children by their peers. It is also important to note than the absence of a large correlation between parents' and children's aggressiveness in such studies minimize the claim that children's aggressive behaviour generates aggressiveness in their parents.

The results of Strassberg and Dodge's study suggest that modelling may have a small but perhaps important effect, but that many other factors must be considered. The authors note several features of the study that may have attenuated the findings. First of all, parents were asked to rate their own conflict resolution strategies. No direct observation of parental conflict was undertaken and individuals may well minimize their own aggressiveness in self-report measures. In comparing this study with others, one must take into account the fact that the normal population studied may reveal less pronounced effects than a population of children known to display problematic aggression.

MacKinnon, Curtner and Baradaran (1991) conducted a cross-contextual analysis of aggressiveness in 7–9-year-old boys and their mothers. The sons' aggression at school was highest in cases where there were indications of aggressiveness in the mother–son dyad *and* there was a high concentration of aggressive youngsters in close proximity at school. Univariate analyses were not productive in identifying familial predictors of classroom aggression. Therefore, this study suggests that it may be productive to considering parental modelling together with "triggers" in the peer culture or school environment.

Social Cognitions of Parents and Children

Reinhold and Lochman (1991) conducted an interesting study with sixty-three teacher-identified aggressive and non-aggressive primary schoolboys and their mothers. The boys were shown twelve videotaped vignettes depicting boys being provoked by peers and reprimanded by teachers. The mothers were interviewed at home and shown a series of vignettes in which the mother was being provoked by her husband or son, or reprimanded by a male authority figure (a superior at work or policeman). Mothers of aggressive boys perceived more negative intent in non-hostile situations involving mothers and sons. They also reacted more strongly and negatively to the vignettes in which the women were being rebuked by authority figures, not giving the authority figure the benefit of the doubt. Reinhold and Lochman concluded that the social information-processing biases of aggressive boys may well be learned in the family. Their contention is bolstered by similar findings by MacKinnon, Curtner and Baradaran, whose study is described above. They reported a significant correlation between hostile attributional bias in mothers and sons.

The Affective Tone of Family Life

The majority of theorists have assumed that it was the parents' behaviours rather than their moods or feeling states, that are reflected in children's social competence. There has been recent attention to the affective climate of the family, with particular attention to two aspects, anger and depression. Coyne's (1976) interpersonal theory of depression emphasized that individuals who are in depressed moods tend to depress other persons in their immediate environments. Therefore, significant others who might serve as sources of support or guide the individual towards more social involvement are discouraged from doing so, avoid the depressed person, and thus aggravate the feelings of depression and despair. While most attention has been devoted to the influence of depression on spouses, there has been more interest recently in the impact of depressive moods on one's children; useful reviews of this literature have been presented by Downey and Coyne (1990) and Gottlib and Lee (1990). Since depression affects many more females than males, it is the sequelae of the mother's depression on her children that is studied most frequently.

The effects of depression on one's children might be direct or indirect. The company of a depressed mother may cause depression in children, which restricts their social interaction and makes them less attractive as companions to other children. Another theory holds that a depressed mother may find it difficult to be positive, warm and consistent with her children, and that children whose needs for nurturance are not met bring their resentments to their relations with others (Bromet & Cornely, 1984; Gottlib & Lee, 1990). Gottlib and Lee believe that the effects of depression may vary according to the child's age at the time of the mother's depressed state or mood. If the mother is depressed while the child is very young, this may preclude a secure mother–child attachment bond (Radke-Yarrow *et al.*, 1985).

Lee and Gotlib (1989a,b) studied the functioning of seventy-five mothers and their 7–13-year-old children. Three groups of participants in the study were recruited from the outpatients of medical and psychiatric clinics: (1) dyads in which the mother was receiving treatment for depression; (2) dyads in which the mother was receiving treatment for another type of psychiatric disorder; and (3) dyads in which the mother was receiving treatment for a non-psychiatric medical problem. A control group of mother–child dyads in which the mother was not receiving medical or psychiatric treatment was recruited through advertisements in local newspapers. Both mothers and children were interviewed by members of the research staff. The more structured Child Behaviour Checklist was also used for mothers' ratings of their children's behaviour. Compared to the three other groups, the children of depressed mothers displayed higher frequencies of a variety of symptoms, including anxieties, fears, sadness and somatic complaints. However, neither parents nor interviewers indicated that the children had social relations problems.

Rubin *et al.* (in press) followed the social adjustment of the children of twenty-one depressed and twenty-two non-depressed mothers from ages 2–5 years. Security of attachment was assessed using the Strange Situation techniques when the children were 2. When they were 5, the children were observed during free play with a familiar peer. Socially withdrawn play was associated with both maternal depression and insecure mother–child attachment.

Emotional regulation in the family. Christensen's (1974) model of interpersonal coping maintains that some individuals grow up with tendencies to over-react to specific expression of emotion—anger, joy, sadness, indifference, etc. Family experiences are seen as contributing to the emergence of these patterns of over-reaction. In the presence of such troublesome emotional stimuli (i.e. expression of these emotions by significant others), one may become "frozen" and anxious and react in ways that are totally disproportionate to the situation at hand. While Christensen and colleagues have studied these reactions most extensively in adults and adolescents, they are thought to occur extensively in children as well.

Building and maintaining a satisfying interpersonal relationship requires appropriate regulation and expression of emotion. Family life is often intensely charged with emotion, and may shape the child's emotional expression in other interpersonal relationships. Butkovsky (1991) studied patterns of emotional expression by the parents of sixty-one 5- and 6-year-olds, who watched their children play a game in the laboratory. The game was rigged to ensure that the child won the game on the first trial, then lost twice, then won on the last attempt. Sociometric measures had previously been collected in the children's classrooms. Parents' expression of positive affect was related to higher peer acceptance of the children by classmates, especially for girls ($r = +0.56$, compared with $+0.20$ for boys). Parents' *appropriate* affect was strongly correlated with peers' acceptance of boys ($r = +0.42$, compared with $+0.14$ for girls). There were no significant correlations between parents' negative expression of emotion and children's peer acceptance. Similar ratings of the children's emotional expressiveness were made, and were not significantly related to peer acceptance. Parents' and children's positive emotional expressiveness were not related, nor were parents' and children's negative affect. However, boys' appropriate expression of affect was positively related to appropriate expression of affect by both their parents, whilst girls' appropriate expression of affect was related to their mothers'.

In a similar vein, Carson (1991) studied the expressions of affect during parents' play with popular and rejected 4- and 5-year-olds. In a laboratory setting, the parents and children were taught the "hand game", the object of which was to grab the other person's hands before they could be pulled away. Parents of sociometrically rejected children displayed more anger and more affective neutrality. The parents of the popular children showed more positive affect, such as happiness and laughter. Of course, it is possible that the parents react to more positive cues from their popular children and more negative cues from the rejected offspring. In any case, these initial explorations indicate that emotional expression may constitute an important part of the family's contribution to children's social competence.

Peer Relations of Children from Abusing Families

As mentioned in Chapter 1, the effects of the environment may be greater at the extremes than across the full range of environmental variation. The recent worldwide concern about child abuse has led to increased research on its effects, including its effects on the abused child's peer relations. Salzinger, Feldman, Hammer and Rosario (1991) studied the peer network of eight-seven non-referred 8–12-year-old children who had been physically abused according to the New York State Child Abuse Register. The results were quite clear. Abused children were of lower social status, were rated by peers as significantly more aggressive and less co-operative than eighty-seven matched non-abused classmates. Most of the findings were significant beyond the probability level of 0.001.

In a more detailed study, Kaufman and Cicchetti (1989) examined the peer relations of abused and matched non-abused primary-school-aged children in a residential summer camp. The abused group represented various types of maltreatment, including neglect, i.e. lack of supervision, nutrition or medical care, emotional abuse, such as insult, and physical injury. Most of the abused participants had experienced more than one of these forms of maltreatment. The children's social behaviour was rated by peers and camp counsellors. The social play patterns of the abused children were far more maladaptive than the non-abused comparison group, characterized by greater social withdrawal and less prosocial behaviour. Children who experienced all three forms of abuse, including physical maltreatment, were rated as extremely high in aggressiveness in particular. The authors based their hypotheses on attachment theory, though other explanations, including faulty modelling, could be invoked. They noted that their findings were very similar to those of other studies conducted with children of the same age as well as younger and older samples. In a similar vein, Fantuzzo et. al. (1991) compared three groups of abused preschoolers with a normal control group. The most severe group were victims of physical and verbal abuse so severe that it required their removal from home to a special shelter. This group displayed restricted social activity (as rated by parents) and impaired social self-esteem, both significantly lower than control children and children who had experienced abuse but who were not removed from their shelters.

Klimes-Dougan and Kistner (1990) observed the social play of eleven abused and eleven non-abused preschoolers at a daycare centre. The observations were conducted during outdoor play by observers who were not informed of the subjects' status (abused or non-abused). The abused youngsters were much more inappropriate in their responses to other children's distress (crying, screaming, expressions of dismay); they either withdrew from the situation or reacted aggressively when it would be appropriate to comfort their peers. The abused participants also displayed more aggression and more withdrawal, and thus caused peers' distress more often. Some other studies have indicated that while the *overall rate* of participation in social play is about the same for abused and non-abused preschoolers, the abused youngsters' play is atypical and indicative of discomfort when they are approached by others specifically (Howes & Eldredge, 1985; George & Main, 1979). Such situation-specific differences could be easily missed by a casual observer or a researcher using an observational grid that did not include sequence analysis.

The consistency and strength of the findings regarding the social competence of abused children lend some credence to the contention that the effects of the family environment are more pronounced at the extremes, or at least at the negative extreme. It is not as easy to ascertain whether there is a type of facilitative family environment associated as strongly with extremely positive social development. However, there has been recent interest in the study of socially gifted children (Abroms, 1985; Schneider, 1987). Since the study of gifted children often includes the study of their family backgrounds, relevant data will hopefully become available.

The Family Within the Community and Culture

As discussed in Chapter 1, Bronfenbrenner and his contemporaries sensitized the research community to the family's ongoing interchange with societal forces. Parenting is affected in many ways by the emotional health of their parents and their ability to deal with stressful life events. An ingenious study by Dumas (1986) illustrated this very clearly. Fourteen mothers who sought professional guidance for child behaviour problems kept logs of their contacts with significant others. It was determined that the mothers were significantly more aversive with their children on days in which they had experienced aversive interactions with adults outside the family.

Economic hardship

Galambos and Silbereisen (1987) demonstrated the interactive effects of family income change and parental acceptance on the social adjustment of adolescents in Berlin. Their sample consisted of 110 adolescents and their families, who were studied longitudinally. In families that experienced a drop in income, those adolescents who felt unaccepted by their parents tended to gravitate towards an antisocial peer context. No such tendency was apparent for youths who felt accepted by their parents. There are several interesting features of this study. First of all, economic hardship is considered together with the affective dimensions of family life. In addition, is was determined that loss of family income was not associated with an overall increase in perceived peer acceptance. This indicates that it might be profitable for researchers to consider not only level of peer acceptance, but also characteristics of the peer associates who are making inferences about a group member's acceptability.

Economic hardship during the Great Depression in the United States occurred while the discipline of psychology was in its early childhood. Longitudinal studies were already underway, including the Oakland Growth Study, which followed 167 California children who grew up in the worst years of the 1930s. Data on income from 1919 to 1933, rating scales of parenting behaviour, self-reports of social competence completed during early adolescence, and mother reports of the children's behaviour, were carefully compiled. Father rejection was associated with lower social competence among girls, but not boys. Elder Jr., Nguyen and Caspi's (1985) interesting path analysis suggested that economic hardship led to the father rejection, which in turn led to the girls' self-rated lack of social competence. In contrast, while the boys became more oriented to the peer group rather than the family, there was no evidence that fathers' behaviour was related to boys' social competence. Economic hardship did not seem to have had similar effects on mothers' treatment of their children.

Family mobility

There has been an increase in population mobility in many countries during recent years. When a family moves, the child's peer network is uprooted as well. This was systematically verified by Vernberg (1990), who studied the peer relations of thirty-six early adolescents who had recently moved into a community and thirty-seven residentially stable peers. Vernberg used observational techniques, maternal reports and self-reports of the children's social interaction. Those who had moved had significantly fewer peer contacts, and those contacts were rated as less intimate, than the residentially stable group. Boys who had moved were also more likely to be actively rejected by peers than boys in the control group.

Social support

Where the parent has resources to cope with a crisis, there probably are fewer disruptions in regular routines for the child, pleasurable activities together and positive home atmosphere. The child may learn how to cope with stress; this coping ability may be mirrored in his management of stressful aspects of concurrent or subsequent interpersonal relations. Therefore, parental social support may be an important indirect influence on children's peer relations. Barrera (1986) distinguished among three broad conceptualizations of social support: social embeddedness, perceived social support and enacted support. Social embeddedness refers to the links an individual has with supportive individuals in their social environments, enabling the individual to experience a sense of connectedness, or, in S. Sarason's (1984) terms, to perceive "a psychological sense of community". Social isolation and alienation are its opposite. Barrera (1986) observed that measures of social embeddedness typically assess only the presence or availability of such potentially helpful significant others, not whether or how they actually provide assistance. This contrasts with the notion of perceived social support, which is based on the adequacy of the support received, or one's satisfaction with it, rather than the mere presence of potentially supportive individuals in one's social network. Finally, enacted support refers to the actual behaviours involved in supporting another person. Barrera implores researchers to make explicit their use of the term social support and to select measures appropriate to the concepts they use.

Krantz, Webb and Andrews (1984) asked the parents of forty-two American 5-year-olds to list the total number of contacts they had with their own friends over the previous 2 weeks, as well as their involvement in community activities. The parents also rated their satisfaction with these contacts. Each of these indices was associated with child social competence as determined by sociometrics, observations and teacher ratings. However, in a study of twenty-five Canadian and fifteen American children with externalizing disorders, Johnson and Pelham (1990) found that reported stress in the mothers' lives was correlated with children's negativty as rated by teachers, but that maternal social support was not associated with children's behaviour. Manetti and Schneider are conducting a longitudinal study in Genoa, Italy, of the links between parental social support and children's social competence using a larger sample of youngsters sampled from the regular school population.

Summary and Conclusions

Not even a decade ago, Stryker and Serpe (1983) offered the following succinct appraisal of theoretical positions regarding the family's influence on children's social competence:

> We have . . . theories stressing the role of the family in socializing its offspring that imply that parents are omnipotent. . . We also have theories suggesting that, at best, famlies are neutral conduits for influences flowing from more basic sources. . . . What we do not have is a theory explaining how it is that families exercise influence on their offspring which at the same time explains how it is that the influence of families is constrained, limited, minimized or even aborted (pp. 47–48).

As evidenced by some of the recent work reviewed in this chapter, even the few intervening years have witnessed considerable progress in these respects. Also, theories which consider the many different mechanisms of family influence and their interactions, as well as the exchanges between the family and its social and cultural context, have benefited from substantial refinement and empirical validation.

One might be left with the impression that researchers have left no corner unexplored in their search for family correlates of children's social competence. However, this is hardly the case. While family relationships are intimate and intense, the social development outcomes explored rarely include children's closer friendships or their more extended social contacts. This is not a minor omission. Other relatively neglected areas include the family's possible contribution to non-verbal aspects of children's social communication, and to the regulation of emotion in exchanges between children.

How is recent different from the host of studies which appeared in this field during the "heyday" of socialization studies a quarter century ago? For one thing, social competence is being targeted more directly as an outcome measure. Nevertheless, some recent studies are remarkably similar to studies completed a generation ago in terms of conceptual underpinning and method. "One-shot" correlational studies with relatively small samples continue to appear, though they have lost respectability. Nevertheless, some of the studies selected for this chapter illustrate promising trends. There is greater recognition of the multiple pathways of family influence. This is somewhat useful in quantifying the total extent of the family's contribution, but of much greater potential value in clarifying the processes by which family influence occurs. In particular, the interconnections of family harmony, externally induced family stress and child-rearing technique have been the subject of both theoretical speculation and systematic research. Non-familial mediators such as social perception and physiological indicators have been considered as well. This emphasis on a multivariate perspective does not imply at all that there is no need for further research on the individual pathways. As discussed at several points in this chapter, there are glaring gaps in the evidence supporting most of the major theories of family influence.

Fortunately, there is increasing awareness of the bidirectional influences in the relationship between a child and his/her parents. As detailed above, there is a trend to consider children's temperament when evaluating the effects of parental variables. More sophisticated explorations of the interactive effects of heredity and family environment will no doubt emerge in the future.

Furthermore, there now seems to be greater attention to the social context of parenting. Researchers now seem to display an enhanced awareness that the parents' disciplinary techniques relate to the parents' own life histories, stress level and social support network. Recent research has also complemented work on general parenting styles with attention to socialization behaviours specific to the facilitation of children's social competence, such as parental orchestration, encouragement and monitoring of their children's peer contacts.

Relatively small samples are still the norm in research on the family, although, as we have seen, there are important exceptions. Working with few subjects is fully understandable in light of the intensity of some of the procedures involved, such as direct observation in homes. As illustrated at several points in this chapter, sophisticated review techniques such as meta-analysis are being applied in order to obtain a more accurate picture of the database. Small effects are not unusual for data in the social sciences and not inconsistent with current understanding of the multiple origins of human behaviour. Nevertheless, our confidence in many of the conclusions reported by researchers studying the family's contribution must be tempered by the size of the effect and the size of the sample, though without forgetting that small effects are not necessarily unimportant.

Longitudinal designs, long a feature of socialization studies, remain in widespread use. The most important studies now underway trace parallel changes in children's relations with their parents and with their peers, instead of basing inferences on correlations obtained at a single point in time. As discussed in Chapter 1, such designs can provide better confirmation or disconfirmation of theoretical models regarding the origins of child social competence in the family. While longitudinal designs themselves are nothing new, recent advances in statistical analysis permit fuller benfits from the data.

Despite the improvements mentioned here, a number of shortcomings remain. First of all, most of the studies have been conducted in the United States, despite the fact that the role of the family may vary greatly by culture. While the socioeconomic status of study participants is being reported more carefully than in earlier reports, there are still very few studies which systematically compare samples of differing SES to see if the effects apply across levels. Too many studies still involve mothers only, despite changes in recent thinking about sex roles.

While the number of studies recently reported or in progress is not small, there is some criticism that the database on parental socialization of children is becoming quite dated, as the children who participated in the "heyday' socialization studies of the 1960s now have children of their own. Child-rearing patterns are known to change over time (Rapoport, Rapoport, Strelitz & Kew, 1977). Some recent research provides useful replication of many earlier findings which have achieved general acceptance, such as Baumrind's (1967) conclusions about the value of authoritative parenting. Additional replications across eras, cultures and socioeconomic levels are still needed for many key studies, including many older longitudinal projects.

In considering the research on the multiple modes of family impact, we might recall Vygotsky's suggestion that different modes of influence might account for different facets of development, or for the development of children of various ages. Despite the huge mass of data that have been accumulated, research has not been comprehensive enough to map avenues of differential family contribution to different facets of children's social competence. Family life may also influence the social competence of boys and girls in different ways. Though Lytton and Romney's (1991) careful meta-analysis of 172 studies revealed little evidence that parents differ greatly in their rearing of sons and daughters, there have been some important differences in other respects, such as the effects of divorce. As researchers move toward more complete research designs, they may provide better answers not only to the question of which modality of family influence is the most potent, but become able to delineate which modalities of family influence are associated with specific facets of social competence and for children of different ages, gender, temperaments and life circumstances.

Whatever portion of the individual differences in children's social competence is accounted for by heredity, parents' decisions about how to raise their children must surely have some bearing. How could the research discussed in this chapter be useful to a parent wishing to enhance his child's social competence? Unfortunately, a simple definitive answer is inconsistent with available data. The limitations, complexities and inconsistencies of our knowledge dictate that any synthesis offered to the public by way of advice be done so as an educated guess and no more. It would seem important to avoid adding to the ranks of the paradoxical parents described by Palacios and to avoid contributing to the practice of blaming mothers gratuitously for all their children's shortcomings. Therefore, such a parent might be assured that the totality of children's social behaviour is not determined by their families, which does not mean that there is nothing a parent can do to help. As well, one might remember that children normally learn much of their social competence by interacting with peers. Therefore, under normal circumstances, the parent as "gatekeeper" might facilitate social contacts for the child, though some data demonstrate that this can backfire. Furthermore, if the child's social behaviour is such that it would alienate the peers in any activity arranged, it would seem incumbent on the parent to employ authoritative child-rearing procedures in order to correct coercive, aggressive behaviours, rather than engender failure by inflicting these behaviours on the child's intended friends. Finally, it may be necessary to bring to mind the studies which suggest that the negative affect and inappropriate learning which accompany hostile, non-affectionate home environments are brought by the child to his/her relations with others. The sequelae of such negative contexts will no doubt outweigh the benefits of any facile effort at promoting children's social activities. Unfortunately, correcting family dysfunction is not easy, though family therapy does have some degrees of success. While future studies will hopefully bring more and better information on the family's contribution to social competence, they are unlikely to result in simple "cookbook"-style prescriptions for parents, but to continue revealing the complexities of the family's contribution to children's social competence as well as the dynamic interplay of familial and extrafamilial pathways of influence.

3

School Climate and Children's Social Competence

Researchers have often found it convenient to collect data in schools regarding children's and adolescents' peer relations and friendships. However, little of this research has taken into account the many ways by which the school itself may influence the peer relations which are studied (Epstein & Karweit, 1983). In sharp contrast, a few scholars in the field of children's social competence assign a primary role to the social skill of adjusting to the reality of the school situation and handling its interpersonal demands in an effective manner (Loranger, 1984; Stephens, 1976, 1981). Vygotsky emphasized the acquisition of literacy as the source of profound changes in the individual's thinking, and attributed considerable importance to the school as a venue for fostering development in general. His research is beginning to spur renewed interest in the school's contribution to children's social competence.

Epstein (1983) contended that until the early nineteenth century, the goals and practices of families usually matched the goals and practices of schools, with clergy often delivering prescriptions for both. However, mismatch between home and school environments is much more possible nowadays. The transition from home to school (or preschool) environments often brings children from family settings which vary considerably to educational settings that tend to be much more uniform. While parents may cultivate, or at least tolerate, a wide range of social behaviour in children, formal education traditionally requires far more circumscribed patterns of social interaction. Where the social norms of the school differ markedly from those of the home, children are thought to have particular difficulty becoming competent at social interaction in the classroom (Florio-Ruane, 1989; Hansen, 1986; Weinstein, 1991). Nevertheless, the consequences of this mismatch in interaction rules seem more serious in classrooms where there is less flexibility in permissible behaviour and where behavioural rules are more strictly enforced (Hansen, 1986).

At what age is it best for children to make the transition from home to the more institutional atmosphere of school or daycare centre? At the time of writing, there is considerable controversy regarding the possible effects of early daycare placement on the attachment bonds between mother and child. As discussed in Chapter 2, insecure attachment during early childhood is thought by some to affect later peer relations. It has been demonstrated that very young children in daycare do in fact exhibit insecure patterns of mother attachment as measured by the Strange Situations Task (see, e.g. Belsky & Rovine, 1988). However, Clarke-Stewart (1989) has pointed out that daycare infants may become habituated to their mother's frequent departures, and, therefore, a seemingly insecure response to the Strange Situation procedure may not have the drastic long-term implications that one might initially suspect. Belsky and Braungart's (1991) recent data indicate that the infants classified as insecure do in fact fuss, whimper and cry during the procedure. Nevertheless, it is by no means clear that peer relations over the long term are affected by early daycare. Indeed, a number of studies have shown that schoolchildren with early daycare experience display higher levels of social competence than classmates without daycare experience (see, e.g. Anderson's [1989] follow-up of Swedish youngsters, Clarke-Stewart's [1991] follow-up studies of Chicago youngsters or Hartmann's [1991, in press] studies of Norwegian schoolchildren).

There are some indications that the impact of daycare on children's social development depends on the quality of the daycare environment (Holloway & Reichhart-Erickson, 1989; Howes & Stewart, 1987; Lamb et al., 1988). Some of Howes's (1990) more recent data indicate that, among children who display patterns of insecure attachment with their mothers at age 1, those who subsequently enrolled in daycare were more socially competent in their play when observed at age 5. Thus, in some situations the caregiver may play an important protective role. In a recent, comprehensive study, Howes, Phillips and Whitebook (1992) demonstrated convincingly that young children cared for in high-quality daycare centres were more likely to become securely attached to their teachers. In turn, securely-attached children were more competent with their peers.

Bates et. al. (1991) found that kindergarteners with previous daycare experience displayed higher rates of problematic aggression. However, their study did not take into account the quality of the daycare environment. Nevertheless, their findings are consistent with Belsky and Rovine's (1988) study of aggressiveness among 5-year-olds who were identified as having insecure attachment histories at age 1. Interestingly, many of these studies show that daycare environments have greater impact on boys than girls. Given these inconsistent findings, it is safe to speculate that further studies—and, presumably, judicious use of the techniques of meta-analysis and causal modelling (see Chapter 1)—will clarify the nature and extent of the effects of early daycare on children's later social competence.

Critics of the schools (see, e.g., Tudge, 1981) maintain that the onset of formal schooling brings the child into an environment over which he/she has little control. Early individual differences in the ability to influence others may thus be solidified, steering an already passive group of youngsters on the path toward feelings of incompetence and alienation. There are some indications that the young child is not a social conformist. Sommer and Langsted (1990) conducted qualitative observations of the play interactions of fifty-eight 5-year-olds, collected as part of a larger study of the social development of children in the five Nordic countries. They divided the children's play into four categories. The first category, *social managing behaviour*, involved making one's own needs and intentions known to other children while recognizing the needs or intentions of others. This was the most typical interaction stance of 48% of the sample. *Self-imposing behaviour* also entailed making one's own wishes known, though without considering the intentions of the other children; it characterized 37% of the children. *Conformity behaviour* involved playing according to the rules of the peer group without playing an active role in creating the rules. It typified only 12% of the youngsters. The final category, *social isolation*, described the extended play pattern of only 5% of the youngsters in these daycare settings. However, the competent social managing behaviours were not uniformly distributed across the daycare settings in the study; they were far less frequent in the Finnish daycare centre. Sommer and Langsted speculated that this may be because adult-structured, specific learning activities are much more common in Finnish daycare. As the children in all countries continue at school, such adult-structured learning activities will no doubt predominate, and perhaps unwittingly reduce the proportion of socially managing behaviours. To some degree, this restriction may be necessary in order for content learning to take place, though many have stressed that a truly effective learner must be an active participant in the learning process (Cooper, Marquis & Ayers-Lopez, 1982).

Thelen (1981) noted that most individuals in Western societies have shared relatively common experiences in schools. In most instances, they have grown accustomed to standard textbooks, didactic lessons, tests and marks. They have adjusted themselves to the vagaries of teachers' styles, personalities and expectations, and have discussed these differences among teachers with parents and peers, spending a major portion of their waking lives—15,000 hours according to a count by Rutter *et. al.* (1979)— engaged in formal schooling. Thelen referred to the shared understanding of the school experience as a cultural archetype, one so well ingrained that it serves as an impediment to change.

The purpose of this chapter is to consider the contributions of the experience of schooling to children's social competence. While it may be more frequent practice to apportion credit or blame for the way children turn out to their parents, it is by no means uncommon to attribute students' successes and failures at least partly to the effects of schools. Edmonds (1986) suggested that the school environment can be so potent in some cases that it overrides virtually all other factors in determining at least the child's social behaviour at school. If this is the case, the school has a more active role to play than is often thought. Edmonds's contention contrasts sharply with other viewpoints according to which the child's behaviour at school passively mirrors the family environment and the socioeconomic conditions that surround it.

In most studies which have explored both school and family influences, family variables tend to explain a greater portion of population variance than school variables (Good & Brophy, 1986). Good and Brophy pointed out that this may be because of restricted range. In most Western countries there are undeniable differences among schools, but there is also a high degree of similarity among them in terms of general organization and the content of instruction. This is not necessarily true in other cultures. Heyneman and Losley's (1983) review indicates that school and teacher characteristics play a far greater role in societies whose economic resources are more limited. A positive school environment may serve as a buffer for children undergoing family stress, though it would be highly naive to expect that a good school will cancel out the negative effects of a poor home. Peres and Pasternak (1991) studied the adjustment of 314 Israeli primary children of divorced parents. In the six traditional schools, youngsters raised by divorced mothers had lower peer acceptance than controls. This effect was totally absent in an experimental school that featured wider student participation as well as a longer and more reverse school day. In most situations, though, children's behaviour at school may not be much different from their behaviour at home. Hinde, Stevenson-Hinde and Tamplin (1985) compared social behaviour observed in preschool with mothers' reports of the children's home behaviour; the children's behavioural style was generally consistent across settings. There has been some suggestion that schools and families influence different aspects of social competence.

School and home may affect different aspects of development. Klindová (1985) speculated that kindergartens may teach children the practical side of social skills, while family life accounted for their social–moral orientation and commitment to others. Berndt and Bulleit's (1985) findings provide some corroboration of this.

An outstanding school could conceivably have much more protective influence than an ordinary one. There are many studies of schools which appear particularly effective, especially schools which work well despite economic deprivation in their catchment areas. However, this research has largely addressed itself to exceptional academic achievement rather than social outcomes.

Educational theorists have referred to two distinct levels of school influence and socialization, the instrumental and the expressive (Bloom, 1977; Isherwood & Ahola, 1981). Isherwood and Ahola (1981) further subdivide the instrumental level into official instrumental and hidden instrumental features. Official instrumental aspects of school life have to do with the accomplishment of the school's stated objectives; for example, the acquisition of academic skill and content. Hidden instrumental aspects pertain to school activities aimed at maintaining the basic structure of the school system, such as subtle teacher reinforcement of conformity to the group structure and sanctions for the violation of school procedures. In counterpoint to such formal, instrumental socialization are the learning experiences afforded by the peer group and peer culture, known as expressive socialization. Isherwood and Ahola maintained that teachers can define classroom environments so that instrumental and expressive socialization either coexist peacefully or compete with each other. In the latter case, the classroom atmosphere is characterized by considerable tension.

At first glance, huge chunks of the school day appear to be devoted to academic lessons during which there is little interaction among peers. This is far from true. Ahola and Isherwood (1981) conducted an ethnographic exploration of two Canadian secondary schools. They found almost constant communication among the pupils, a host of opportunities to form friendships, compare oneself to others, delineate boundaries of social acceptance and rejection, worry about social acceptance and rejection, etc. The social life of the students permeated almost every part of the day, dominating intervals between lessons but also subtly but definitely present during lessons.

Coleman (1961), in his comparison of the student culture in ten highly heterogeneous American secondary schools, concluded that pupils' attachment to the peer group is crucial to their involvement in the entire process of schooling. Having no friends at school leads to disengagement and alienation, which in turn may precipitate premature school leaving. Kagen (1990) observed that such disengagement may ensure early patterns of poor communication with teachers, differential treatment by teachers, rejection by successful peers, forcing the child to gravitate towards a sub-group of alienated peers. Thus, even if academic failure is caused by forces external to the school, an unfavourable school experience may exacerbate the risk of social and vocational maladjustment for children already vulnerable (Kagan, 1990). The theoretical contributions of Piaget, Vygotsky and others have sensitized us to the importance of peer interactions in facilitating children's cognitive development, and thereby their academic success (Doise & Mugny, 1984).

A Taxonomy of School Influence

Just as family interaction and family effects have been conceptualized in many different ways (see Chapter 2), there are many ways in which the school environment can be described and can affect children's development. Anderson (1982) clarified the concept of school climate by recalling Halpin and Croft's analogy that "climate" is to an organization what "personality" is to an individual, as well as Nwankwo's definition of school climate as the general "we-feeling" or group sub-culture of the school. Anderson evoked the metaphor of a beast in portraying the variations in attitude towards the concept of school climate. The albatross regards school climate as something which can be defined and which has an impact on children, but does not consider school climate a worthwhile focus of enquiry because it is not amenable to manipulation. Another group of critics takes on many characteristics of the unicorn—the study of school climate is seen as desirable in theory, but not likely to be successful, like a beautiful beast which can never be found. Such pessimism about being able to measure and study school climate is partly based on the observation that the climate of each classroom within a school may be very different, precluding any meaningful generalization about the overall "we-feeling" of the organization. Furthermore, any measurement of school characteristics will be hopelessly confounded by student background characteristics.

As researchers overcome the shortcomings of earlier efforts, the image of a phoenix (Anderson, 1982) is becoming more prevalent. Earlier studies often used measures that were convenient but grossly inadequate, and looked at a few isolated aspects of school functioning, leading to few findings of significance (Brookover *et. al.* 1979). Their contemporary counterparts have adopted more comprehensive depictions of the workings of schools, yielding more encouraging indicators that schools do indeed make a difference.

Conceptual models developed by Tagiuri (1968) and Moos (1979) will be used to structure the remainder of this chapter. There are several salient dimensions useful in delineating the climate or atmosphere of a school or organization. The first dimension is the physical ecology of the school, its building, furniture, maintenance, lighting, equipment, utilization of space, etc. The *social system* or *social structure* refers to the implicit or explicit patterns or rules of social interaction in the school. The term *school culture* is used in this literature to refer to the beliefs or values of the individuals involved. In all major studies, these variables are studied in light of *intake* or *milieu* variables, i.e. the socioeconomic and educational background of the pupils and staff. Theoretical models differ as to whether these variables operate in a simple additive fashion or whether they interact to influence the outcomes of schooling. Anderson (1982) also described a useful *mediated* model, portrayed in Figure 3.1. The figure depicts three pathways of influence. The first is a direct input–output pathway: intake or background characteristics have major and direct impact on the dependent variable. In the two other pathways of influence, these background variables affect the social structure and culture of a school, which in turn affect the student outcome.

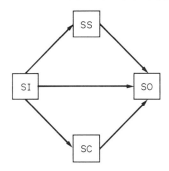

FIG. 3.1. Mediated model, with School Social Inputs (SI), School Social Structure (SS), School Social Climate (SC) and Student Outcomes (SO). From Anderson, Carolyn S. (1982). The search for school climate: A review of the research. *Review of Educational Research*, **52**, 368–420. By permission.

Physical Ecology of the School

Psychologists have long been aware that the physical arrangement of a school or workplace influences the nature and extent of the social interaction that occurs within. Tracing the history of this notion, Getzels (1975) noted that as part of the intellectual climate prior to World War II there was extensive reflection on ways of facilitating leadership qualities and co-operation and preventing problematic aggression. Attention to the physical ecology of the classroom was an integral part of this concern. Moreno (1953), the grandfather of peer relations research (see Chapter 1), administered the "oldest version of the sociometric test" (p. lxxi) to a New York City primary school class in 1937, with the idea of substituting a more "democratic" pattern of seating chosen sociometrically by the children for the "authoritarian" pattern imposed by the teacher who assigned seats. Kurt Lewin (Lewin, Lippitt & White, 1939) conducted a series of "group climate" studies, in which physical ecology was an important element. He introduced the metaphor of a "circular class-room"—as opposed to the traditional "square" or rectangular arrangement of pupils in rows—as a way of encouraging everyone to face each other and interact more co-operatively. Lewin's theories of context were quite complex (Lewin, 1954), emphasizing the interaction of an individual's personal characteristics, personal characteristics of peers and characteristics of the physical setting.

Borrowing concepts from the field of ethology, some consideration has been given to the child's identification with physical space, in parallel to other species' notions of territoriality, and to the need for privacy as part of the emergence of an individual's sense of identity. However, Prohansky (1974) called for more refined concepts of space identity which go beyond simplistic notions of privacy and territoriality. He noted that if, as part of the socialization process, the child internalizes representations of significant others, of the roles he must play in groups and of unique interpersonal experiences he/she has encountered, there must also be some internalization of the places which help define socialization behaviours. Interactions with the physical setting in which satisfactions and frustrations occur and in which feelings of competence or incompetence are nurtured must be salient features of the individual's experience of important life events. Prohansky argued that if individuals *express* their identities in the ways they structure, decorate and maintain important physical settings, the converse must be true: the contexts which have helped define an individual's development must be expressed in the structure of that person's identity.

Size of the school. Early research on school climate (McDill & Rigsby, 1973; Weber, 1971) explored the link between the size of schools and the academic achievement of pupils and their general satisfaction with schooling. These studies yielded largely non-significant findings, and have been criticized for their simplistic methodology and failure to look at the human ecology of the school together with the physical ecology. Similarly, Rutter and his colleagues (1979), studying the school climates of ten inner-city London secondary schools, found that the size of the school had little to do with the pupils' attention, achievement, attendance or with the delinquency rate of pupils. Thus, school size has, on the whole, been dismissed as a productive variable in school climate research.

The specific instance of school size in relation to children's social competence may warrant an exception. LaFreniere and Sroufe (1985) compared the social competence (as measured by sociometrics and direct observation of classroom behaviour) of forty 4- and 5-year-olds in two preschool classrooms. One of the classrooms enrolled fifteen children, the other twenty-four. This study is particularly interesting because it explored the fifteen effects of class size in conjunction with the children's attachment history. In the larger class particularly, children with histories of anxious attachment with their mothers were more likely to be "swept away in the contagion of activity . . . and judged . . . to be out of control" (p. 66). Thus, LaFreniere and Sroufe's study, among others, illustrates the importance of considering individual child differences in assessing the impact of the school's physical ecology.

Coleman (1961) observed that in larger schools a student's sociometric status may tend to "blur". In other words, the social hierarchy of the school is less well-defined, and it is more likely that larger numbers of social subgroups will form, each of whom will have its own leaders and rejects. Thus, there will be less consensus with regard to who is most and least liked, and it is more likely that a given youngster will be well-liked in one particular social sub-group, which is defined by specific interests (athletic, artistic, social), though not well-liked in another, dissimilar sub-group. As part of a longitudinal study in which sociometric measures were readministered at 1-year intervals in the same schools, Caulfield (1980) interviewed a number of children whose social adjustment had improved over several years. The youngsters whose sociometric status had improved were asked to speculate about the reasons. They very often cited a move to a larger school. In contrast, direct interventions by parents, teachers and counsellors seemed to have had little impact on their improved social status, at least according to the children's own perceptions.

Grabe (1981) noted that in smaller schools there tends to be greater participation in extracurricular athletic, social and artistic activities. Therefore, there is greater identification with the school and its social group, at least for those who participate. However, as such extracurricular activities dominate the atmosphere of a small school, there is also a heightened sense of alienation and rejection among those who do not identify with the somewhat uniform general atmosphere of the small school. Similar findings were obtained in the classic study by Barker and Gump (1964).

Coleman (1961) found that the impact of school on one's peer relations may depend on the size of the community. In a smaller community, all potential friends are likely to attend the same school. Therefore, one's social interaction at school will determine one's peer group status to a much greater extent. This appears to be especially the case for girls. Presumably, in a smaller community, the consequences of being rejected by a particular social group are also greater because there are not many other social groups available.

The widespread concern in many countries about violence in inner-city schools might suggest that larger, urban schools are characterized by higher levels of aggression. However, Olweus's pioneering studies of bully–victim problems in Sweden, Norway and Finland suggest otherwise. Data are available from over 700 schools, ranging from tiny, rural schools (the smallest of which enrolled forty-three students) to large urban schools. There is no indication at all of any relation between school size (or class size) and the frequency of bullying (Olweus, 1991).

As children progress in their studies, they are transferred to large, less personal schools in most countries. In the United States and Canada, "junior high schools" have become widespread in an effort to avoid the former drastic transition from a small, intimate primary school to a complex large secondary school. Junior high school starts at different ages indifferent communities, but typically begins at about age 12. Thus the transition to a larger school occurs more or less at the onset of adolescence, normally a very difficult time. As discussed by Simmons (1987), this transition to the larger school setting, while intended to prepare pupils for the transfer to secondary school 2 or 3 years later, often has negative consequences, including disruptions of friendship networks, lower participation in school activities and more aggressive behaviour. In her large cross-sectional study of students' choices of best friends, Epstein (1983) found that important changes in the children's friendship networks ensued school transition years (American Grades 6 and 9—approximately ages 12 and 15 years). While best friends still behaved like best friends after the transition—there were no changes in the reciprocity of best friends' esteem—the pupils' ratings indicated fewer reciprocated friendships than they did the years prior to the transition, or indeed a year later once they had settled into their new school.

It has been shown that there are negative effects in the large junior school where efforts are made to maintain smaller sub-group units (Hawkins & Berndt, 1985; Lipsitz, 1984). Ladd (1989) studied the school transition experiences of younger children, and suggested that well-developed social skills, as well as the availability of a social support network at home and in the community, are important protective factors which facilitate school transitions. It would be useful to explore these variables at other ages and in different countries.

Arrangement of space

Lewin's context theory, mentioned above, emphasized the effects of the arrangement of the learning setting as well as the interaction between the arrangement of space and individual characteristics. Optimal organization of physical space has received considerable attention, culminating during the debate between open and close-space classrooms. In contrast, there has been relatively little systematic study of the interface of space arrangements context and individual differences among pupils. Theorists in the area of environmental psychology have emphasized the need for "transactional" models which capture the bidirectional relationship between environment and behaviour (Bronfenbrenner & Crouter, 1983; Legendre, 1989). However, most available studies use a far more restricted conceptual framework. The technique of behavioural mapping (Ittelson, Rivlin & Proshansky, 1970) has greatly faclitated the study of links between arrangement of space and social interaction among its occupants.

Many schools in disadvantaged neighbourhoods may have relatively bare, poorly equipped outdoor playgrounds. Parents and teachers may hope that the provision of play structures and gymnastic equipment will help correct problematic social interactions in these schools. However, this is not supported by the limited data available. Johnson's (1935) early study suggested that where extensive playground equipment is provided, social interaction actually decreases, though there is an increase in physical exercise and other desirable behaviour. These results were replicated by

Weinstein and Pinciotti (1988) who conducted extensive observations of primary schoolchildren at play before and after an empty blacktop play surface was replaced by a tyre playground. After the playground was built, there were many changes in the children's play behaviour, most of them positive: increases in active and pretend play decreased roughhousing and less uninvolved play. However, there was no significant change in social interaction or conversation, which actually decreased, though not significantly. Thus, interactions with the play apparatus appear to replace interactive play with peers to some extent. If enhanced social interaction during outdoor play is the desired outcome, it may be necessary to design play equipment in a way that would maximize co-operative play.

Play and classroom settings may be divided into separate compartments or feature no visual boundaries. Manetti and Campart (1987, 1989) conducted an experimental study of the use of space during indoor play by preschoolers in a disadvantaged area of central Genoa. The study was conducted in a single classroom with eighteen youngsters whose ages ranged from 3 to 5 years. In the first part of the study, the classroom was left the way the teacher had arranged it, with all play equipment arranged along the outside walls, leaving open space in the middle. The researchers observed the children's interactions in the four quadrants of the classroom, which at this point were not divided physically. The rate of social interaction in the three of the four quadrants was essentially the same, whereas there was little social interaction in the fourth quadrant, which was relatively bare. The overall rate of interaction was similar for boys and girls, though girls interacted much more frequently in the quadrant which contained the play house. The furniture was rearranged for the second part of the study in order to physically divide the classroom into four sectors; storage shelves were used as dividers. This division resulted in a dramatic increase in social interaction. This may be because of the greater provision for privacy or because the monolithic and relatively barren open space was converted into more useable play areas.

Pellegrini and Perlmutter (1989) conducted a multidimensional observational study in order to determine whether certain types of play occur more frequently in certain areas of the preschool classroom. Separate groups of 3-, 4- and 5-year-olds participated in the study. In general, the type of play props provided influenced the social level of play. More solitary play occurred in art areas and block areas, while interactive play was more frequent in the replica area. The presence of both adults and peers also affected play patterns. As might be expected, solitary and parallel play occurred in areas remote from adults and other children. This may mean *either* that interactive play is more likely where playmates are in close proximity *or* that children who are less inclined to social play choose to play away from others.

Droege and Howes (1991) conducted an observational study with

California preschoolers to determine whether *social pretend play* occurs in certain areas of the daycare centre. Pretend play is a very frequent and important component of the social play of preschoolers, which may prepare them for subsequent real-life social roles (see Rubin, Fein & Vandenberg, 1983). For both boys and girls, indoor play areas that were structured and had suitable props available (such as men's and women's dress-up clothes, pretend cutlery and crockery, telephone, doll's house, etc.) were the location of the greatest amount of pretend play. This applied especially to play involving themes of family life. Girls engaged in much more pretend play than boys in all locations. Boys engaged in hardly any pretend play in areas other than those set up specifically for it. Droedge and Howes suggested that planners of daycare environments provide for children's apparent needs for a physical setting in which this type of play seems likely to occur.

Other data strongly suggest that young children's use of space depends heavily on certain individual child characteristics, including social competence, as well as the simultaneous use of space by the teacher or caregiver (Legendre, 1989). Legendre (1987) found that in preschools where there were many visual boundaries, children generally spent more time in close proximity to adults. Children who were socially competent exhibited greater security in venturing more frequently to areas separated by visual boundaries from the adult caregiver. Nevertheless, there was relatively little dyadic interactive play in parts of the room without visual contact with the caregiver. Thus, in the very young child, autonomy from spatial constraints may depend heavily upon other aspects of the child's development. Visual obstacles may have a marked effect on children's social interaction. Presumably, the absence of visual obstacles would permit children to play in all areas without sacrificing proximity to the adult caregiver (see Neill, 1982). Thus, there are inconsistencies between these results and those of Manetti and Campart, discussed above, which will hopefully be resolved as more studies appear.

Most primary schools have by now rejected the "open-space" architecture which was advocated energetically in the 1970s as a vehicle for enhancing interpersonal interaction within schools. This "innovation" is now seen by many as creating distractions and disorganization, even though systematic evaluations of open education have revealed small mixed effects. Giaconia and Hedges's (1982) review indicated that, on the whole, pupils in "open concept" schools (implying openness in both physical structure and programming) made slightly less academic progress than others, but scored a bit higher on measures of self-concept and feelings about school. Hallinan's (1976) large-scale study on friendship patterns in open and traditional-concept classrooms did indicate that in open-arrangement primary-school classrooms there were fewer social isolates. Nevertheless, the failure of open-concept schools to revolutionize education as promised may stem from inattention to the interaction between the physical and human ecology of the schools. In retrospect, it may have been naive to expect that simply removing walls and rearranging furniture would bring about fundamental change in the activities which take place within the school. Fortunately, the co-operative learning movement has featured rearrangement of space and furniture as an adjunct to the redirectional of the goal structure of the school's programme of academic instruction, not as an isolated intervention. Research on co-operative learning experiences is discussed later in this chapter.

Charlebois *et al.* (1992) studied the seating arrangements of Montreal primary-school classrooms over a 3-year period. They found that boys identified as socially at-risk were almost always seated either at the very front or very rear of the classroom. When the same subjects were located in classrooms 2 years later, a striking 84% were assigned seats in the same zones. Unfortunately, a high proportion of teacher attention and feedback was directed at the middle rows. This study illustrates the importance of considering the interaction of physical ecology and subject characteristics.

In summary, research documenting the effects of the classroom setting on children's social interaction has not only shown that the physical ecology of the classroom can have an important impact, but has begun to consider the interaction between the physical and human ecology. Both descriptive and experimental methods have been put to good use. However, these studies are still fragmentary in many respects. Further work is needed to clarify the interactive effects of the classroom setting and teacher leadership style as well as the differential influence of physical ecology on children of various ages, backgrounds and levels of social competence.

The School as a Social System

Does the teacher make a difference?

When reflecting on one's school career as a whole, it may not be uncommon to remember a single exceptional teacher whose impact appears to have been more enduring than the others. As well, most of us can probably remember at least one teacher we disliked and whose influence may have been negative. Nevertheless, the contribution of teacher characteristics to children's social competence has not been very widely studied. Thelen (1981, p. 2) insisted that the "teacher's fundamental function is to monitor the quality of life in the [school] society". However, her portrayal of the quality of life in most schools depicts an unimaginative series of routines. The pupil is required to adapt to a variety of teaching styles and teacher personalities, rather than experience teacher styles adapted to his/her own learning needs. Thelen sees our unchallenging acceptance of this cultural "archetype" for the school experience as an obstacle to progress.

Personal contact with pupils. During the primary school years, children typically have extended contact with a single teacher or small number of teachers, who may therefore become very salient elements of their interpersonal field. In secondary school years, children may or may not establish meaningful personal contact with their teachers, depending upon the structure of the school, teacher and pupil attitudes, time and other facors. In the study by Rutter and colleagues (1979), teacher availability for personal contact was associated with several positive indices of school outcome, though these were more academic than social. Some more recent data also indicated that the benefits of personal contact may not be that clear-cut. Kasen, Johnson and Cohen (1990) interviewed 300 New York pupils aged 16 years to obtain descriptions of the climate of the 250 schools they attended. Their parents were interviewed regarding the participants' problem behaviours; these interviews were repeated 2 years later. Contrary to expectations, children attending schools rated as high in social facilitation (i.e. where teachers arrange personal discussions) displayed *greater* increases in depression and anxiety, though no change in conduct problems or oppositionality. These results suggest that the effects of personal teacher–pupil contact vary according to the general level of hostility and conflict in the environment. In schools characterized by high levels of conflict, discussions about interpersonal problems may provide an opportunity to express feelings, but not eliminate the hostility in the environment nor mitigate its effects. In any case, it is important to remember that the specific effects of these personal contacts on children's social competence were not explored in either of these two interesting studies.

Teacher feedback to pupils. White, Smith and Kuzma (1991) conducted an interesting analogue study in which children were shown videotapes of teacher–child interaction. Different versions of the videotape displayed different amounts of positive and negative teacher feedback. Positive teacher feedback did influence the subject's ratings of liking of the child actors to some extent; negative teacher feedback influenced the ratings more heavily. It is not clear whether these findings might be replicated in an actual classroom.

These has also been some suggestion that certain types of children react more favourably to teacher input. Byrnes (1985) discussed this in connection with the specfic needs of socially neglected children, who are not actively rejected by peers, but forgotten and isolated. Research is needed to corroborate her observation that these pupils are in particular need of individual teacher attention, an assertion which intuitively seems quite valid.

Flanders and Havumakis (1960) conducted an interesting analogue study of the effects of praise on peer perceptions of liking. In discussion groups formed for the purpose of the study, half the previously unacquainted adolescent participants were praised by the adult group leader for their contributions. Those who had been praised received higher sociometric ratings of popularity from other group participants. A small-sample study by Medinnus (1962) provides some confirmation that, in a real classroom, teacher praise is linked to patterns of peer liking. The sociometric status of the 6-year-olds studied was highly correlated with both frequency of teacher praise and teachers' ratings of their preferences among pupils.

Feshbach (1967; Portugues & Feshbach, 1972) conducted a series of studies in which primary schoolchildren were shown films of either rewarding, positive teachers or hostile, negative ones. Following the films, the children's imitation of the modelled behaviours was observed. Many of the children imitated the behaviours of the positive model, though some important social class differences were noted. The tendency to imitate positive teacher behaviours may be limited to middle-class subjects, and not extend to lower-class schools, where, unfortunately, critical authority figures may be more familiar to the children. Thus, Feshbach's results depart somewhat from the general pattern of research findings, which clearly indicates that teacher enthusiasm is associated with positive student outcome. As Feshbach's findings may relate to some idiosyncratic aspect of the black American subculture in which his lower socioeconomic status participants were raised, it is important that future studies conducted with that and other minority cultures specifically compare results across socioeconomic levels. Furthermore, it may be more profitable to assess teacher praise and encouragement *in vivo* rather than use either Feshbach's videotaped analogue technique or Flanders and Havumakis's somewhat contrived group discussion task. These analogue studies are not without heuristic value, but cannot capture the full atmosphere of a classroom, and may seem unfamiliar or contrived to the subjects.

Teacher empathy. By subjecting his intriguing theoretical views to systematic empirical research, Carl Rogers succeeded in convincing a generation of psychologists that warmth, empathy and unconditional positive regard are "core conditions" which facilitate interpersonal relationships. Rogers's theory had profound impact on education. Most studies indicated that in a more student-centred learning environment, the learners' self-concept is enhanced, while academic progress is, at the least, not decelerated in comparison to a content-centred setting. However, fewer data are available regarding the impact of student-centred schooling on children's social competence. Several authors regard empathy as a core variable in the development of positive relationships.

Warmth and enthusiasm. Much of the teacher's own social interaction style must be quite evident in the course of their everyday teaching activities and routine interactions with pupils. As detailed by Brophy and Good (1974), the effects of teacher warmth and enthusiasm have been widely studied. In general, warmer teachers have more positive classroom atmospheres. Several studies have established that teacher warmth, while probably of some importance to all students, is particularly important to some, particularly alienated members of minority groups (see, e.g., Kleinfeld [1972] or St. John [1971]), pupils in schools where the culture emphasizes interpersonal relationships rather than achievement (Della-Piana & Gage, 1955) and students with high dependency needs (Amidon & Flanders, 1961).

Serow and Solomon (1979) conducted in-depth observations of American primary school classrooms in order to make more explicit the links between teacher style and social interaction between pupils. Their primary interest was interaction between children of majority and minority group origin. They found that in classrooms where the teacher was warm, easygoing and accepting, there was much positive social interaction. In more businesslike, task-oriented atmospheres, there was little contact between children of different cultural backgrounds.

Ziv's studies focused on the teacher's enthusiasm and sense of humour (e.g. Ziv, 1979). His results demonstrated that an enthusiastic teacher with a keen sense of humour may be not only well-liked, but may facilitate the academic productivity of pupils. It would be interesting to find out whether these teacher characteristics help children learn to relate to each other with the same energy and humour.

Teachers' leadership style and organization of the classroom. Brophy and Good (1974) provided the most comprehensive review of research on the inerplay of teacher and pupil characteristics. The teacher's interpersonal style tends to remain stable from year to year, class to class, whilst there is a greater tendency for the pupils to adjust to the teacher's style (Anderson, Brewer & Reed, cited by Brophy & Good, 1974). Attempts at modifying the teacher's leadership style often meet with only partial success. In Rubin's (1971) study, teachers did not respond well to efforts to train them in an interpersonal style highly dissimilar to their own. In their review, Brophy and Good found that a democratic teacher leadership style (as opposed to either authoritarian or laissez-faire) is associated with more positive classroom atmosphere, greater co-operation and pupil enjoyment, less competitiveness and frustration. However, research regarding the influence of this democratic classroom leadership style on academic achievement has yielded conflicting results. Therefore, Brophy and Good concluded that it may be more productive for researchers to consider the interactions of teacher leadership style and child variables. They maintained that there are two conceivable ways of matching teacher and pupil interpersonal styles. The first involves assigning children to teachers whose interpersonal styles are similar to theirs, whereas the alternative approach entails matching children whose behaviour is problematic with teachers whose leadership style might engender modification of the children's undesirable social behaviour. Bergmans (1983) suggested that boys may experience a greater range of teacher behaviour than girls, as teachers react to boys' proneness to restlessness and resistance to structure. It is quite conceivable that age as well as sex differences (i.e. teacher as well as child sex) mediate the impact of teacher variables. Hopefully, this will become clearer as more studies are conducted. Thomas and Chess (1977), as well as other scholars interested in children's temperament, have often advocated an optimal fit between the child's temperament and an appropriately matched school environment. Fischbein (1987) proposed a related concept, speculating that hereditary factors determine greater degrees of behaviour variation in school environments which are permissive and stimulating as opposed to restrictive and unstimulating. Fischbein is collecting longitudinal data regarding the school adjustment of large samples of twins in Swedish primary schools and Israeli kibbuzim in order to support this contention.

Wright and Cowen (1982) studied the associations between classroom atmosphere and students' acceptance of their peers. Upper primary school pupils in five suburban schools in Rochester, New York, were the participants. In classes where students perceived higher order and organization, as well as greater socialization, pupils indicated higher overall levels of acceptance of each other. These correlations were higher for students with social behaviour problems than for the whole group. In contrast, classes highest in perceived teacher control were characterized by lower levels of pupil popularity ratings. The data indicates the importance of considering the difference between a class that is well organized and one that is dominated by attempts at achieving control. Wright and Cowen's findings for order and organization were replicated with younger primary school pupils by Toro *et. al.* (1985). Both studies feature analyses of classroom effects both for the whole class and for subjects experiencing social adjustment problems. Both perspectives are essential to an understanding of school effects on social competence.

Teacher involvement in pupils' social relations. Teachers, like parents, vary in their involvement in social relations among their pupils. Bonino

(1991) observed very young children (aged 18–36 months) in two Italian daycare centres which adhered to two very different philosophies. In centre A, the caregivers believed in and practised very extensive involvement in their charges' social play. Centre B subscribed to an almost opposite philosophy, one of as little intervention as possible. The two centres enrolled children from similar socioeconomic milieux. While Bonino provided little detail of the exchanges between the caregivers and children, a systematic, reliable observational code was used for observations of the children's social play. The results were unambiguous: The youngsters in Centre A were far more aggressive and engaged in much less co-operative play. Presumably, children of this age learn much more about social relations by experience.

Bonino's conclusion does not necessarily apply to older children. Olweus (see below), who dealt with older Norwegian pupils who displayed severe problematic aggression, found that increased supervision of the children's play led to a marked reduction in bullying. Replications of some aspects of Olweus's work are underway in the United Kingdom and Canada.

Teacher introversion–extroversion. The very extensive research literature on the fundamental personality dimension of introversion–extroversion leads logically to the expectation that the extroverted teacher would bring many valuable attributes to the classroom, with positive impact on the pupil's social development. Jones (1971, cited in Brophy & Good, 1974) conducted the most complete study of the dimension of teacher introversion. Sixteen female teachers in training participated in the study along with a sample of the students they taught. Jones hypothesized that extroverted teachers would interact more frequently with extroverted pupils, whereas introverted teachers would establish more contact with introverted children. The results provide clear indication that introverted *children* received far higher amounts of teacher attention of all kinds. However, the pattern of findings among Jones's many dependent measures revealed only weak, inconsistent evidence for a link between teacher introversion and classroom interactions. Jones's study is limited by the fact that it was conducted with teachers in training, whose apprentice status may have attenuated proclivities toward extroversion or introversion.

Summary: teacher effects. The limited data available on teacher effects have only partially confirmed that the teacher's own social competence has an enduring influence on children's peer relations. This does not necessarily mean that teacher characteristics do not make a difference, but that their effects may depend on how they structure their classrooms for interpersonal interaction, or the "goodness of fit" between teacher and pupil characteristics. Much more research is needed to support both of these speculations. Hopefully, researchers will respond more fully to Brophy and Good's insistence on studying teacher variables in conjunction with pupil variables. As well, more studies targeting teacher effects on child social competence specifically are needed.

Age and gender composition of the student body

The age range and gender distribution of pupils in a school may both contribute to the social relations of students. A wide range may provide for modelling by older children. When students remain in the same school for a longer time period, groups may be more cohesive than where promotion to higher forms or grades leads to transfer to a new and inevitably larger school. There has been little systematic study of these effects for primary or secondary school pupils. However, Baudonnière (1988) compared the social interaction of youngsters in two different types of preschool which are prevalent in France. In one type, there is a wide age range; the other is limited to an age span of a year or two. No significant differences in children's social interaction were found between the two.

Administrative structure and cohesiveness

The cohesiveness of the school's teaching staff may be communicated to the pupils in both obvious and subtle ways. Regardless of what advice teachers may give children about the proper ways of interacting, the adult interactions observed may constitute a highly salient instructional medium. In Rutter *et. al.*'s (1979) study of secondary schools in Inner London, staff relations emerged as a powerful predictor of several types of school outcome (though peer-related social competence was not measured specifically in that study).

At least one ethnographic study confirmed that co-operative interactions among the school staff do have some connection with children's peer relations. Batten and Girling-Butcher (1981) used a combination of interview techniques and rating scales to compare the quality of seven Australian secondary schools. In one of the seven, a Catholic religious school, the staff were seen by the pupils as working together like a family and displaying a keen sense of commitment toward each other. In that school, peers were seen as particularly friendly and supportive. The students interviewed spoke of one particular case in which a classmate who had experienced marked difficulty getting along with others in a previous school was learning to adapt well in this more cohesive environment.

Grouping students by academic ability

Kagan (1990) discussed a number of ways in which schools alienate children who are at risk for psychological difficulty. These include isolating them to sub-groups which do not identify with the school and with the process of learning. It has been shown that once students within a classroom have been grouped on the basis of academic ability, social boundaries form and are rarely crossed (Putallaz & Gottman, 1981), though the increased contact with individuals within one's own track may facilitate friendship formation within it (Hansell & Karweit, 1983). When classroom assignment itself is based on academic ability, an alienated peer subculture may crystallize among low-ability pupils. Since individuals' academic and social competence tend to correlate (see below), ability grouping (tracking) may lead to differential access to competent peer models as well as differential peer reinforcement of social skills. However, in mixed-ability groups or classes, high academic achievement may serve as the ticket to group participation and peer acceptance (Asher, Oden & Gottman, 1977). Experimental attempts at fostering interaction between high-ability and low-ability pupils are discussed below.

Co-operative vs. competitive goal structures

The promotion of co-operative learning experiences has been probably the most active and best-accepted effort to date at restructuring the social ecology of the school. Co-operative learning techniques were developed as an alternative to the competitive goal structure of most schools. A system in which pupils compete with each other for marks allows no incentive for children helping each other; helping another child is usually considered cheating. Where there are official or unofficial restrictions on the proportion of high marks which can be assigned, a student who provides assistance to classmates may lower her own mark as a result (Johnson & Johnson, 1975; Slavin, 1987). Thomas (1984) maintained that competitive goal structures have replaced harsh discipline as a tool used by urban schools to maintain a modicum of control over pupils. In his view, competition is no more productive a tool in the long run. It causes profound alienation of disadvantaged youth, who escape the situation by not achieving their potential and by leaving school early.

Proponents of co-operative learning have developed a variety of specific procedures and empirically documented their effects. Co-operative learning does not mean simply telling children to work together. In order for co-operative goal structures to meaningfully influence the social system, incentives must be made contingent on group rather than individual achievement. Accountability must also be built in if the pupils are to take the co-operative learning experience seriously (Slavin, 1987). One important challenge in modifying the competitive goal structure of the traditional school is to provide each child or group with an equal opportunity to succeed and obtain rewards. Johnson and Johnson (1975) organized children into work teams. Before being assigned to work teams, children were pre-tested on their mastery of a given content area. Following instruction in that area, the children worked together on exercises designed to promote mastery of the content and were encouraged to assist team-mates having difficulty. The students were then post-tested; A collective mark was given each team based on each member's *improvement* since the pre-test, not on their final level of mastery. Thereby, weaker students do not handicap the team, while stronger students are most advantageous if they share their knowledge with team-mates. Johnson and Johnson do not advocate that the co-operative learning modality completely take over the school day, but discuss the nature of lessons for which it is most suitable.

The "jigsaw classroom" (Aronson *et. al.* 1978) is another innovation designed to promote co-operative goal structure, one which is perhaps more applicable to material that is less circumscribed than the discrete, testable chunks better used in Johnson and Johnson's co-operative learning. In the jigsaw model, work is divided into sections which logically fit together. Each member is assigned one part of a project on which he/she is to become proficient. In order to complete the project, the team members must co-operate to integrate the sections into a coherent whole.

While there has been a great deal of research on the effects of these co-operative learning experiences, cognitive outcome measures have been far more prevalent than measures of social competence. Thorough reviews of this literature were presented by Johnson and Johnson (1975), Johnson *et. al.* (1981) and Slavin (1987). The majority of findings indicate that children achieve greater academic gain in co-operative learning experiences than in control conditions of various types, while in most of the remaining studies the experimental and control groups appear to have learned the material equally well. This optimistic picture has been challenged because of the methods used both in the reviews and some of the original studies (Vedder, 1985). Vedder (1985), whose own experiment on co-operative learning of geometry in a Dutch high school yielded inconclusive results, was unsuccessful in his attempt to replicate Johnson *et. al.*'s (1981) findings regarding the effects of co-operative education on academic achievement. It is perhaps important to note that since American children, particularly Anglo-American children, have been found to be more competitive than most (Madsen & Shapira, 1970), co-operative learning experiments may be more successful in that culture than elsewhere.

Johnson and Johnson (1981) conducted an experiment to determine whether co-operative learning would facilitate the social integration of youngsters with learning and behaviour problems into a regular classroom setting. This is an important question, because school systems in many countries have invested abundant energy in accommodating pupils with various types of handicaps within the regular class. One obstacle that must be overcome is the lack of contact between handicapped and non-handicapped pupils after integration (Gresham, 1982). Fifty-one American fourth-grade students (age approximately 9-10 years) participated in Johnson and Johnson's (1981) study. Of these, twelve were pupils with severe behaviour and learning problems. The pupils were randomly assigned to either co-operative or individual learning conditions for one lesson (45 minutes) per day for 16 days, team taught by the regular classroom teacher and a teacher specially engaged and trained for the study. Each daily lesson was followed by 10 minutes of free play, during which the children's interactions were systematically observed. The results support co-operative learning most impressively. Interactions between handicapped and non-handicapped averaged thirty-three per hour in the co-operative condition, compared with five per hour in the individualistic condition. The number of students involved in these interactions between handicapped and non-handicapped pupils was also higher. There was significantly less off-task behaviour in the co-operative condition. The children in the co-operative condition also reported more reciprocal help between handicapped and non-handicapped children.

Tryon and Keane (1991) conducted a study to determine whether competitive and co-operative goal structures differentially affect children who are socially successful and unsuccessful. Pairs of children were invited to a university research laboratory where they were videotaped while playing the "Word Naming Game". The rules of the game were varied in order to create co-operative and competitive situations. A third child was asked to join the games in progress. This third child was of either rejected or popular social status according to sociometric assessment previously conducted in their primary school classrooms. As would be expected, the rejected youngsters were far less effective than the popular children in their group entry strategies in all goal structures. Furthermore, entering a game under competitive conditions was far more difficult for them than entering a game under other conditions. A more complex array of social skills seemed needed to enter the competitive game, which the rejected subjects did not appear to have. Thus, Tryon and Keane's results suggest that competitive situations may augment the difficulties faced by socially rejected children in getting along with their peers.

Active participation by pupils

Teachers have the choice of a traditional "lecture" format in which pupils play a passive listening role, or a teaching style which more actively involves the pupils and encourages their participation. Epstein's (1983) comprehensive study of friendship choices among adolescents in high-participatory and low-participatory secondary schools revealed many advantages of a participatory style. Sociometric measures indicated that in high-participatory schools more students were selected as best friends and fewer were left out. Students selected more friends from classrooms other than their own and there was less evidence of small "cliques" with tight boundaries. Presumably, these social advantages are the result of greater contact with other pupils during school activities.

Teachers also have the option of setting all rules and making all decisions, or involving pupils in decision making as their maturity permits. Jennings and Kohlberg (1983) found that participation in the governance of a school enhanced the moral judgements of adolescent delinquents. Since juvenile delinquents may well be of rejected social status, it would be interesting to explore the impact of such participation in decision making on the peer group's acceptance of rejected children.

Humphrey (1984) conducted a large-scale study of primary school pupils' perceptions of the structure of their classrooms and the degree that they felt involved in their environment. Children and teachers seldom shared perceptions of their classrooms, but it was the children's perceptions which were correlated with ratings of the children's behaviour and their own ratings of self-control. Where classes were seen as well organized (see above) *and* children felt highly involved, children's self-control was highest. Humphrey's findings underscore the importance of simultaneously considering multiple aspects of an environment and of tapping multiple sources of information on its effects.

Peer tutoring

Peer tutoring is another method for enhancing social interaction among pupils, promoting helping behaviour and improving academic achievement. As with co-operative learning, there is a large body of quantitative research documenting its effectiveness. Here again, most of these studies were conducted in the United States, with academic achievement the most frequent outcome variable (Cohen, Kulik & Kulik, 1982; Goodland & Hirst, 1989; Kalfus, 1984; Kalfus & Stokes, 1987; Loranger, Tremblay & Parent, 1986). Goodland and Hirst (1989) outlined some of the challenges inherent in evaluating the effects of peer tutoring. The first problem is that it is extremely difficult to achieve peer tutoring and control conditions (usually traditional teaching) that are equivalent in time and salience. Peer tutors may develop relationships with each other, and seek more extended contact with each other both inside and outside of school. This is unlikely to occur where a child is tutored by a professional, as occurs typically for the control group. Secondly, any interaction between members of a tutored group and control group (e.g. in the same class or school) can make it more difficult to assess the long-term outcome of changes. As well, the research design must control the effects of the tutor's (and tutee's) own personality and social competence, perhaps by switching tutors systematically during the course of the study.

While research overwhelmingly has documented the effects of peer tutoring on academic achievement, its benefits for children's peer relations have not been established as clearly, though they are depicted graphically in many qualitative accounts (Goodland & Hirst, 1989). Pigott, Fantuzzo and Clement (1986) arranged peer tutoring for primary school pupils weak in arithmetic. In this study, the children experiencing academic difficulty tutored each other; peer "experts" were not used. The instructional roles to be assumed by the children within their study teams were assigned designations associated with athletic teams ("coach", "scorekeeper", "referee" and "manager"). They were allowed to select their own roles from among these each week. The children were assigned to groups of four, in which each role would be assumed by one student. Each team also selected its own goal for improvement in arithmetic. The team's "score" was determined by its attainment of its own goal. Pigott, Fantuzzo and Clement found that accurate tutoring in arithmetic occurred, despite the children's deficiencies in that subject, and that this procedure resulted in improved arithmetic achievement. As well, there were dramatic gains in the peers' ratings of the social acceptance of the study team members.

In contrast, a "jigsaw" model (see above) was used for a peer teaching study by Wright and Cowen (1985). Each pupil was assigned the task of learning a different section of an assignment and teaching it to other students. In comparison with control subjects who received traditional instruction, the peer teaching group achieved better academic results and perceived the classroom as a more positive atmosphere. However, the groups did not differ in self-esteem change, and the control subjects assigned higher ratings of acceptance to peers than those in the peer teaching condition. Wright and Cowen speculated that the peer teaching condition might unwittingly have set up a competitive situation, with children trying to impress each other with their knowledge.

In a series of studies, Strain and his colleagues (Strain, 1985) instructed non-handicapped classmates to prompt mentally handicapped peers in such appropriate social behaviours as initiating play or conversation, sharing toys, helping others and expressing affection. Within-subjects, multiple-baseline designs were typically used. Results showed dramatic increases in the prompted behaviours. Perhaps Strain has been better able to demonstrate the impact of peer prompting than the peer tutoring studies because of his focus on specific behaviours, precisely defined and measured by means of direct observation, as opposed to assessing group changes in such global constructs as self-concept and peer acceptance, which are affected by a wide range of life experiences in addition to the peer interventions. Recent results obtained by Christopher, Hansen and MacMillan (1991) lend support to this conjecture. They trained classroom peers to prompt the social interactions of three socially isolated boys aged 7–8 years. Multiple baseline analyses confirmed sharp increases in the specific behaviours prompted, whereas more global sociometric measures, teacher and self-ratings provided inconsistent corroboration of the success of the intervention.

Tutoring by adults. One might wonder whether the benefits of peer tutoring accrue because of the experience of interacting with peers or because of the actual gain in academic skill. It has been frequently reported that socially rejected children tend to be deficient in academic achievement (Coie, 1985; Green *et. al.* 1980; McMichael, 1980; Schmuck, 1963; Wiener, 1987), though these correlations are not usually very strong (0.20 to 0.40; Coie, 1985). There may be several reasons for this link. An underlying pattern of neurological dysfunction may cause both academic failure and deficient social perception or social behaviour. Alternatively, poor school performance may lead to negative feedback from teachers and concomit-ant reductions in self-confidence and self-esteem (Coie, 1985).

Coie and Krehbeil (1984) conducted an experiment with primary school children who were experiencing both social and academic failure. There were four experimental conditions: social skills training alone, academic tutoring (provided by adults) alone, social skills training plus academic tutoring, and no-treatment control. While social skills training did engender some degree of improvement, it was short-lived. By the time of follow-up 1 year later, it was clear that the academic tutoring had brought about the most substantial gains in both academic and social competence. While replication of this study is needed, its outcome suggests that one should not discount the value of academic capability itself as an asset in peer relations.

Peer relations taught as part of the school curriculum

Up to this point in the chapter, pupils' social competence has been considered as a function of the physical or human ecology of the school. In addition, the need for specific instruction in social competence as part of the regular programme of study has been widely recognized. Moreno (1953) intended to follow his sociometric testing in classrooms with a therapeutic group intervention called spontaneity training, but, curiously, the school principal (head) of the first school approached thought that the role-play intervention would meet resistance within the schools.

E. Lakin Phillips (1978) articulated perhaps the most eloquent theoretical proposal for a social competence curriculum. He called on schools to help children build some degree of tolerance for adverseness and annoyances, but learn to solve the interpersonal differences which will inevitably arise. Such a curriculum should feature a realistic sequence of clearly-stated goals with the development of competence in the long term, not just the resolution of immediate issues. It should strive to reduce hostility toward others and impulsive reaction, and emphasize one's ethical obligations to others.

While there have been a fair number of reviews of the research on children's social skills training, Weissberg and Allen's (1986) synthesis focuses most specifically on preventive work in the schools. They presented a number of compelling justifications for teaching social competence to all students who are in schools where a high risk of psychological disorder can be ascertained. They also advocated secondary prevention programmes which attempt to enhance the social competence of individual children who are already showing signs of dysfunctional social behaviour. The established fact that social maladjustment during childhood often predicts adult psychological disorder (see review by Parker & Asher, 1987) is sufficient reason for intervening as early as possible when troublesome social behaviour emerges as a stable behavioural profile. However, Weissberg and Allen recalled that many children who display no maladjustment problems remain vulnerable to psychological disorder and may benefit in the long term from social competence education. In addition, Schneider (1989) remarked that learning these skills may be beneficial to less vulnerable individuals in solving the interpersonal difficulties which emerge as part of everyday living, even if these do not develop into an enduring pattern of psychopathology.

Weissberg and Allen argued that schools are a logical site for preventive interventions. First of all, school-based interventions are accessible to all children, and avoid the stigmatization which may occur if a child with minor difficulties is referred to clinics or hospitals. Hopefully, the school setting also affords better opportunities for the immediate practice and reinforcement of the social skills taught as part of the curriculum.

One of the best known modalities for teaching social competence as part of the school programme is social problem-solving. The rationale for social problem-solving lessons stems from studies which indicate that aggressive, socially unsuccessful youngsters tend to respond impulsively to situations without considering alternatives (Camp, 1977). Spivack and Shure (1982) introduced a forty-six session programme for 5-year-old youngsters. Using a variety of stories, songs and discussion material, the children were taught to use strategies which typify effective problem solvers, such as "brainstorming"—generating a series of possible solutions rather than just one's typical response pattern, contemplating the consequences of a given solution, effective planning of desired responses and others. Many other social problem-solving interventions have been developed, including some for older primary schoolchildren and adolescents (see Caplan & Weissberg, 1989). Many of these recent programmes are more careful in presenting social problems relevant to the context in which the pupils are experiencing social difficulty.

There have been many empirical studies of the effectiveness of social problem-solving. These have been the subject of detailed reviews by Durlak (1983), Pellegrini and Urbain (1985), Urbain and Kendall (1980) and others. The general consensus of these reviews is that social problem-solving has a mixed record of success; similar conclusions are reported in review articles which compare social problem-solving with other types of social skills training (e.g. Michelson & Mannarino, 1986; Schneider, in press).

Feshbach (1983) researched school-based interventions designed to enhance children's ability to understand the perspective of other persons and empathize with them. Such programmes were found quite beneficial in comparison with control groups that received no social competence intervention. However, Bonino (1989) randomly assigned youngsters to either an empathy training or social problem-solving condition. The social problem-solving intervention proved more beneficial. It should be noted that the participants in the two studies were quite different. Aside from possible differences between Italian and American children, Bonino's subjects were older than Feshbach's. In a younger population, a higher proportion of subjects may be deficient in perspective-taking, which might be a more profitable intervention. Schneider's (1992) meta-analytic review indicated little difference in effect size between the two interventions, though relatively few perspective-taking studies were included.

Adalbjarnardottir (1991) conducted a particularly interesting intervention designed to enhance children's ability to negotiate with classmates and teachers. Eight Icelandic primary school classes were randomly assigned to either treatment and control conditions. The intervention consisted of focused training in solving interpersonal conflicts, and was administered to four classes as a whole. A semi-structured interview was conducted at the beginning of the school year and repeated at the end. The children's interpersonal negotiation style was also observed directly in the classroom. Their interactions were rated, first of all, as either submissive or assertive. They were also coded according to the degree to which the actions reflected a sophisticated understanding of other persons' perspectives regarding the situation observed. Subjects who had received the intervention developed more mature negotiation strategies over the school year according to both the interviews and observations. It is interesting to note that the observational data indicate improvement for situations involving classmates but not teachers, suggesting that youngsters may have more difficulty understanding the perspectives and needs of adults even after intervention. Abalbjarndottir's study is of particular value because its outcome measures, which included both an interview and direct observations, were devised to assess very directly the specific outcome targeted by the intervention.

More direct coaching and modelling techniques also have potential utility in school-based prevention programmes. In a coaching procedure, the "coach" provides ideas or concepts about social interaction, asks the child to generate specific behavioural examples of each, and encourages the child to use the concepts and monitor his/her own behaviour (Asher, 1985). Obviously, this approach is more suitable to secondary prevention with children known to be experiencing social difficulties. Modelling approaches feature either filmed (Schneider & Byrne, 1987) or role-play (Goldstein & Glick, 1987) models of skilful behaviours.

Schneider's (1992) meta-analytic review indicated that these school-based direct instruction approaches have a significant influence on children's social behaviour. The effect sizes for school-based social problem-solving are small to moderate, though, as discussed previously, such small to moderate effects are known to have real-life importance for many children. The effects are much more pronounced for withdrawn children than for others. Coaching, modelling and combined approaches seem more successful than problem-solving, though the technique used explained much less of the variance in effectiveness than the type of child (withdrawn youngsters responded much better than aggressives). However, there are many reasons to suspect that existing studies underestimate the potential contribution of school-based social competence promotion. For one thing, most of the social competence lessons were taught by teachers participating in these studies having little experience in providing instruction of this type, and who often receive little training (Schneider, 1989; Weissberg, 1985). In most of the studies, there is no systematic verification that the intervention was actually conducted the way the researcher intended (Schneider, 1988, 1992). The newest instructional technology is rarely applied (for some interesting exceptions, see Margalit and Weisel's [1990] use of a computer program to teach social problem-solving skills to mentally-retarded adolescents or videotaped social skills materials developed for adolescents by Hazel et. al. [1985]). Perhaps most important, few interventions have been planned to take into account the interaction of the intervention content with the classroom or school ecology. Should we expect a lesson on co-operation to have any substantial bearing on behaviour in a classroom with a highly competitive goal structure? If effective problem-solving is taught as an isolated instructional unit, but infractions are handled in an impulsive, angry fashion, is there any benefit derived from the abstract tutelage on how to deal with irritants? Hopefully, educational planners will adopt a multipronged approach in adding social competence to the curriculum while attempting to provide a competence-enhancing environment.

Olweus's (1990) nationwide multidimensional intervention was quite effective in reducing the instances of bullying behaviour across Norway. His approach featured a combination of classroom discussion and role-play, individual counselling, teacher training, closer supervision of recess play and co-ordination with the parents of both bullies and victims. Thus, didactic lessons were supplemented with improvement of the school environment. Efforts at replicating this type of intervention in other countries will help determine the potential of this approach in reducing problematic aggression in countries where bully/victim incidents may involve children of different cultural backgrounds, and where there is less precedent for national policy to direct specific school practice. Olweus's results confirm the benefits of combining didactic lessons with efforts at improving the environment.

Figure 3.2 illustrates how interventions can be planned with awareness of the ways by which various context factors may facilitate them. As shown, different avenues of intervention relate to different levels of social reality. The juxtaposition of levels in the figure does *not* imply that intervention at a "higher" level is more valid than intervention at the individual level. However, as indicated by the vertical arrows, effects at one level have implications for the others. For example, an individual trained in social problem-solving and empathy may be a better candidate for relationship intervention, such as pairing with a peer "buddy" in school. If one attempts to change the individual's social network without addressing his impulsive, self-centred behavioural style, the effort might backfire as the peer "buddy" is exposed to egocentrism and impulsivity. Helping reticent children improve their conversational skills may be of little benefit if the surrounding goal structure places them in competition with potential conversation partners for available rewards. Conversely, changing the goal structure of a classroom may not teach conversation skills to a child with a genuine deficit in that area.

School Culture

Schools can be characterized according to the predominant emphases or the concerns which pervade communication within them. Some place heavy emphasis on academics, others on sport or club activities. In some schools, logistics dominate the atmosphere—co-ordinating classes, class-rooms and personnel. Some schools emphasize the pupils' personal growth while others devote much of their energy to the establishment of school rules, disciplinary procedures, etc. (Anderson, 1982). While there are few solid data on the subject, the school culture may well have an impact on students' peer relations.

Bossert (1979) conducted an in-depth study of the cultures and activity structures of different classrooms within an American primary school. In some of the classrooms, an academic emphasis predominated. The "recitation" style of instruction was most often employed and academic achievement was highly emphasized. In these classrooms, children tended to form friends with peers whose levels of academic competence was

LEVEL OF SOCIAL REALITY   INTERVENTION

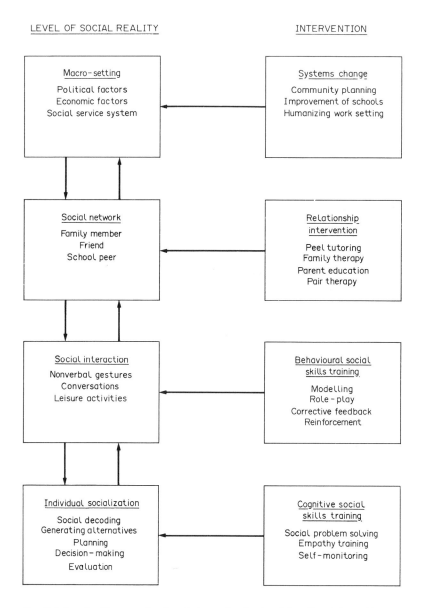

FIG. 3.2. Levels of intervention in relation to levels of social reality. Adapted from Gaylord-Ross, R. (1992). Issues and research in special education, Vol. 2. (New York: Teachers College Press © 1992 by Teachers College, Columbia University. All rights reserved). Figure 5.3—p. 223. By permission of the publisher.

similar to their own. These academically homogeneous peer groupings may be influenced by the children's heightened awareness of each others' levels of academic performance. Other classrooms featured more emphasis on social development and had less competitive atmospheres. There was less use of discrete, structured academic tasks and recitation, which were replaced by more integrated, multitask learning activities. In these classrooms, children formed friendships across levels of academic achievement. As well, friendship groupings were more fluid during the school year. Thus, Bossert's results are consistent with those obtained by Serow and Solomon, who, as detailed earlier in this chapter, found that in structured, academically-orientated classrooms, there was little social interaction among children of different cultural origins. In addition to elucidating the influence of academic culture on children's friendship formation, Bossert's study demonstrates the importance of considering the culture of each classroom, not just the culture of the whole school.

While Bossert's results suggest that an academic culture may in some ways impede social interaction among pupils, Rutter *et. al.* (1979) demonstrated that a business-like academic atmosphere may have other beneficial effects. As mentioned at the beginning of this chapter, Isherwood and Ahola (1981) maintained that it is quite possible for teachers to define classroom environments so that the instrumental aspects of schooling and the school's task of expressive socialization co-exist rather than compete.

Teachers' beliefs about children's social development

As discussed in Chapter 2, children's social competence may be affected in several conceivable ways by their parents' beliefs about social development and its origins. Similarly, some teachers may consider that pupils' social development is a priority, while others may place greater emphasis on other areas, such as intellectual development, creativity or adjustment to school routine. Some teachers may feel that their social behaviour in the classroom can have a substantial impact on peer relations among students, while others may see children's social relations as a product of parenting, heredity or cultural influence. Such differences in teacher beliefs may well have direct or indirect effects on children's social interaction, though there is relatively little research which documents their importance. However, there are some indications that teachers tend to attribute responsibility for children's social behaviour problems to family influences. For example, Quadrio, Saita and Iezzi (1991) presented descriptions of hypothetical children whose classroom behaviour was moderately maladjusted to a sample of teachers in Milan, who were asked to speculate about the causes of the problem. These teachers cited poor family background most frequently, and discounted the possibility that a poor school environment caused or exacerbated the difficulties. This tendency was most pronounced when parental divorce was included in the description of the hypothetical case. In a similar vein, Schneider, Kerridge and Katz (in press) asked teachers to rate the desirability of several interventions for aggressive and withdrawn youngsters. Fifty-three Canadian teachers participated in the study, of whom thirty-one were teachers of classes for youngsters with special learning and behavioural needs. Two different hypothetical cases were presented on audiocassettes. The first was a 6-year-old girl named Sally, whose behaviour was extremely aggressive; the other case was that of Craig, a 10-year-old boy characterized by extreme withdrawal and depressive features. Commonly-used psychological interventions were described on audiotapes: modelling, social problem-solving, coaching, token reinforcement, time out (only for Sally), family therapy, play therapy and pharmacotherapy. The interventions were presented in eight different sequences, using a Latin-square design. The teachers were asked to indicate their preferences among the interventions. The authors expected that the teachers would identify most strongly with classroom-based approaches that featured a didactic, positive approach in increasing children's social competence (modelling, coaching and problem-solving). As illustrated in Figure 3.3, these interventions received relatively high ratings. However, the teachers endorsed family therapy over any intervention involving changes in the classroom or direct therapy with the child, with *post-hoc* Tukey tests indicating that it received significantly higher ratings than all other treatments, whilst the ratings for pharmacotherapy were signficantly lower. Male teachers were slightly more inclined to favour all interventions (see Figure 3.4). Bar-Tal (1979) found that teachers shared the credit with parents for pupils' academic success, but attributed students' failures to deficits in the home environment. Perhaps this pattern of attributions applies to children's social success and failure as well. Schneider, Kerridge and Katz's study is limited by the fact that, in an effort to avoid stereotypes, they presented relatively unfamiliar stimuli, i.e. an aggressive girl. Researchers interested in pursuing this work might use several exemplars of both sexes if possible.

Conclusions: School Life and Children's Peer Relations

In sharp contrast with the literature on the family's impact on peer relations, research on the possible contribution of the school appears limited and highly fragmented. This chapter has brought together selected gleanings from highly diverse literatures, which are not easy to combine and synthesize. Hopefully, the next generation of research will tackle the school climate "beast" head on, and attempt to document the multifaceted influence that a school's climate may have on relationships among pupils. Perhaps we shall be able to determine, for example, how beneficial warm,

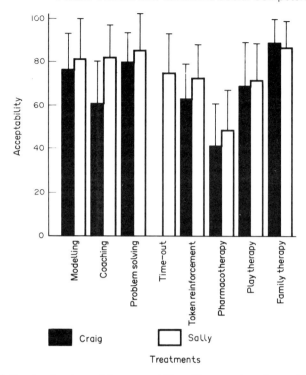

FIG. 3.3. Teachers' ratings of the acceptability of interventions for a withdrawn boy (Craig) and an aggressive girl (Sally). From Schneider, B., Kerridge, A., & Katz, J. (in press). Teacher acceptance of psychological interventions of varying theoretical orientation. *Schools Psychology International*. By permission.

enthusiastic teachers are if they also engineer co-operative goal structures and sound acquisition of academic skill. At the moment, we might speculate that the available data underestimate the potential impact of schools, because they are based on fractions of the school experience.

Nevertheless, in light of the many other influences on children's social development, one might expect that the school's impact is a small one. However, as discussed in Chapter 1, such small effects can be more important than they first seem, and perhaps of particular importance to children at risk for social maladjustment. The interaction of school climate with children's temperamental predispositions and social behaviour patterns merits further exploration. Corroboration is needed of the possibility that schools may have greater effects—socially as well as academically—in developing countries.

The aspects of school life discussed in this chapter vary in their amenability to change. There have been serious efforts to enhance only some of the influences discussed. It has been noted that the general

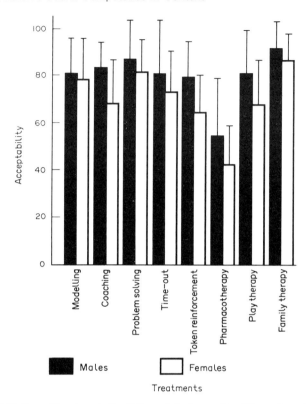

Fɪɢ. 3.4. Ratings of treatments (for Sally and Craig combined) by male and female teachers. From Schneider, B., Kerridge, A., & Katz, J. (in press). Teacher acceptance of psychological interventions of varying theoretical orientation. *School Psychology International*. By permission.

structure of schooling is firmly ingrained within societies. Therefore, in attempting to enhance children's social competence by modifying the school environment, one would confront long-established notions of the ways children should be educated. Perhaps for this reason, teachers have not fully put into practice many of the changes which psychologists have proposed as means of enhancing children's social behaviour at school (Witt, 1986). In spite of our firmly-entrenched "archetype" for schooling (see above), efforts to improve schools are perennial. While some "innovations" reflect little more than the vagaries of fashion, others seem to have at least the potential to bring about more enduring change, including facilitation of pupils' social development. The ultimate success of any attempts at constructing school environments that enhance social competence will help ascertain the importance of the school's contribution to children's interpersonal relations.

4

Cultural Imprints on Children's Social Competence

Chapters 2 and 3 outlined many of the pathways by which families and schools may impact on children's peer relations. However, both families and schools operate within a broader framework as representatives of the surrounding culture. The sociocultural context is an important guide essential for understanding the meaning of any individual's social behaviour. Cross-cultural psychologists see culture both as a result of human social behaviour and as a causal agent which shapes human behaviour (Segall, 1979). Whiting and Edwards, principal investigators of probably the largest and best-known cross-cultural study of children's social behaviour, have remarked that the settings frequented by adults and children strengthen, if not create, behavioural dispositions far beyond the conscious intent of the parents and teachers who supervise children's lives within them. The nature of the setting is largely determined by culture, most often in terms of patterns of economic activity, division of labour, patterns of settlement, etc. They propose that the most salient features of settings are the other individuals present–their number, age, kinship relation, etc. An important task undertaken by the cross-cultural researcher is to identify whether there are stable modes of peer interaction whch are associated across cultures with particular patterns of interactions between children and specific categories of individuals in settings (Whiting & Edwards, 1988). Whiting and Edwards's own work (1988) illustrated impressive cross-cultural similarity in children's social development, leading them to conclude that social behaviour is intentional and driven by a maturationally-related striving to become competent. However, patterns of economic activity, differential child-rearing patterns and different propositions of time spent with various kinds of people are interrelated mechanisms by which culture seems to modulate this seemingly inherent striving; more detail on these influences appears later in the chapter.

Comparisons of social behaviour in different cultures serve many purposes in elucidating the origins of social competence. While one important contribution of cross-cultural research is to trace links between various characteristics of a society and the social behaviour of its members, cross-cultural research is also useful in demonstrating that certain aspects of social behaviour are replicated in virtually all cultures. Indeed, cross-cultural researchers have discovered that there are a relatively small number of "scripts" for peer interaction which appear to recur in many cultures around the world which have little possibility of mutual contact (Whiting & Edwards, 1988). Discovery of such parallels across cultures helps identify the features of behaviour which may be genetically transmitted species-wide. As Segall aptly put it: "human beings are sociocultural animals—This is not to say that we are not, first of all, biological creatures (p. 5)". However, Argyle (1983) has pointed out that, since humans have greater capacity for learning than other species, they are more likely than other species to acquire at least some of their social competence by means of learning experiences. Margaret Mead (cited in Eisenberg & Mussen, 1989, p. 42) similarly accentuated the malleability of human nature in responding with accuracy to changing cultural conditions.

In all cultures, children display an apparently inherent motivation to become competent and to construct knowledge about themselves and about social interactions (Edwards, 1986). This implies that we should not seek to study only the imprint of culture on the child's social behaviour (i.e. "how society gets inside the individual" [Corsaro, 1988]), but how such cultural influences impinge upon the child's own inherent propensity to make sense of her world. Reflecting the dramatic impact of the contributions of Piaget and Vygotsky, many scholars have recognized in principle the need for such a constructivist approach. In exhorting developmentalists to move beyond linear models of childhood socialization, Corsaro (1988) advocated increased attention to the role of language and discourse. However, this tacit acceptance of the child's active role has for the most part not been translated into new research strategies.

Since culture influences interpersonal relations, as will be illustrated below, the results of virtually any study of children's social competence cannot be readily generalized outside of the culture in which they were obtained. However, this does not mean that psychologists must now begin replicating all studies of children's development one by one, culture by culture. Such mass-production, atheoretical cross-cultural research is obviously not feasible, and in any case would likely be less productive than it might seem at first. Research which considers culture systematically as an independent variable holds much more promise, as this would enable a more informed understanding of the reasons for cultural influences and the mechanisms by which they operate (Gudykunst & Ting-Toomey, 1988). Anthropologists working in the field have compiled literally thousands of descriptions of social interaction in societies around the world (cf. Triandis & Berry, 1980). These have been catalogued and compared for many purposes, including comparisons of parents' socialization of aggression (Barry et al. 1976). Nevertheless, systematic, theory-driven investigations of cross-cultural differences in children's social competence and its origins remain rare.

Classification schemes for cultures

Considering the ways cultures vary is one promising way of developing hypotheses about cultural effects of children's social competence. Theorists from several disciplines have developed typologies of cultural variation; the reader is referred to Gudykunst and Ting-Toomey's (1988) articulate explication of cultural classification systems for more detail.

Individualism/collectivism. The distinction between collectivistic and individualistic societies has been widely considered the most fundamental dimension of cultural variation (Triandis, 1986). Parsons (1951) used a related terminology, namely self vs. collectivity orientation. Triandis (1986) discusses a similar distinction between allocentrism as opposed to idiocentrism, as does Tajfel (1978), whose concept of social identity refers to the portion of an individual's self-concept which derives from his knowledge of membership in a social group or groups. In a collectivistic culture, one's identity as a member of a group moves to the forefront. Compared with an individualistic culture, the group's goals achieve greater importance, with individual goals becoming concomitantly less important. Members of a collectivistic society assume greater responsibility for each other's welfare. In many if not most cases, this responsibility includes shared concern for each other's children, and, very often, collective child-rearing arrangements.

The major English-speaking countries, U.S.A., Great Britain, Canada and Australia, are virtually the most individualistic societies known (Hofstede, 1983). Therefore, children in our cultures are surrounded by a belief system which emphasizes a sense of individuality to a far greater degree than almost all Third World cultures or even those of Continental Europe. Their beliefs about others are more likely to be idiosyncratic, rather than common beliefs shared with others. Within a given culture, rural milieux may be more collectivistic than urban centres (Madsen & Shapira, 1970). The many differences between individualistic and collectivistic societies are no doubt profoundly manifest in both the nature of the children's peer relations and the importance they and adults assign to relations with others.

One's group membership is thought to be a more essential part of one's identity in stuations where there is extensive contact between groups, as in multicultural societies (McGuire *et al.*, 1978), particularly among minority groups (e.g. Hewstone, Bond & Wan, 1983; Hofman, 1985). As documented later in this chapter, the social adjustment of minority children has been explored in a number of countries, including several where the basic strucure of the minority culture differs profoundly from that of the surrounding majority. There are theoretical grounds for predicting two opposite tendencies when a collectivistic minority interacts with a more individualistic majority. One argument would hold that the minority parents cling steadfastly to the orientation of their culture of origin, energetically inculcating its values in order to maintain group identity. However, it has also been proposed that parents actively attempt to transmit to their children the competences necessary for the children to succeed within that culture (Ogbu, 1981). If this is the case, parents who emigrate to a more individualistic society might emphatically alter their parenting styles in order to accommodate their perceptions of the competences needed by their children to adapt.

While individualism/collectivism is commonly seen as the most important dimension in cultural variability, as well as the dimension which seems likely to affect children's social competence to the greatest extent, several of the other dimensions reviewed by Gudykunst and Ting-Toomey suggest important cultural differences in the social rules that must be mastered by the child as part of the process of becoming socially competent. For example, Hall (1976) observed that in certain cultures individuals explicitly communicate information about relationships to each other (as may be the case in the English-speaking countries), whereas in others (for example, China, Japan or Korea) the message is largely inferred from the context. In high-context cultures, the socially-competent child must become particularly adept at making inferences based upon knowledge of situations rather than from precise messages received from others at the time of each social transaction, though the ability to understand and interpret social situations has been seen as crucial even in relatively low-context cultures (see, e.g., Argyle, Furnham & Graham, 1981).

Gudykunst and Ting-Toomey (1988) maintained that the dimensions of cultural individualism/collectivism and high/low context together influence the extent to which interpersonal relations are characterized by a need to "save face" as an individual, or maintain a positive public image of oneself. In individualistic, low-content cultures, there may be a greater need to maintain one's own public image, whereas in collectivistic, high-context cultures, it may be more important to maintain the mutual face of one's group. However, it can also be argued that it is important in a collectivistic culture to cultivate an individual public image that is not at variance with the group's norms and beliefs. Loss of face is often seen as particularly devastating by adolescents even in the highly individualistic North American culture. In this and many other areas, increased attention must be given to the interaction of developmental differences and cultural differences, as cultural differences may be more evident at certain levels of development.

Tolerance for ambiguity and diversity. Different cultures also have divergent thresholds for ambiguity in relationships and for tolerating diversity in behaviour (Hofstede, 1979). Where there is little tolerance for adversity, there is greater pressure on the child and his/her parents to eliminate social behaviours which depart from the norm. As well, the child learning about peer relations in such an environment may learn to reject potential companions whose social behaviour is atypical. In a cultural context where uncertainty is avoided, a child may come to expect more formal rules for social behaviour and less informal negotiation. Where there is a need to avoid uncertainty, interpersonal relations may be characterized by more frequent displays of emotion and higher levels of stress.

Hofstede (1980, 1984) also established that individuals in certain cultures more easily accept that power is unevenly allocated. In high-power-distance cultures, children may be more likely to value social conformity and to assume authoritarian beliefs. Children's relationships with adults would be based on unquestioned obedience.

Rules. Argyle (1983, p. 123) defined a social rule as "a shared belief that certain things should or should not be done" within the confines of a particular setting. All social situations have rules; failure to follow them inevitably leads to some degree of rejection by peers. Within a given culture, rules differ from one setting to another, i.e. there may be fewer rules governing some types of relationships than others. Cultures are known to differ somewhat in terms of the rules which apply to different settings. For example, Japanese adults are expected to restrain the expression of emotion and defer to others far more than their counterparts in Britain (Argyle *et al.* 1986). There are also rules for relationships among children and between children and adults; these probably vary according to age, culture and setting. However, few data are available regarding cross-cultural differences in rules for children's relationships.

Research strategies for studying cultures

As might be expected, cross-cultural researchers have invested heavily in drawing links between such variations among cultures and aspects of individuals' personality or development. However, any attempt to link these cultural variables with aspects of children's social behaviour must be undertaken with considerable caution. To begin with, most of the data available are contained in global ethnographic accounts designed to portray a culture in its entirety, depicting not only distinct aspects of the culture but their interrelations as elements of a whole system. In order to use these ethnographic data in cross-cultural comparisons, they must be dissected into smaller parts. Shweder (1979) reviewed some of the shortcomings inherent in doing this. Any given norm, convention, custom or ritual will lose some of its significance when it is separated from its position in space and time in order to be compared with parallel features of other cultures.

Selection of measures. Shweder's remarks also suggest some standards for sound cross-cultural research. He exhorted researchers to refrain from inferences based on trait measures of personality, for example. The validity of these measures has been questioned because social behaviour is known to vary considerably within cultures from one setting to another. Shweder also questioned the facile assumption often made in cross-cultural research that specific child-care practices lead to stable patterns of social behaviour which persist into adulthood. The data collected rarely suffice to prove either the hypothesized causal link or the hypothesized stability of the "outcome" behaviour over time.

It is often tempting to draw causal inferences from cross-cultural comparisons without due regard to the correlational nature of the research. In most situations, correlational designs are more or less inevitable, but must nonetheless be interpreted appropriately. Moreover, the links between a given predictor variable in a culture and a "resulting" child behaviour variable will in most cases constitute a statistically small effect, though this does not mean that they are unimportant—see Chapter 1. Because of the nature of the data, the research design and the size of the effect, the same "resulting" child behaviour could in almost any case be caused by another aspect of the culture, or indeed by some other variable. For example, Eron and Huesmann (1987) remarked that while the United States has a much higher homicide rate than Poland, no observational field study can clearly demonstrate which of the many differences between Polish and American culture are responsible for this difference in people's behaviours. It would be easy to attribute the differences to the fact that Poland did not have a competitive market economy at the time of their data collection, but the methodology—or any conceivable refinement— could not allow conclusive delineation of this aspect of Polish society as the causal factor. *This limitation applies to all the studies reviewed in this chapter.*

Weisfield, Weisfield and Callaghan (1984; see below) speculated that the item "acts grown up" in a peer rating instrument may have been interpreted differently in their two samples, with Hopi Indian children perhaps understanding it to mean the performance of useful labour, whilst Afro-American girls may have understood it to mean wearing makeup, using profanities and insulting people.

At the very least, these methodological and conceptual considerations indicate that, in drawing inferences from cross-cultural studies of children's social behaviour, we should assign greater weight to studies that employ a variety of measurement strategies, as this will help avoid unwarranted generalizations based on a single source of information. As well, items on a questionnaire may be interpreted differently in different cultures.

Studies that include direct observation of children's behaviour as one of the techniques also inspire greater confidence, especially if the observers attend adequately to situational factors influencing the target behaviour. It is important for the observer to understand the social significance of the behaviours observed, not just record their presence. Nevertheless, it may be important to work with observers who are members of the culture studied, or very familiar with it (Whiting & Edwards, 1988). In any case, it must be remembered that direct observations of behaviour are costly, though many would consider them a wise investment of resources.

An example of a well-designed study in which multiple methods were used judiciously may help us appreciate what might be missed in studies employing a more restricted range of measurement tools. Van der Kooij and Neukater (1989) compared German, Dutch and Norwegian parents in terms of their directiveness in supervising their children's play. Three basic measures of parental directiveness were used. The first was a self-report scale on which parents rated their own directiveness. The parents were also asked to watch a series of videotapes which depicted increasing levels of parental directiveness, and rate the degree to which their own style corresponded to the tapes. Finally, the parents were observed in a play situation with their children; their directiveness was coded by independent raters.

When the parents' self-reports were considered, the Dutch sample appeared to be the most directive, significantly more than the Norwegians, who rated themselves as significantly more directive than the Dutch. However, the direct observations of the parent–child interaction yielded exactly the reverse pattern, with the Dutch parents rated significantly *less* directive than either of the two other samples. There were no signifcant differences among the countries in the parents' codings of the videotapes. Because of these inconsistencies in measurement, van der Kooij and Neukater could not present definitive conclusions about the extent cross-cultural differences in parents' directiveness or about how directiveness affects children's social play in the countries studied. Had the researchers failed to use multiple measures, they might have presented a more simple, but highly questionable, set of conclusions.

Some researchers have attempted to standardize the measurement of children's propensities toward co-operative behaviour across cultures by developing standard games or tasks. Madsen's (1971) marble-pull game, portrayed in Figure 4.1, is an example. This game involves a table on which an eyelet has been screwed into each end. A marble is held at the centre of the table by a weight, which is held together by a two-part magnet. The

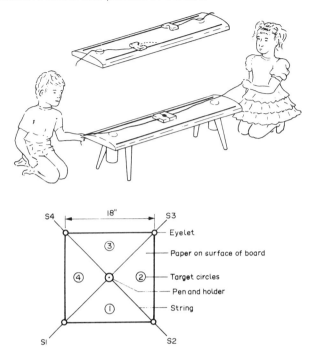

FIG. 4.1. Co-operation board. From Madsen, A. C. & Shapira, A. (1970).
Co-operative and competitive behavior of urban Afro-American, Anglo-
American, Mexican-American, and Mexican village children. *Developmental
Psychology*, **3**, 16–20. By permission.

object of the game is to have the marble drop into a pocket. The apparatus
can be set up by rigging from the eyelet to the weight in the centre in such a
way that the marble will drop only if it is pulled in one direction, making
co-operation more adaptive. If the string is pulled simultaneously in both
directions, the two parts of the magnet separate, and the marble rolls away.
While this type of game does permit efficient quantitative comparisons
across cultures, removal of play behaviour from its naturalistic context
may be problematic. Therefore, this tool is perhaps best used as one of
several measures of co-operative or competitive behaviour. Nevertheless,
Madsen's tool facilitated cross-cultural comparison by providing something of a common metric. As discussed later in this chapter, the task has
been used in the U.S.A., Latin America, Israeli kibbutzim, Communist
countries of Eastern Europe and many other societies.

Selection of sample. Sampling procedures also colour the findings of any
study to a very marked extent. Selection of the cultures to be studied may
be largely subject to the vagaries of acquaintanceship patterns among

researchers rather than systematic sampling. In addition, efforts should be made to document that the individuals who participate in a study are reasonably representative of their culture. Special care must be taken in studying countries characterized by sharp internal variations in socio-economic level or ethnic affiliation. Socioeconomic differences within countries may turn out to be at least as salient as differences between countries. Lambert, Hamers and Frasure-Smith (1979), in their study of parents' child-rearing values in ten Western cultures, found cross-cultural differences on virtually every dimension. However, there were also many important social class differences within cultures on most of these dimensions, with participants from lower socioeconomic levels tending to be stricter and more demanding with their children. Despite this cleavage within cultures, cross-cultural research is clearly predicated on the assumption that the cultural unit studied displays a coherent mode of structuring the social lives of children. Even if one is satisfied that such coherence exists, this mode will often vary according to the children's ages. In any study, it is preferable to obtain information on children at various developmental levels and, ideally, at different historical eras, though such data are quite rare. Size of sample is another basic consideration. This does not refer only to the number of individual participants, which determines the statistical power of a particular analysis in this as in all areas of quantitative research, it is also important to consider the number of cultures sampled (Eron & Huesmann, 1987; Lambert, Hamers & Frasure-Smith, 1979). Many cross-cultural studies are comparisons of two cultures. With just the two data points, it is impossible to know whether the groups studied represent the extremes of a continuum, whether one is typical of most cultures while the other is idiosyncratic, or whether the aspect of behaviour studied is one characterized by large variations across cultures.

Cognitive and behavioural measures. Most psychologists and anthropologists engaged in cross-cultural research have, predictably, been interested in establishing cross-cultural differences in the behaviour of adults and children. Less energy has been invested in exploring the differences in people's understanding of others, their internal mental organization of social experience, even though theorists have long held that cultures function in many ways, often unconscious ways, to influence one's perceptions, cognitions, psychological dispositions and motivations. Szalay and Maday (1983) noted that these subtle modalities of cultural influence, which they call "implicit culture", have variously been referred to as "subjective lexicon" (by Miller), "meaning systems" (by Osgood and colleagues), "cognitive map" (by Tolman and colleagues), "world view" (by Black) and "thought world" (by Whorf). In all cases, these terms refer to what Campbell (1963) defined as a sensory/cognitive representation of the world whose organization exerts various degrees of influence on behaviour. Szalay and Maday have studied implicit culture among adults by means of a verbal free association technique. It would be interesting to trace the developmental unfolding of these meaning systems in children. Therefore, an ideal cross-cultural study would provide information on both observable behaviour and the mental events which help mould it.

Few if any of the studies in the literature would measure favourably against the methodological yardsticks implied above. However, it must be remembered that the obstacles inherent in conducting research in different cultures are myriad, and impose considerable practical limits on the scope of any given study. In light of their limitations, the conclusions of all the studies reviewed below must be considered somewhat tentative.

Modes of Cultural Influence

Much cross-cultural research has been criticized for being atheoretical and haphazard, for demonstrating that cultures may or may not differ in a particular respect with little thought as to *why* or *how* these difference come about. However, a scan of some recent sources reveals considerable reflection as to the mechanisms which may intervene in determining cultural impact on social behaviour. Super and Harkness (1986) proposed a framework useful in conceptualizing the various aspects of cultural structuring of child development, and the variety of hypotheses which underlie the studies discussed below. Their construct of "developmental niche" features three components: physical and social setting, norms and customs regarding the rearing of children, and the psychology of caretakers. Each component has distinct relationships with other features of the larger culture. Homeostatic mechanisms provide for balance among the three components of the model and for harmony with the child's age and individual characteristics.

Patterns of economic activity and land use

The ways adults earn their livelihoods may define an atmosphere of either competition or co-operation. For example, in societies where animal husbandry is a predominant economic activity, children are often taught to be competitive. Anthropological descriptions of such societies contain more frequent mention of aggressive behaviour among children. Furthermore, children tend to be involved in adult work, the tending of livestock, and therefore the adult social world, from a very early age (Whiting & Edwards, 1988). Where agriculture is the principal economic activity, children are involved in a variety of ways, though not as early as in cultures where there are flocks to tend. This may permit more extended interactions among children, perhaps diminishing somewhat the eventual imprint of adult models on children's social behaviour, while making more room for peer, sibling and other influences.

Industrialized Western societies feature many different patterns of economic activity, with competition the basis for upward mobility in many cases. One might speculate that this results in increased aggressiveness. However, Segall (1983) observed that ethnographers have described remote, small, nonliterate cultures characterized by levels of aggression that would be considered "natural" in most Western countries, as well as other remote, small, nonliterate cultures with very low levels of violence. Though this was hardly the case at the beginning of the twentieth century and earlier, children in most contemporary industrialized Western countries are probably initiated into adult work far later than children in communities where agriculture or animal husbandry are the means of earning a living. This may make it even easier for a children's culture to develop that is more independent of the adult social world, making room for even greater influence by socialization agents other than parents— sibling caregivers, peers, media, daycare centres and schools.

A generation of researchers invested heavily in the study of both individuals' and societies' need to achieve economically (McClelland *et al.*, 1958). It seems logical to expect that individual children and adults raised in societies or homes with high needs for achievement would engage in more competitive social behaviour. However, the need to achieve may also be a collective one, which might result in co-operative behaviour within the national unit in order to compete with other countries. The actual social behaviour of individuals received little attention in the research literature on need for achievement, which placed a premium on projective techniques and dream analysis as tools for studying motivation.

Differential contact with adults and peers

Whiting and Edwards (1988) emphasized cultural differences in the permission given to young children to roam about their neighbourhoods. This obviously increases children's opportunities for social contact with others, and decreases concomitantly the proportion of time they spend with their parents. Children may be restricted from venturing away from their homes for a variety of reasons, including parents' perceptions of neighbourhood safety. Cultures are known to differ in terms of the proportion of time children spend in the company of other children and of adults for other reasons. Parents may keep their children close at hand because their economic activity makes this possible or desirable. Parents in some cultures may believe that it is important for children to spend time with them, while others may believe that peer association is beneficial to their children's development. In addition, there are potentially important differences in terms of how adults spend their time with children. For example, adults may tend to become involved in children's games or, conversely, children may be involved in routine adult activities. In many societies, children are passive observers of adult life. Bronfenbrenner (1970) discovered that Russian adults were far more involved than Americans in their children's group activities. Other studies indicate that American children and children in several less technological societies spend approximately the same proportion of time in contact with adults (Rogoff, 1981; Whiting, 1977). Presumably, extensive contact with adults, especially pleasurable contact, would enhance the salience of the adult as a socialization agent. Peers might exert greater influence in cultures which afford children more unsupervised peer experience. Some recent developmental theorists particularly attuned to the role of peers in socialization (e.g. Youniss, 1980) might argue that this is an advantage.

At the opposite extreme, certain cultures are characterized by very intensive contact with the mother during infancy. Very often, these same societies inculcate values of fortitude and strength, especially in boys, perhaps as a compensation for their extensive early contact with their mothers. This has been shown to correlate with higher societal rates of aggressive behaviour during later childhood (Barry *et al.*, 1980).

Opportunities for interaction with same-age peers is obviously limited in isolated communities where there are literally few or no other children of the same age. This obviously determines to a great extent the nature of children's social interaction. In these situations, children must necessarily play with a wider age group and with adults, and may not therefore develop skill in interacting with peers. Descriptions of such isolated communities include the winter camps of the Paiute Indians of Oregan (Whiting, 1986), the Kung Bushmen of the Kalahari Desert (Draper, 1973) and isolated Norwegian farm communities (Hollos, 1974).

Child caretaking

Children in most non-Western societies are assigned considerable responsibilities in caring for and instructing younger siblings (Rogoff *et al.*, 1975; Werner, 1979; Whiting & Whiting, 1975). This occurs in both industrialized nations (e.g. Japan; cf. Caudill & Plath, 1966) and in less technological societies. There may be a number of implications for the development of social competence. Caring for a younger sibling may mean becoming more caring, tolerant and empathic, as well as more responsible, though perhaps more domineering at the same time (cf. Werner, 1979).

Different reinforcement paradigms

Madsen (1971) observed that the nature of economic activity in a community may relate to differential reinforcement of co-operative and competitive behaviours. In a subsistence agriculture setting, co-operation is more likely to be reinforced. Any competitive or aggressive behaviour towards one's family members, who are often also one's co-workers, would be punished, since it would serve no useful purpose. In contrast, the urban middle-class parent may come to impart the values on which the urban work setting places a premium. Such settings are often far more competitive. Competition may also be fostered in agricultural communities where there is limited availability of land or water (cf. Paddock, 1975; Greenberg, 1981, cited in Fry, 1988).

Cognitive processing and semantic influences

As mentioned above, individuals in different cultures come to have different understanding of other persons, their behaviour and their social relationships. This has been documented in research with adults as well as children. When understanding or explaining the social behaviour of others, adults in non-Western cultures generally place less emphasis on the psychological dispositions of persons and more emphasis on the impact of the social context of behaviour than members of Western societies (Miller, 1984). The study of cross-cultural differences in children's attributions regarding others' social behaviour must take into account developmental changes in the cognitive capacities that permit increasingly sophisticated understanding. Using an interview technique with middle-class children of various ages, as well as adults, in Chicago and Mysore, India, Miller (1986) found that children's attributions for others' social behaviours appeared to evolve in a largely similar way in the two countries while the children were young. In both countries, young children tended to explain others' behaviour by referring to concrete events which occurred in its immediate vicinity. However, by adolescence, important cultural differences emerged. The Indian sample displayed a marked shift toward context-related explanations of social behaviour such as references to social norms and the obligations of particular social roles. Differences between the American and Indian samples in terms of the use of "psychological" explanations, e.g. attributing a behaviour to another person's mood, state or personality, did not emerge until adulthood. Thus, this study provides some evidence for both the self-constructive processes of development operating across cultures as suggested by Piaget, and for some degree of culture-specific social transmission of attributions for social behaviour. It also demonstrates graphically the importance of providing for developmental differences in the design of cross-cultural research.

Religion

Religious teachings also influence an individual's expectations of others, understanding of their social behaviour and tolerance for diversity in social behaviour. As described more fully below, Buddhist teachings may relate to greater tolerance among Thai adults for social behaviours considered unacceptable by many Americans. Bachtold (1984; see study described below) attributed much of the staunch individualism of Anglo-Saxon Californians in a rural community to their Calvinist heritage. Western religions and many others provide more or less specific direction to parents as to how children should be reared.

Media

Children in most cultures are exposed to the mass media to some degree. Television has become a perhaps unwilling vehicle for transmitting the basic precepts of a culture as well as for providing models of social interaction. The role of television in propagating children's aggressive behaviour has received widespread attention. However, the portrayal of friendship on television may also have an influence on children's social competence. For example, many American police dramas, while conveying a highly violent content, also portray a largely amicable style of interaction between policemen working as partners, reflecting considerable intimacy, concern and empathy towards one's partner and friend. The effects of these portrayals of friendship—as well as the consequences of the combination of friendliness and aggression—appear not to have been explored empirically to date. While much television programming is exported internationally, access to television does vary, as does the availability of television programmes and related toys.

In summary, cross-cultural research has been widely criticized as atheoretical, with some justification. However, it must be recognized that differences between the social behaviour of individuals in different cultures are probably attributable to a complex interaction of intervening mechanisms that is not easy to trace. Perhaps cross-cultural researchers opt to provide far more description than explanation of the phenomena they study because they recognize the multiplicity of the intervening mechanisms at work within cultures.

Peer Relations in Collectivistic and Individualistic Societies

Warm Springs children: Divergent rules for speaking in group situations

Philips (1972) studied the use of speech by native Indian and non-native children in rural Oregon, inspired by teachers' remarks that Indian children tend not to speak or participate in class. At the time of the study, the Warm Springs Indian tribe numbered about 1,500. Income from the sale of timber had greatly altered the economic context, which was previously one of abject poverty. An observational procedure was used to compare the use of speech in all-Indian classrooms on the reserve and non-Indian classrooms for pupils of the same age at an Oregon school off the reserve. Classes for two age groups were observed: 6 and 12 years old. Differences between the Indian and non-Indian groups were striking, and depended greatly upon the *participant structure* of the particular activity. Indian children eschewed involvement in activities wherein a child had to speak in the presence of a group, such as lessons directed by the teacher or teacher-appointed student leader. They would almost never volunteer an answer and, if called on, would respond, if at all, as briefly as possible in a soft tone of voice. Their behaviour was markedly different during portions of the day when children were assigned tasks to work on at their desks, with the teacher available for help. While the younger Indian children initiated little contact with the teacher at the beginning of the school year, such contact increased after a "warm-up" period of several weeks, reaching the same frequency of initiation as in the non-Indian classrooms. In the classrooms for 12-year-olds, pupils initiated contact with the teacher far more frequently than in non-Indian classrooms. When the children were assigned projects to complete in small groups, the Indian children participated eagerly, with sustained attention that far exceeded the level observed in non-Indian classrooms. When an Indian pupil was reprimanded for not following classroom procedures, classmates would begin to defy as well. If one child was rebuked for putting his or her feet on a chair, others would immediately place their feet on the furniture. During outdoor play activities, the Indian youngsters would organize themselves into groups and teams without adult or peer direction, and persist at such activities without incident far longer than in non-Indian schools. If teachers tried to structure the outdoor activity, no child would volunteer to be the leader, and if one were appointed, he/she would hesitate to give instructions to the others until prodded. In contrast, non-Indian children would plead to be appointed to such positions of authority.

Philips identified a number of parallels between the Indian children's social behaviour in school and the structure of the Indian society on the reserve. The youngsters' "peers" or play companions on the reserve tend to be their siblings and cousins; thus the bond with play companions tends to be stronger than in other cultures, and to endure for extended periods of time. Children learn many skills by an extended process of observation, then demonstration, then trial. By the time they are 10 or 11 years old, they are considered capable of spending afternoons or evenings with their age-mates in groups; specific permission to leave the home or to participate in a particular activity is not required. All social events are community-wide, not organized by individuals and families, with participation by both adults and children. During tribal councils, anyone may speak. There are nominal leaders, but they wield little absolute authority. If one person does contribute more, it would be because he knows more about the subject at hand; this would vary from topic to topic.

In terms of the typologies introduced above, the Warm Springs culture is emphatically collectivistic, with low-power distance in interpersonal relationships. Philips observed that the more experienced, flexible teachers at the reservation school adapted themselves by reducing formal lessons and competition among pupils. Less successful teachers might attempt to confront the culture of their charges head on, ignoring the intense bonds among the children and the style of learning to which they were accustomed. The likely result was poor mastery of content due to inadequate instructional communication, as well as alienation from the school experience.

Philips's study presents a more fine-grained analysis than most others of differences in the interpersonal communication between the more collectivistic atmosphere of North American Indian communities and other settings within North America. Similar findings are reported by other researchers using other tools. For example, Miller and Thomas (1972), using Madsen's Co-operation Board, found that Blackfoot Indian children aged 7–10 years, residents of Canada's largest Indian reserve, worked co-operatively even on a task in which rewards were to be dispensed on an individual basis, whereas the comparison group of Canadian urban children were engaged in competitive behaviour which impeded their success on the task.

Does peer rejection occur in a collectivistic cultural ecology?

As discussed in Chapter 1, measures of peer reputation have often been regarded as the "marker variable" of children's social status. Most recent research on children's peer status has been conducted in English-speaking countries, especially the United States. In the absence of widespread cross-cultural replication, one might wonder whether in a more collectivistic society, where individuals are theoretically more committed to group identity, one would find similar dimensions and proportions of children regarded as popular by others, or children rejected by their peers.

Kupersmidt and Trejos (1987) administered a group sociometric interview to 328 primary schoolchildren of three different age groups in Costa Rica. Costa Rica shares the collectivistic orientation of most Latin American countries, but is also somewhat unique in that region because of its 40-year history of political neutrality, non-violent changes of government and lack of a formal standing army. Thus, it could be argued that Costa Rica is a collectivistic society on several different levels. Like most Hispanic cultures, Costa Rican society tends to emphasize family relations as opposed to peer relations, and clearly defined traditional sex roles (Biesanz, Biesanz & Biesanz, 1982; DeRosier, 1989).

Kupersmidt and Trejos's results indicate that on identical peer nomination instruments the percentages of children nominated as popular were quite similar to American samples (11% versus 13%), as was the case for peer rejection (11% versus 15%); similar results were reported by Young and Ferguson for their study of southern Italian adolescent boys, as discussed later in this chapter. However, the specific behaviours associated with peer rejection were slightly different. For example, in Costa Rica, withdrawing from social interaction was associated with peer rejection; this has not been clearly demonstrated in American studies. Therefore, it may be useful for future cross-cultural comparisons to focus on the impact of social withdrawal on rejection by peers. In a collectivistic society, social withdrawal may mean non-participation in the collective experience which is so fundamental to identity formation. In contrast, such non-participation may be seen in a more individualistic culture as an individual's prerogative and, as such, may be much more acceptable to peers. On the other hand, despite the greater commitment to the group, children in more collectivistic cultures seem to have likes and dislikes for specific individuals which appear as marked as those of youngsters in less collectivistic cultures.

DeRosier (1989) studied Costa Rican children's perceptions of their network of close relationships. She administered the Network of Relationships Inventory (Furman & Buhrmester, 1985) to 148 Costa Rican primary school pupils from predominantly working- and middle-class home. Comparative American data were readily available in Furman and Buhrmester's original article. The Costa Rican children assigned more positive rating than American children of the same age to most persons in their networks (i.e. parents, siblings, grandparents, best friends and teachers), and indicated that these relationships were less conflictual. DeRosier speculates that these positive attitudes towards others are connected with the prosocial, co-operative nature of surroundng culture.

The Costa Rican children reported that, of the individuals in their social networks, mothers and siblings provided the highest levels of companionship, a function which American children attribute to their best friends. In both countries, teachers were reported to provide the lowest levels of companionship. The relationship with the best friends was described as the least affectionate of all, a position assigned by American children to their teachers. In contrast with American youngsters, the Costa Ricans reported that relationships with their best friends were characterized by higher degrees of conflict and lower levels of affection; they were also less satisfied with their relationships with their best friends. Thus, cultural ecology may impact upon the relative importance of peer relations and the relative functions of supportive individuals. DeRosier's study is of particular importance because, in contrast with most others mentioned in this chapter, it deals with closer, more intimate relationships rather than peer relations in larger groups.

The result of these Costa Rican studies are fully consistent with extensive other data documenting the collectivistic nature of Latin American society and children's culture in comparison with the Anglo-Saxon North American society with which it frequently interacts. Space precludes extensive consideration of all relevant studies, but it is reasonable to conclude that the collectivistic orientation of Latin American children has been demonstrated at a wide range of ages using a wide spectrum of measures. These have included Madsen's Co-operation Board (Madsen, 1971), as well as semi-structured interview used by Hart, Lucca-Irizarry and Damon (1986) to illustrate the extent to which Puerto Rican children and adolescents focus on the social qualities of the self in defining themselves as individuals.

The effects of early collective experiences in rural Hungary

Hollos (1980) studied the co-operative/competitive tendencies of youngsters in rural Hungary who were reared in settings characterized by different degrees of collectivism during the 1960s and 1970s. The socialist reorganization of agriculture was being implemented at the time of data collection in 1976. The study was conducted with two samples from the same area of the Central Hungarian Plains. Collectivism was more fully implemented in the village, whose total population was 12,000. From the age of 2 years on, village children spent the entire day in the company of others, in group daycare or school, during which collective ideology was emphatically inculcated. The children on farms in the surrounding area received a very different upbringing. As preschoolers, they were left at home in the care of older siblings, grandmothers or neighbours, or else taken with their mothers into the fields. School-age children went home immediately after school, and helped raise younger siblings or engaged in work around the farm. Hollos also noted several fundamental differences between village schools and farm schools. The village school was larger and better equipped; children were separated by age. Teachers at the farm school felt overburdened. Children of several school levels were grouped together in the same classes. According to Hollos, these teachers had no time to organize special group extracurricular activities or to engage in extra ideological instruction.

A total of forty-eight children aged 6–8 years, including twenty-four farm children and twenty-four village children, participated in the data collection. By the time they were 8 years old, village children were slightly better at understanding the feelings of other characters in a cartoon story, and significantly better at adjusting their verbal communication in accordance with the needs of the listener. According to Madsen's Co-operation Board task, described above, village children were more competitive than the farm children.

These data seem at first to contradict the findings of other studies described in this chapter about the influence of collectivistic ideology on children's co-operative behaviour. However, a clearer understanding of the two settings indicates that it is very difficult to interpret the results of this study. While the village setting was officially more collectivistic, the joint enterprise of running what was still essentially a family farm may in fact have been the setting which, of the two, placed more genuine emphasis on co-operative interaction.

There have been a number of other interesting portrayals of children's orientation towards the norms of emphatically collectivistic societies during the Communist era. Bronfenbrenner's (1970) comparison of children's experiences in the Soviet Union and the United States is probably the most complete account available, and describes how collectivism totally permeated the school atmosphere and children's lives. He documented the emphatic nature of the prescriptions for the behaviours of parents, teachers and children. Such prescriptions were aimed at inculcating collectivism and obedience simultaneously. Children were to become obedient in order to foster "self-discipline"—internaliza-tion of rules. Tendencies toward independence were to be curtailed, as these were seen as leading to "anarchistic behaviour", in the words of a best-selling manual for Soviet parents. In any case, children's development was to be moulded, so that the children's future was not placed at risk "by allowing their upbringing to be determined by spontaneous drift" (p. 13). Daycare centres for young children were fitted with special complex toys that required co-operation. Children were taught to criticize each other's behaviour from the perspective of the group. Even 2 and 3-year-olds were taught to serve others at table, clean up, care for the premises, etc. Schools were to teach "character" as well as content. The schools were decked with posters extolling collective ideology. Classrooms were divided into teams called links whose members were responsible for regulating their peers' behaviour. In an effort to promote altruism, links of older children were expected to help links of younger pupils. Link membership was a predominant feature of a child's school life. Similar features characterized other Communist countries. Ekblad (1984) reported that Chinese children identified more extensively with the collectivistic norms of their culture than Swedish children. That study was conducted at a time when both the Communist movement in China and the Social Democratic party in Sweden were clearly the dominant political forces in their countries. While the Communist-inspired environments probably fostered a strong internalized collectivism, it is not clear whether their emphasis on compliance related to its internalization.

Correlates of peer acceptance by Hopi Indian and Afro-American children

Some additional insight into the specific behaviours associated with peer acceptance in different cultures is provided by Weisfeld, Weisfeld and Callaghan (1984), who compared peer reputation patterns among Hopi Indian children in north-eastern Arizona and Afro-American children in Chicago. The Hopi live in desert areas. This matrilineal subculture is known for its non-violence and collectivistic orientation. Community decisions are taken by a tribal council whose procedures are very democratic. Aggression among children is totally unacceptable to parents, and leads to punishment. The Afro-American children studied were predominantly of middle socioeconomic status. Urban centres in the United States are known for high incidence of violence.

There were dramatic differences in the social play of the two samples. The Afro-American boys played competitive football and softball; the girls played jump rope (skipping). In comparison, the Hopi boys changed the rules for the game of basketball, so that the object of the game was for the group (rather than the individual team) to score as many points as possible. (In other accounts, Hopi children have been found to play basketball without keeping score [Thompson, 1950].) The observers' records indicated that fights occurred in the Chicago playground about once per hour, whereas there was only one incident of shoving in several hours of play in the Hopi playground, and this was stopped by other children. (Unfortunately the report contains little detail of the observation procedure, definition of "fight", etc.) In contrast, sociometric ratings of the two groups were very similar, with athletic ability associated with popularity in both cultures. These data, together with other findings discussed throughout this chapter, suggest that observational data may be more sensitive to cultural differences than peer reputation measures. Status among peers is more based on relative position along a particular dimension. Even in a non-violent culture, one child is likely to be more aggressive than another. That child may be rejected by peers because of his aggression, though he may be much less aggressive than age-mates in most other cultures.

Hupa Indian and Anglo-American preschoolers in California

Bachtold (1984) conducted another study of co-operative behaviours among American Indian populations. The Hupa Indians live in a remote valley in California, whose isolation limited the penetration of the majority culture until World War II. After the war, traditional ways of earning a living were largely replaced by a wage economy. Like those of most other American Indian tribes, Hupa values emphasize co-operation rather than non-co-operation. Bachtold's comparison group was Anglo-American preschoolers in the Davis region, where the population is composed of two main groups, the descendants of early settlers, whose religious orientation she described as Calvinist, and university students and faculty associated with the University of California at Davis. Hupa patterns of child rearing are permeated by the parents' needs to instil respect for the group and its rules, far more than the more individualistic Anglo-American socialization practices. Observations of the twenty-six 2–4-year-olds in the study were recorded on videotape for analysis. While there were many similarities in the play behaviours of the two groups, the Hupa preschoolers were significantly more sociable and intimate with each other, whereas the Davis children were significantly more authoritarian and aggressive.

Preschoolers' relations with the "neighbours" in America and Italy

Corsaro (1985, 1988) used a combination of observational techniques to study the peer culture of nursery schools in the United States and Italy. His observations are of particular value because they were conducted over extended periods of time (10 months in the U.S.A., 6 months in Italy) in each case, and combined passive observation, videotaped recording and participant observer techniques. The American study was conducted at the laboratory preschool at a university, whilst the Italian study was conducted in a nursery school in a northern Italian urban centre.

Corsaro defined peer culture as "a stable set of activities or routines, artifacts, values and concerns that children produce and share" (1988, p. 3). His cross-cultural comparisons have focused on selected routines or rituals which re-occur frequently in the children's play. Examples of such routines include insult and teasing sequences, mimicry and mockery of adult-imposed rules and approach-avoidance of an attractive but threatening stimulus. The data reveal that a great many of these play sequences are similar in both countries. For example, coming close to, then fleeing, a pretend "monster" is a common routine within the peer culture of both Italian and American preschoolers. Should these routines be observed in yet other cultures, one might infer that they are a universal feature of social development.

However, there were some differences in routines between Italy and the United States which may have potential theoretical importance. Corsaro (1988) detailed differences in territoriality routines, for example. These occur when a group of youngsters playing together delineate an area of the playroom as belonging to them. Groups of both Italian and American children displayed this tendency to protect their interactive space in this manner. In some cases, Italian children were similar to their American counterparts in their displays of hostility when their "territory" was invaded. However, in some of the examples, Italian children were much less defensive and, in fact, sometimes even accommodating when an "outsider" attempted to gain entry to a group's playspace. They might explain the play to the newcomer, or impose conditions on his or her entry. Corsaro remarked that this mirrors the greater concern in Italian city life with "relations in public", brief meetings and greetings with casual acquaintances, neighbours, etc. In both countries, the territoriality ritual may be understood as part of the children's efforts at understanding interpersonal relations and their preparation for later roles in their communities. The fact that the differences between Italian and American play patterns may not be as dissimilar as, say, between an Oriental and an American culture is not surprising given the fact that the adult societies which surround are not as dissimilar. However, the very high degree of individualism known to characterize American peer culture may be reflected in these subtle differences even when compared with Italy, which is still considered relatively high in individualism in relation to non-Western societies (Hofstede, 1983, 1984).

An explicitly collectivistic subculture: the Israeli kibbutz

The psychosocial adjustment of children growing up on Israeli kibbutzim has been subjected to exhaustive investigation. The kibbutz is unique in a number of respects. The ideology is emphatically collectivistic, but there is continual and active contact with the less collectivistic surrounding Israeli society. Those who join kibbutzim freely elect to share belongings and work responsibilities with other members. They or their offspring are free to leave the community, which does regularly occur. The fact that kibbutzniks join a collectivistic subculture by choice makes the kibbutz probably the best setting for research on the effects of collectivistic ideology.

Kibbutz schools are structured to foster much more co-operative behaviour than the European-style schools of surrounding Israeli cities. Children traditionally live together in a children's house, though they would maintain regular contact with their families. In recent years, however, there has been a clear trend toward family-style living arrangements. There are a number of possible implications for children's peer relations. First of all, the collective upbringing and extensive contact with caregivers rather than their parents may affect their early parental attachment relationships, which, as discussed in previous chapters, may in turn have repercussions in subsequent interpersonal relationships.

Secondly, it is interesting to chart the degree to which the surrounding collectivistic atmosphere is mirrored in the children's play relations and social contacts.

Infant–adult attachments of kibbutz infants (see Chapter 2) and their sequelae have been studied, focusing on attachment relations with the *metapelet*, or caregiver, as well as with parents. Oppenheim, Sagi and Lamb (1988) conducted a follow-up study with fifty-nine kibbutz infants. They reported that insecure, resistant attachments are quite frequent in kibbutzim, but it is not clear that these attachment histories have the same implications in the kibbutz as elsewhere. Early results suggest that insecure attachment relationships with the *metapelet* foreshadow less mature social development patterns in the community at large at age 4, while the nature of early attachment with parents had far less predictive power than in research conducted in other cultures. Most research on the social competence of kibbutz children has, fortunately, included comparison measures obtained from their age-mates in Israeli cities. Differences between these two populations are very apparent from early childhood. For example, kibbutz children of kindergarten age already display a relatively crystallized sense of how well they are accepted by peers, which matches teacher ratings of their peer acceptance to a moderate degree (Priel, Assor & Orr, 1990); these findings did not characterize Israeli city youngsters.

A number of observational studies have included systematic comparisons of the social play of kibbutz and non-kibbutz preschoolers. Levy-Shiff and Hoffman (1985) compared the social play of urban and kibbutz youngsters in free-play settings. All participants in both settings were Israeli-born children of European cultural origin. Kibbutz children displayed far more developed group interaction skills, and much less competition, than their city counterparts. At the same time, kibbutz children displayed far less emotion and less warmth. They replaced physical aggression with verbal confrontation. Levy-Shiff and Hoffman suggested that these play patterns foreshadow the social adjustment patterns of adult kibbutzniks, which are stereotypically characterized as more group-orientated in general, with a certain degree of emotional distance.

According to an observational study conducted by Hertz-Lazarowitz *et. al.* (1989), kibbutz primary school children display similar high levels of interactive behaviour. Their level of social interaction was higher than that of city children in both traditional classrooms and classrooms which afforded greater opportunities for active participation by pupils. Shapira and Madsen's (1974) study involved kibbutz and city youngsters aged 4–11 years. They used the marble-pull task described earlier in this chapter. Kibbutz children at all age levels were less competitive than their city counterparts. While they did become more competitive as they got older, this increase occurred later than in the city children. At age 11, kibbutz children were still extremely co-operative while performing this task. Sharabany (1982), using a questionnaire method, determined that while kibbutz preadolescents had many more social contacts than Tel Aviv youngsters of the same age, the kibbutz group displayed less concern regarding peer group sanctions and lower identification with the peer group. Another study in which structured self-report instruments were used indicates that anxiety with regard to social relations—or, indeed, general manifest anxiety—appears to be no higher or lower among kibbutz children and preadolescents (Ginter et. al., 1989). These findings further corroborate the general picture of greater peer involvement but also greater emotional distancing from peers by kibbutz children that several researchers have portrayed.

The collective economy of the kibbutz may not be the only aspect of kibbutz culture which impacts on children's social competence. For instance, Eron and Huessman (1987) studied the relations between children's television watching, peer ratings of aggressiveness and peer popularity among Israeli kibbutz youngsters and Israeli city youngsters, as well as children in Australia, the United States, Finland and Poland. There were many findings common to all these samples. Children's aggressiveness as rated by peers was highly stable over a 3-year period, and was a negative correlate of popularity in all samples. On the other hand, there was considerable cross-cultural variability in the degree to which exposure to television, particularly violent television, predicted aggressiveness. This correlation was particularly weak for kibbutz children, quite possibly because the kibbutzim regulate the amount of violent television the children watch. *Metaplot* typically discuss the social implications of violence after the children watch television programmes of this sort. Another plausible explanation of the findings is that the effects of violent television are attenuated by the general collectivistic nature of the kibbutz.

Early observers of peer interaction on the kibbutz discovered a clear "incest" taboo. For instance, Spiro (1958) reported that none of the children who grew up together in the kibbutz he studied had married another member of the same group, nor, to the best of his ability to determine, was there a single incidence of sexual intercourse among members of the same kevutzah. While theorists offer differing theoretical interpretations of this (see Spain, 1988), it is clear that fellow members of the same kevutzah assumed characteristics of peers and siblings at the same time. It would be interesting to determine whether such incest taboos have remained despite the recent trend towards family housing in the kibbutz, as well as the decline discussed by Cohen (1978, cited in Spain, 1988) in taboos in modern, industrial societies.

Value judgements as to whether kibbutzim produce children with better or worse social development contribute little to our understanding of the influence of this collectivistic setting. However, the kibbutz research strongly suggests that such an emphatically collectivistic subculture has profound effects on the peer relations of children raised in it.

While the kibbutz is probably the best known and stable venture of its type, it is certainly not the only experiment in voluntary communal living. The American counterculture movement of the 1960s spawned many efforts at achieving ideal small communities. These communes were relatively small and often short-lived. Young, alienated single people were the main participants (Allen & West, 1968), but there were some children. Plattner and Minturn (1975) conducted a small-sample comparison of commune preschool children and youngsters in a neighbouring traditional community, using mainly observational measures. Unfortunately, the very small sample precluded meaningful statistical treatment of the data. Nevertheless, the commune children were much more self-reliant and perhaps a bit more sociable. Plattner and Minturn attributed the commune children's self-reliance to their greater exposure to the collective work activities of the commune, as well as their more frequent contact with many adults (all female commune members took turns working in the preschool). The emphatically non-competitive, even *anti*-competitive, atmosphere of the commune was also reflected in the commune children's markedly lower scores for achievement motivation.

Peer and school experiences of Pumehana adolescents

In addition to the above-mentioned studies conducted with pre-schoolers, the social behaviour of adolescents raised in subcultures more collectivistic than the surrounding majority culture has received attention. One of the most dramatic examples is Gallimore, Boggs and Jordan's (1974) study of the adolescents of 'Aina Pumehana, a community in Hawaii. This study employed a combination of in-depth interviews and observations of the children's behaviour at school.

There may be few cultures in which adolescents assign a fundamental importance to peer relations as do the Pumehana youth. Only two of the fifty adolescents interviewed expressed the desire to spend their leisure time on their own. Half could think of *no* leisure-time activity that they would enjoy doing by themselves. Conversations appear to focus almost exclusively on shared activities and acquaintances, with little mention of non-shared experiences or one's own perspective. The peer network is a highly supportive one. An individual could easily drift away from contact with a friend or group of friends, but be fully accepted should he decide to drift back. Displays of inequality were scrupulously avoided. A football coach noticed that younger players did not really try their best in order to avoid depriving the football heroes of the school's graduating class of their last year of glory. Friends were expected to be helpful, friendly and modest.

In fact, when asked by the interviewer what qualities they admired or "looked up to" in friends, many of the respondents indicated that they did not think friends should be admired or looked up to; everyone should be equal. They considered friendliness as among the most important qualities. While some of the youths, particularly boys, were physically aggressive, much of their aggression, indeed all the aggression which they regarded as serious, would be directed at outsiders or their property. Outsiders were seen as meriting little kindness.

Peer group discussions were characterized by much participation and latitude. The youths maintained that they were free of pressures to conform, though, as discussed above, belonging to the peer group was crucially important to them. In most groups, there was only an identifiable leader in very exceptional circumstances. Nonetheless, there were some cases of bullies dominating by force. Those youths who had gravitated to the more delinquent sub-groups nonetheless subscribed to the common premium placed on friendship and mutual support. They conceived their superficial roughness as horseplay occurring among potential friends.

As one might imagine, the teachers of these children, who were not members of the Pumehana community, were among the outsiders who served as targets. Pumehana high schools were virtual battlegrounds. Even one of the researchers was physically attacked. Some teachers managed a modicum of control by being highly authoritarian but emphatically fair, others by adopting a stance similar to that of an older brother or sister left in charge of younger siblings. In either case, strict consistency and avoidance of hostile verbal interactions—or even nonhostile but protracted negotiation procedures—were the only roads to peaceful coexistence with the class.

At home, total, unquestioned compliance with parental authority was expected. Sanctions for disobedience by children or wives might include physical beatings, though domestic violence seems to have been more talked about than practised. Discussion or negotiation with parents were rare. Older children were very heavily involved in raising their younger siblings; this may well relate to their propensity toward affiliative behaviour. It would be simplistic to attribute the complex social behaviour of Pumehana adolescents at school solely to a clash between a collectivistic subculture in an individualistic context. The highly cohesive adolescent peer group can be seen as engaging in collective rebellion against both the strict authoritarianism of its parents and the incursions of other cultural groups. The adolescent peer culture has norms for aggression which differ markedly from those of the school authorities. This may in some way relate to the fact that authoritarian relationships at home were cemented with at least the spectre of physical violence. The youngsters bring to school little experience with authority figures who are reasonable and compromising, and unfortunately often leave school early, having gained little skill at dealing with authority figures in more mature ways. If there is a single enduring message to be learned from this study, it is that prediction of behaviour from broad cultural characteristics must take into account the interplay of a variety of environmental forces, and must be fine-tuned enough to account for differences across situations. While most collectivistic societies are non-aggressive, collectivism may also be expressed as collective aggression in some situations.

Cultural Dimensions of Childhood Aggression

Adult and child aggression in Zapotec communities

Just as cultures and subcultures differ in terms of normative levels of co-operation, there are important differences in levels of violence and aggression. The Zapotec communities in Oaxaca, Mexico, provide interesting opportunities for examining the possible links between adult aggressiveness in a community and children's aggressive behaviour in peer contexts. Most of the Zapotec are engaged in agriculture and live in relatively small communities. Interestingly, there are enormous differences between the communities in terms of the rates of adult aggression, with annual homicide rates reported to range from under 4 to 123 per 100,000 inhabitants in the twenty-four communities which have been studied (Paddock, cited in Fry, 1988). Attitudes toward violence differ markedly from community to community. In the non violent communities, young children are discouraged from even play fighting. In the more aggressive communities, there is frequent horseplay even among adults and greater use of corporal punishment with children.

Fry (1988) conducted an observational study of the behavioural interactions of children in two Zapotec communities that differed markedly in normative violence. Twenty-four children in each community participated in the study; their ages ranged from 5 to 8 years. The observation code was limited to serious fighting, play fighting and threats. The rate of play aggression was fully twice as high in San Andres (a pseudonym), the more violent community, than La Paz: an average of 6.9 incidents per hour in comparison with 3.7. There was far less serious aggression in both communities, but, again, the rate was twice as high in San Andres, 0.78 incidents per hour versus 0.39. Perhaps more important are the age differences. In San Andres, the older children engaged in more serious play fighting than the younger ones, whereas in La Paz, serious aggression was lower for the older children in the sample. Correlations between serious and play fighting were marginal.

Fry's results suggest that while aggressive behaviour among childhood peers occurs across cultures and may have some evolutionary function, the immediate cultural context plays a striking role in at least the maintenance of aggressive tendencies. The findings also lend credence to Smith's (1989) contention that play fighting is a means by which children prepare for the roles they will assume in their cultures as adults.

"Gentleness" in Tahitian culture and Tahitian children's peer relations

The classic example of a culture characterized by low levels of hostility is that of Tahiti. Levy's (1978) ethnographic research was based on interviews with Tahitian adults during the 1960s, but he chronicles the pervasive gentleness of the Tahitian culture as mentioned repeatedly in historical writings since the eighteenth century. There are a few exceptional accounts of hostility during transitional periods in which Tahitian society adjusted to new European inroads, but these brief interludes of violence abated as the traditional Tahitian culture reasserted itself. According to Levy, Tahitians believe in a cult of "passive optimism"—that individuals should accept the "natural ordering" of things, rather than strive to influence the status quo. Aggression is defined as an attempt to upset the natural ordering of things. Timidity is actively encouraged. While children may express aggression at times without excessive sanction, they may be warned that nature will get even with them. Tahitians believe that hostility is dangerous to one's body, but by expressing it briefly and appropriately one will minimize the somatic consequences. Wrestling is a very popular pastime. However, anything more enduring than a transient display of anger is considered a shameful indicator of weakness.

According to Levy, Tahitian infants are fussed over, coddled and spoiled. Adoption is very normal—Levy's observations indicate that approximately half of all children were adopted, when their biological parents felt unready to raise them. In early childhood (3–5 years), limits are abruptly set and the child is thrust into a social world of other children and a variety of caretakers and siblings. Given the norms for adopting children and group caretaking, children in Tahiti during the 1960s were very much children of their whole communities. Levy implicitly attributes the gentleness of the Tahitians to this collective socialization, the collectivistic economy and to the culture's reverance of "natural" forces over individual impulse. Unfortunately, his account does not include any specific data regarding aggression and prosocial behaviour in children's groups or schools. Tahitian society has changed since the 1960s, with greater Western inroads and some degree of political unrest. If these recent tensions have in any way compromised the gentleness of Tahitian peer relations, this may be a transitory phenomenon as in previous periods of collective stress. It should be noted that a number of other Polynesian societies have been studied and are characterized by the same co-operativeness and helpfulness (Graves & Graves, 1983; Tietjen, 1986).

Differences within cultures compared to differences between cultures

In contrast with many studies reporting and explaining significant cross-cultural differences in children's co-operativeness, Charlesworth and Nakra (1991) found that the individual differences within cultures in terms of children's co-operativeness were enormous compared with little difference between cultures. Their study compared Indian, Caribbean and North American 5–7-year-olds during a standard situation in which a cartoon could only be viewed by one child if the other children helped by operating the apparatus containing the cartoon. These results were interpreted as supporting an evolutionary view that the ability to co-operate while competing for resources is universal at this age. Nevertheless, the results of this study must be interpreted in conjunction with the many findings indicating important cross-cultural differences in the extent of children's co-operative behaviours, including most of the studies reviewed above.

Different Priorities for Children—Cultural Differences in the Perceived Importance of Peer Relations

Socialization of adolescent boys by southern Italians and their emigrant cousins

Young and Ferguson (1981) conducted a careful and comprehensive study of 120 adolescent boys in southern Italy, as well as emigrants from the same communities who had settled in Rome ($n=123$) and Boston ($n=96$). The subjects in all three sites shared essentially a common cultural heritage, though their immediate social, economical and family environments varied considerably. According to the authors (p. 11), the relatively homogeneous Italian regions of Sicily, Calabria, Puglia, Campania, Lucania and Abruzzi were selected because there is some indication that these regions are characterized by fairly homogeneous genetic composition, as established by distribution of blood groups, prevalence of colour blindness and gene frequency of A, B and Rh D, and are thought to differ from the rest of Italy in these respects. The researchers elected to study males only because they believed that in a culture which maximizes protection of adolescent girls, there might be some difficulty in generating an appropriate female sample. The subjects were followed from early adolescence through early adulthood. At the time the data were collected in the 1950s and 1960s, economic conditions in southern Italy were markedly less favourable than in Rome or Boston for individuals of similar socioeconomic level. The southern Italian communities lagged behind in terms of nutrition and health care, opportunities for physical exercise at school, extracurricular activities at school, psychological counselling and many other services.

A structured interview regarding parents' socialization of their sons was conducted at all three sites. The Boston parents were clearly more permissive in almost all respects than either Italian sample, allowing their adolescent sons significantly more freedom in choice of friends, activities and school programme. There were some interesting differences in the parents' instructions regarding the boys' aggression toward peers. The Boston parents tended to advise that their sons defend themselves physically against an aggressive peer, while the Italian parents tended to allow the child to decide how he would respond or, alternatively, exhort the child to respond in a non-aggressive fashion. The Italian-American families were characterized by a more reciprocal communication style, with sons discussing their own needs and participating in group decisions to a far greater extent. The Italian-American parents regarded their sons' friendships as immensely more important than both parent samples in Italy. Fully 40% of the Boston parents mentioned aspects of human relations as among the most important things a boy should learn to do; this response was rare in Italy. There was far more participation in group activities with other adolescents by the Boston boys (64%) than either Italian sample (26% in Rome and 10% in Palermo). Virtually all the Boston parents (99%) indicated that they were pleased that the boy had friends, while as many as 34% of the Palermo parents were not pleased; many Italian parents preferred that their son spend his free time at home.

These differences in the parents' values with respect to peer affiliation and aggression were very clearly mirrored during interviews with the boys at age 14–16 years. The Boston boys were overwhelmingly more oriented to social relations than the Italian adolescents, a third of which expressed a preference for having a few friends rather than many, compared with only 4% in Boston. Only 2% of the boys interviewed in Boston said that they had no friends or only one, compared with 20% of the Italian boys. About one-sixth of the Palermo boys indicated a preference for playing alone, a response which was virtually unknown in Boston or Rome. Eight per cent of the Palermo boys felt that their parents did not wish them to have friends, another response virtually unknown among the other samples. Despite these differences in affiliativeness, the samples were quite similar in patterns of liking and disliking of peers. Classroom sociometrics revealed similar proportions of classmates nominated for positive and negative roles.

With regard to their responses to a physically aggressive peer, there were differences in the boys' responses as to what they were *expected* to do. The vast majority of the Italian boys said that their parents expected a non-violent response, as did a smaller majority of the Boston boys. A sizeable minority of the Americans indicated that their parents expected them to hit back. In any case, hitting back is what most of the boys in all three sites said they would in fact do, regardless of parental dictates.

There were interesting differences among the three samples in the correlates of parental involvement in boys' peer relations. Boston parents who intervened to some degree in their sons' peer relations had sons who, according to their personality inventories, displayed higher warmth, sociability, ego strength, emotional maturity and, according to the interviewers' ratings, aggressiveness. There were very few significant correlates of parental intervention in their sons' peer relations among the Rome or Palermo samples, and in fact when there was higher parental involvement in the peer relations of a Palermo youth, this tended to be slightly related to social withdrawal. Young and Ferguson speculated that the Boston parents' involvement in their sons' peer relations must be supportive in nature. Such parental intervention may be very different in Italy, where it may occur in response to the son's loneliness and need for support.

Parents' Valuing of Social Competence in Different Cultures

Another, though less comprehensive, study of parental valuing of social competence was conducted by O'Reilly, Tokuno and Ebata (1986) in the Hawaiian islands. They compared parents of Japanese and European origin in terms of their priorities for their children. The Japanese-Americans placed highest emphasis on "behaving well", followed by self-direction, then sensitivity to others. In contrast, the two highest-ranking values among American parents of European ancestry were self-direction and sensitivity to others' feelings. The researchers interpreted these findings as indicating the importance of the values of the culture of origin, especially since Japanese-Americans in Hawaii are known to constitute a distinct community within which children must initially function. Unfortunately, some potentially interesting data points were not included, such as comparisons with parents in Japan or Japanese-Americans living in communities where they constitute a proportionally smaller minority. It would also be interesting to know whether and how the parents attempt to transmit these values to their children, and whether such attempts are successful. Quite possibly, parents living in cultures where social competence is highly valued may make greater efforts to "set the stage" for children to get together (see Chapter 2), arrange opportunities for children to interact, provide guidance and actively encourage their children in initiating social contacts. Cross-cultural comparisons of such parental behaviours would be very interesting.

Cultural Differences in Tolerance of Atypical Social Behaviour

As introduced earlier in this chapter, one fundamental dimension of cultural difference is the latitude of acceptable social behaviour. Different thresholds for tolerable child behaviour will likely lead to differential efforts by adults to reinforce or extinguish comparable withdrawn or aggressive behaviours by children. Weisz *et. al.* (1988) systematically compared Thai and American parents' tolerance thresholds for both overcontrolled behaviour (i.e. shyness and fear) and undercontrolled behaviour (e.g. aggression). Thailand was selected because the core teachings of Thai Buddhism emphasize that everyone experiences some degree of dissatisfaction or unhappiness, but that these conditions should not be considered permanent or indicative of one's enduring personality. Two vignettes, each describing an exemplar of the behaviour patterns studies, were read by both Thai and American teachers and parents. They were then asked to rate the seriousness of the behaviour, how unusual it is, how concerned they would be if they were the protagonist's parent or teacher, and how likely it was that the behaviour would change. Respondents were also asked to indicate what they believed to be the likely cause of the behaviour and what they would do about it.

In comparison with American parents, Thai parents and teachers rated both over- and undercontrolled behaviours as less serious, less worrisome to a teacher or parent, less unusual and more likely to improve spontaneously. Importantly, these effects held up after statistical correction for the effects of age and education, a methodological safeguard often overlooked in cross-cultural research. Interestingly, Thai and American psychologists were about equally concerned about the "problem" behaviours (more concerned than Thai parents and teachers, but much less concerned than American parents and teachers). Thais tended to attribute both the undercontrolled and overcontrolled behaviours to faulty child rearing more frequently than Americans, who more often attributed them to environmental stressors or internal conflicts. In both cultures, undercontrolled problems were considered more worrisome than overcontrolled behaviours. It would be most interesting to see if Thais and Americans—and individuals from other cultures—actually react differently in their homes and schools to similar child social behaviour.

A number of studies documenting cross-cultural differences in parents' child-rearing beliefs and practices have been less venturesome in speculating as to the theoretical origins of this diversity. Lambert, Hamers and Frasure-Smith's (1979) study of parenting is perhaps the most comprehensive and sophisticated methodologically. However, the ten nations studied were all highly literate and relatively advanced technologically. Therefore, the generalizability of the results is somewhat limited.

Less attention has been devoted to cross-cultural differences in school and teacher thresholds for acceptable social behaviour. Walker and Lamon (1987) compared the behavioural standards and expectations of American and Australian primary schoolteachers. Though most behaviours rated as problematic in American schools were also somewhat problematic to the Australian sample, American teachers were far more concerned about disruptive behaviour in their classrooms than about children's lack of positive social skills; this gap was not as wide in Australia. In comparison, Australian teachers seemed more preoccupied with the continuity of their lessons. They assigned very negative ratings to pupils' off-topic remarks during lessons. They assigned very negative ratings to pupils' off-topic remarks during classroom conversations. In both countries, teachers who work with handicapped or behaviour-disorded pupils were more accepting of atypical child social behaviour. While the comparison of these two countries is of interest, it would be useful to see these methods applied in a wider spectrum of cultures.

Cultural Differences in Gender Segregation

North American studies of children's friendships have clearly illustrated a preference for same-sex friends from early childhood throughout adolescence (see reviews by Daniels-Beirness, 1989, and Hartup, 1983). This finding emerges from studies using sociometric as well as observational methods. In addition, it has been found that school-age boys tend to play in larger groups while girls play in groups of two and three.

There are some indications that such gender segregation in children's groups is less marked in other cultures. Harkness and Super (1985) conducted an observation study with 152 children aged 18 months to 9 years in a rural community in Kenya. Agriculture is the major economic activity in Kokwet, Kenya. Children assist in looking after the cows, removing weeds and caring for younger siblings. This more collective upbringing may be related to the finding that gender segregation in children's play groups was less pronounced than in an American comparison sample, with the shift towards greater gender segregation occurring at later ages. Presumably, adolescent experiences foster the transition to the largely gender-segregated adult world in Kokwet, though the social development of adolescents in that community has not been systematically studied.

Cross-cultural comparison of sex differences in early social development was a major thrust of the very comprehensive Six Culture Project (Whiting & Edwards, 1988; Whiting & Whiting, 1975). This ambitious project featured very careful direct observation of children aged 2–10 years and their mothers in India, Okinawa, the Philippines, Mexico, Kenya and the United States. The precise observation scheme used by researchers familiar with each culture contributes greatly to the value of the study;

mother–child interaction was coded as well as interaction among children. The two volumes describing the study detail each culture in terms of living arrangements, economic activity, children's responsibility, child-rearing norms and beliefs and social support network.

There were some important differences in social development among the cultures studied. For example, there was more extensive peer contact, with same-sex peers primarily, among school-age children in cultures with universal education. In contrast, interaction with peers was lowest in Nyansango, Kenya, where only one of the twenty-two children studied attended school. Aggression among peers during the observation intervals was rare in all samples, especially among girls, but the highest frequency of aggressive behaviour occurred in Khalapur, India, where children were subjected to the most physical punishment, and in Mixteca, one of the Mexican Indian communities characterized by high levels of adult aggression. Rough-and tumble "horseplay" among boys was most typical of cultures which provided sex-segregated competitive school experiences. Nurturant behaviours with same-sex peers were highest in cultures where children had the most experience caring for younger siblings.

Despite these differences, there were a great many cross-cultural universal features of children's social interaction. School-age children in all cultures associated mainly with peers of the same sex. Behaviours characterized as sociable were the most important aspect of the social play of both girls and boys. Rough-and-tumble games as well as dominance-related behaviours were the next most frequent categories for boys. In all cultures, girls were more nurturant than boys with same-sex peers, while boys engaged in more dominance-related behaviour. There were also a great many cross-cultural similarities in the ways mothers respond to their children. In their conclusion, Whiting and Edwards (1988) emphasized the role of universal biologically-prepared "scripts" which interact with culture-specific environmental influences to determine children's social development. Nevertheless, one cannot conclusively determine from these data whether the sex segregation of children's groups is attributable to genetically-based aspects of children's social behaviour or to seemingly universal sex-role socialization by parents.

Cultural Differences in the Relative Influence of Context Elements

As illustrated above, investigators have compared the values, beliefs and practices of parents of various cultures in socializing their children's peer relations. There has also been some cross-cultural comparison of schools and of peer group values. Research rarely accommodates the very genuine possibility that the total impact of the family, school or peer group context may be much greater in some cultures than others, depending upon the structure and value system of the society. The relative importance of these contexts may vary somewhat across cultures as well. There may also be cultural differences in children's overall susceptibility to the influences of other persons. Chu (1979) compared the responses of 180 elementary schoolchildren in Taipei and 180 New Mexico children of the same age to a task designed to measure sensitivity to interpersonal influence. Two classmates participated in the study at the same time—one designated as model, the other as recipient of modelling. In one experimental condition the model's "status" was raised by the experimenter, who passed on compliments which supposedly had been heard from the teacher. In another condition, the model's "status" was enhanced in the same way. The subjects were asked to select a picture to represent the best answer to a series of questions whose solution was ambiguous. The designated model completed the task first. In a competence-manipulation paradigm, the model was told that his or her answers were right or wrong for the model-competent and model-incompetent conditions, respectively. In some conditions, a token prize was added for "correct" answers. The modelling recipient completed the task after the designated model was finished. Imitation of the model's choices was used as a measure of susceptibility to peer influence.

Chu's results were somewhat complex. Chinese students gave answers indicative of either complete imitation of the model or total anticonformity, i.e. giving the opposite responses. American children displayed a pattern of responding more independent of the model. Chu interpreted these differences as indicating that Chinese children are more susceptible to peer influence—with such influence operating both ways. The various manipulations of reward and "status" yielded non-significant findings. It would be interesting to see whether children of these and other cultures respond to parent or other adult models in the same way. As well, it would be useful to determine whether these processes operate outside the confines of a contrived laboratory situation. Nevertheless, Chu's findings do confirm at least that there may be important cultural differences in susceptibility to peer influence.

Cultural Differences in Nonverbal Dimensions of Children's Social Behaviour

Most cross-cultural research with children has focused on rather molecular aspects of social behaviour, such as the general character of the children's play (e.g. co-operative, aggressive, etc.), or the number and nature of play partners they choose. However, Argyle (1988) has sensitized us to the importance of a more micro-level analysis of social competence, and to the very substantial impact on interpersonal relationships of seemingly subtle non-verbal behaviours. Most of the available data regarding cross-cultural differences in non-verbal communication were collected with adults. However, there is some evidence of cross-cultural differences in children's non-verbal social behaviour. For example, Aiello and Jones (1971) found that Puerto Rican 6- and 7-year-olds tended to place themselves closer together than American children of Anglo-Saxon origin. Moore and Porter (1988) noted that certain non-verbal behaviours influence perceptions of a person as a leader. Individuals with higher status use more personal space, touch more and intrude more into others' personal space. In Moore and Porter's study, 202 Anglo and Hispanic American primary schoolchildren were videotaped while playing a co-operative board game. Both observers of the videotapes and classroom teachers rated the pupils as leaders. There was little difference between the non-verbal behaviours associated with ratings of leadership for Hispanic and Anglo study participants. However, Hispanic females were significantly less likely to interrupt others, to intrude on their physical space or to use enhanced horizontal space—the very behaviours which were found to be associated with leadership in both their ethnic group and the majority Anglo group. Thus, these girls' status both as members of a minority ethnic group and as females within that community may be reflected in their non-verbal behaviour in game situations. Parallel situations may emerge in many other parts of the world where different ethnic groups come into contact because of emigration or other reasons. Given the current mobility of populations in many parts of the world, this area of research seems worthy of increased attention.

Conclusions: Culture and children's social competence

On the whole, the evidence for cultural influences on the emergence of children's social competence appears quite fragmented. Also, the methodology used in many of the scattered studies inspires only limited confidence in the findings. Robust, multimethod assessment of social competence is relatively rare in the literature. In considering many if not most of the studies discussed above, it is very appropriate to wonder whether the results would replicate if an attempt at replication were made. Where larger, more complex societies are studied, there is little compelling reason to believe that the conclusions are valid across socioeconomic strata and other internal distinctions.

Nevertheless, some of the studies do appear to document logical links between characteristics of cultures and patterns of children's social behaviour. There would seem to be enough data to accept, at least, that the broad dimension of cultural individualism/collectivism is associated with more co-operative interaction of children. Of course, the argument might be raised that these cross-cultural differences in both adult collectivism and children's co-operativeness are both attributable to genetic influence.

However, some of the studies provide clear refutation of this hypothesis. For example, there is little reason to suspect a substantially different gene pool for Israeli children raised in kibbutzim and in cities, for southern Italians in Italy and immigrants from the same regions in Boston, or for Zapotec Indians in different villages within the same Mexican state.

If one subscribes to the view that development is a function of both cultural influences and universal aspects of maturation, it is imperative to consider both in designing research. At the very least, it would be useful to track developmental differences when conducting cross-cultural comparisons, the importance of which has been illustrated at several points in this chapter (cf. Young & Ferguson, 1981). Whiting and Whiting (1975) inferred that by age 6, children have internalized many important elements of the value system of the adult culture. While this does suggest that the study of the socialization of younger children is of paramount importance, socialization does continue and may change as both children and parents encounter new developmental challenges. Furthermore, the adult values internalized by age 6 may have different impact on the social behaviour of individuals at different stages of development.

This literature has been repeatedly criticized as atheoretical. Shortage of suitable theoretical vantage points cannot possibly be responsible for atheoretical forays into the cross-cultural comparison of children's social development, if this criticism is indeed valid. Most of the studies reviewed in this chapter did specify a theoretical rationale, often quite elaborate. However, the link between the theory and the data may be quite weak. For example, the finding that the correlates of children's sociometric acceptance and rejection tend to be similar across cultures has been invoked to support a number of theoretical positions. Weisfeld, Weisfeld and Callaghan (1984) suggested that the tendency of boys in different cultures to value physical prowess may relate to an inherent need to preserve the species by selecting the best hunters. This position cannot be reconciled with the repeated finding that aggressive children are socially rejected by their classmates (Coie, 1985). Another explanation of the cross-cultural similarities in the correlates of peer acceptance might emanate from social learning theory, because children could come to internalize an appreciation of behaviours they have seen reinforced in others. That might well have occurred for both the Hopi and Afro-American samples in Weisfeld, Weisfeld and Callaghan's study, both of which had access via the media to American professional sport. A social-learning explanation would equally suit other correlates of peer acceptance, such as academic achievement, which would seem to have few ethological implications. Several other theories can and have been used quite validly in explaining cross-cultural similarities in distributions of sociometric data. While multiple explanations of findings are interesting, research that is only superficially informed by theory is only slightly more valuable than atheoretical research. Hopefully, more sophisticated research designs will be developed to better differentiate among explanations for cross-cultural similarities and differences in children's social behaviour.

Life-span developmentalists are increasingly focusing on cultures, social contexts and historical cohorts in explaining specific developmental patterns as opposed to general, universal patterns of development (Silbereisen & Eyferth, 1986). Many of the societies which have welcomed researchers in the past are undergoing profound change at this moment. Collective ideology is waning in Eastern Europe and elsewhere. Impending changes within the European community will result in increased contact between highly different peoples. North American Indians, whose culture has been widely studied, are becoming increasingly conscious of their identities and insisting on educational environments that will foster them. Israeli kibbutzim are largely abandoning collective housing for children in favour of more traditional family sleeping arrangements. Each of these changes represents an important opportunity for researchers to document the impact of societal change on children's social relations.

Our knowledge about cultural influences on children's social competence may also have implications for improving relations between diverse cultural groups brought into contact because of migration. Collett (1971) found that sharing this information was useful in enhancing Englishmen's understanding of Arabs and their culture. A parallel approach might help teachers, neighbours and children understand the social behaviours of culturally different children new to their communities.

5

The Next Generation of Socialization Studies

As the preceding chapters have hopefully illustrated, there are many antecedents of social competence evident in family life, school life and the cultures that surround. Despite the many universals in social behaviour and child socialization that have been identified, it is very reasonable to expect that a child might turn out quite different if she grew up in a very different home, school or culture, though the evidence for these antecedents is far from complete, far from consistent and by no means easy to interpret. As we have seen, the available data emanate from divergent theoretical frameworks, making them difficult to synthesize.

Researchers who choose to continue tracing the origins of social competence will hopefully profit from what we have learned to date. Theorists and practitioners can no longer naively assume that the child's behaviour is the mere mirror image of the way she had been reared by parents, nor the direct imprint of his school climate, nor just the product of the culture in which the family and school operate. Furthermore, we cannot assume that families and schools operate in the same way in all cultures and subcultures. We must also recognize the possibility that the various social worlds in which the child grows—family, peer group, school, neighbourhood, culture—may have different effects when considered together as compared with studying the unique effect of any one of them. Once we begin to recognize the child as an active participant in the process, to recognize the complex interplay of intra-individual and interpersonal factors, our understanding of this research endeavour must be fundamentally different from that of early researchers in the field. We can be particularly encouraged that some researchers are beginning to attempt to include both genetic and environmental factors in their designs for the exploration of family, school and cultural influences. The few studies that have demonstrated the importance of these influences above and beyond the apparent impact of constitutional variables are worthy of particular attention.

Before proceeding any further, it is important to comment on the level of confidence that is appropriate to place in the studies reviewed. A large portion of the extant psychological literature is devoted to litanies of methodological weakness and to trading accusations of flawed methodology. While I have mentioned many of the problems with the studies reviewed in the previous chapters, I have tried to avoid making this all too familiar methodological *mea culpa* the central theme of this book. The precise methods of the laboratory cannot be readily packed up for use within the confines of the home, the complexities of the school or the unpredictable domains of distant, unfamilar cultures. However, the fact that research is conducted in the field has too long served as an all-purpose excuse for almost any shortcoming. In many if not most of the studies reviewed, samples were small where they could probably have been larger, measures were poorly described or poorly developed where better descriptions or better measures could have been provided and samples were generated casually where more careful sampling procedures could have been implemented. At times, studies labelled qualitative yield results expressed essentially in terms of the relative frequencies of behaviour. The potential richness of a qualitative study is thereby not fully attained, while the scientific methods necessary for adequately establishing the relative frequencies of behaviour in a family, school or culture are not used. For all these reasons, our confidence in the existing database must be limited, and our conclusions must remain tentative until more studies of higher quality appear.

This review was qualitative rather than quantitative in nature. Therefore, little has been said about the *strength* of the various findings beyond the dichotomy of significance versus non-significance. A quantitative review of this highly fragmented literature would most likely prove unsatisfying even if it were possible. This is unfortunate, because it precludes me from conveying anything more conclusive than my global impression that the effects of family, school and culture constitute small effects in the statistical sense. At the risk of sounding repetitive, I will provide one last reminder that small effects can be very important in certain situations. I have attempted to include studies reported in book chapters and at conventions, where one is more likely to encounter non-significant findings than in professional journals (Light & Pillemer, 1984). Nevertheless, there may be many unpublished studies in these areas that are difficult to retrieve; these may contain non-significant results.

In my work in a psychology department, which emphasizes applied work with children exhibiting maladaptive social behaviour and their families, I observe that many of my colleagues and students operate as if these effects were overwhelming. If this review serves to correct an occasional excessive expectation, they would be interpreting it far better than by invoking these chapters to obliterate their zeal.

Most of the studies considered above do not encompass the element of time. However, families do change somewhat over the course of their own histories, as do schools and cultures. If researchers capture these changes, the impact of context factors in children's social development will become clearer. Some degree of change in these contexts does occur over the life cycle of a family and the history of a culture. Perusal of parallel changes in children's social development will help determine how important these contexts are in its facilitation.

It is very true that most parents rear their children the way they themselves were raised. Most schools teach children according to our society's well-ingrained schema for schooling, and most cultures provide scripts for the socialization of their young. In addition, as Scarr (1987) has pointed out, the child's inborn disposition determines to a large degree his/her psychological environment. In spite of the repeated evidence that we rarely exercise our option to determine the complexion of the settings in which we raise our young, that option does exist. Whatever the genetic contribution to behavioural outcome for children, parents and schools do have some degree of conscious choice in their methods of raising their children, and members of a culture do have some degree of impact on its future precepts. For many parents and teachers, the value of this area of research is its implications for the enhancement of children's social competence through the improvement of children's environments. There are some suggestions that such "artificial" improvement in these environments may bring about some of the better outcomes desired, though here again our expectations must be realistic and we must recognize that the data are far from conclusive.

Feinman and Lewis (1991) remarked that as notions of the role of socialization agents become more sophisticated and bidirectional, enthusiasm for this research endeavour may wane. Researchers must decide for themselves whether they can be satisfied exploring effects which are probably not large, or causes which are probably partial. The fact that we must ask ourselves these questions bears witness to the emerging maturity of this field. In conclusion, I offer the hope that this book, while imparting a note of realism, will nonetheless inspire others to continue the story.

References

Abramovitch, R., Pepler, D., & Corter, C. (1982). Patterns of sibling interaction among preschool-age children. In M. Lamb & B. Sutton-Smith (Eds.), *Sibling relationships: Their nature and significance across the lifespan* (pp. 61–86). Hillsdale, NJ: Erlbaum.

Abramovitch, R., Corter, C., Pepler, D., & Stanhope, L. (1986). Sibling and peer interaction: A final follow-up and a comparison. *Child Development, 57,* 217–229.

Abroms, K. I. (1985). Social giftedness and its relationship with intellectual giftedness. In J. Freeman (Ed.), *The psychology of gifted children* (pp. 201–218). Chichester: Wiley.

Adalbjarnardottir, S. (1991). *How children negotiate with classmates and teachers: Development in thought, action, and style.* Paper presented at the biennial meeting of the Society for Research in Child Development, Seattle, WA, April 1991.

Ahern, F. M., Johnson, R. C., Wilson, J. R., McClearn, G. E., & Vandenberg, S. G. (1982). Family resemblances in personality. *Behaviour Genetics, 12,* 261–280.

Ahola, J. A., & Isherwood, G. B. (1981). Social life: A student perspective. In J. L. Epstein (Ed.), *The quality of school life* (pp. 153–172). Lexington, Mass.: Lexington Books.

Aiello, J. R., & Jones, S. E. (1971). Field study of the proxemic behaviour of young school children in three subcultural groups. *Journal of Personality and Social Psychology, 19,* 351–356.

Ainsworth, M. (1991). *Past and future trends in attachment research.* Paper presented at the XIth biennial meeting of the International Society for the Study of Behavioral Development, Minneapolis, MN, July 1991.

Ainsworth, M. D. S., Bell, S. M., & Stayton, D. J. (1971). Individual differences in stranger-situation behaviour of one-year-olds. In H. R. Schaffer (Ed.), *The origins of human social relations* (pp. 17–57). New York: Academic Press.

Albersheim, L. M., & Carter, T. N. (1991). *Influencing the quality of attachment: An early preventive intervention model.* Paper presented at the XIth biennial meeting of the International Society for the Study of Behavioral Development, Minneapolis, MN, July 1991.

Allen, J., & West, L. (1968). Flight from violence: Hippies and the green rebellion. *American Journal of Psychiatry, 125,* 120–126.

Amato, P. R., & Ochiltree, G. (1986). Family resources and the development of child competence. *Journal of Marriage and the Family, 48,* 47–56.

Amidon, E., & Flanders, N. (1961). The effects of direct and indirect teacher influence on dependent-prone students learning geometry. *Journal of Educational Psychology, 52,* 286–291.

Anderson, B. E. (1989). Effects of public day care—a longitudinal study. *Child Development, 60,* 857–866.

Anderson, C. S. (1982). The search for school climate: A review of the research. *Review of Educational Research, 52,* 368–420.

Anderson, S., & Messick, S. (1974). Social competency in young children. *Developmental Psychology, 10,* 282–293.

Ansbacher, H. L., & Ansbacher, R. R. (Eds.), (1956). *The individual psychology of Alfred Adler.* New York: Harper & Row.

Argyle, M. (1967). *The psychology of interpersonal behavior.* Harmondsworth, Middlesex, England: Penguin.

Argyle, M. (1975). *Bodily communication.* London: Methuen.

Argyle, M. (1983). *The psychology of interpersonal behaviour.* New York: Penguin.

160

Argyle, M. (1988). *Bodily communication.* New York: Methuen.

Argyle, M., & Furnham, A. (1982). The ecology of relationships: Choice of situation as a function of relationship. *British Journal of Social Psychology,* 21, 259–262.

Argyle, M., Furnham, A., & Graham, J. A. (1981). *Social situations.* Cambridge: Cambridge University Press.

Argyle, M., Henderson, M., Bond, M., Contarello, A., & Iizuka, Y. (1986). Cross-cultural variations in relationship rules. *International Journal of Psychology,* 12, 287–315.

Armentrout, J. A. (1972). Sociometric classroom popularity and children's reports of parental child rearing behaviors. *Psychological Reports,* 30, 261–262.

Aronson, E., Blaney, N., Stephan, C., Sikes, J., & Snapp, M. (1978). *The jigsaw classroom.* Beverly Hills, CA: Sage.

Asher, S. R. (1985). An evolving paradigm in social skills training research with children. In B. H. Schneider, K. Rubin, & J. E. Ledingham (Eds.), *Children's peer relations: Issues in assessment and intervention* (pp. 157–174). New York: Springer-Verlag.

Asher, S. R., & Parker, J. G. (1989). Significance of peer relationship problems in childhood. In B. H. Schneider, G. Attili, J. Nadel, & R. P. Weissberg (Eds.), *Social competence in developmental perspective* (pp. 5–23). Dordrecht: Kluwer Academic Press.

Asher, S. R., Markell, R. S., & Hymel, S. (1981). Identifying children at risk in peer relations: A critique of the rate-of-interaction approach to assessment. *Child Development,* 52, 1239–1245.

Asher, S. R., Oden, S. L., & Gottman, J. M. (1977). Children's friendships in school settings. In L. G. Katz (Ed.), *Current topics in early childhood education* (vol. 1, pp. 33–61). Norwood, NJ: Ablex.

Attili, G. (1989). Social competence versus emotional security: The link between home relationships and behavior problems in preschool. In B. H. Schneider, G. Attili, J. Nadel, & R. P. Weissberg (Eds.), *Social competence in developmental perspective* (pp. 293–311). Dordrecht: Kluwer Academic Press.

Attili, G., Travaglia, G., Alcini, P., Vermigli, P., & Felaco, R. (1988). *The difficult child: Cultural determinants of a difficult concept.* Paper presented at the 3rd European Conference on Developmental Psychology, International Society for Behavioral Development, Budapest, Hungary, June 1988.

Austin, A. M. B., & Lindauer, S. L. K. (1990). Parent–child conversation of more-liked and less-liked children. *The Journal of Genetic Psychology,* 151, 5–23.

Bachtold, L. M. (1984). Antecedents of caregiver attitudes and social behavior of Hupa Indian and Anglo-American preschoolers in California. *Child Study Journal,* 13, 217–233.

Bakeman, R., & Gottman, J. M. (1986). *Observing interaction: An introduction to sequential analysis.* Cambridge: Cambridge University Press.

Baltes, P. B. (1979). Life-span developmental psychology: Some converging observations on history and theory. In P. B. Baltes & O. G. Brim, Jr. (Eds.), *Life-span development and behavior* (pp. 255–279). New York: Academic Press.

Baltes, P., Reese, H., & Lipsett, L. (1980). Life-span developmental psychology. *Annual Review of Psychology,* 31, 65–110.

Bandura, A. (1978). The self system in reciprocal determinism. *American Psychologist,* 33, 344–358.

Bandura, A., & Walters, R. H. (1963a). *Social learning and personality development.* New York: Holt, Rinehart & Winston.

Bandura, A., & Walters, R. H. (1963b). *The social learning of deviant behavior: A behavioristic approach to socialization.* New York: Holt, Rinehart & Winston.

Barker, R. G., & Gump, P. V. (1964). *Big school, small school.* Stanford, CA: Stanford University Press.

Bar-Tal, D. (1979). Interactions of teachers and pupils. In I. H. Frieze, D. Bar-Tal, & J. S. Carol (Eds.), *New approaches to social problems. Applications of attribution theory.* San Francisco: Jossey-Bass.

Barrera, M., Jr. (1986). Distinctions between social support concepts, measures, and models. *American Journal of Community Psychology,* 14, 413–445.

Barry, H., III, Josephson, L., Lauer, F., & Marshall, C. (1976). Traits inculcated in childhood: Cross-cultural codes. V. *Ethnology,* 15, 83–114.

Baskett, L. M. (1984). Ordinal position differences in children's family interactions. *Developmental Psychology*, **20**, 1026–1031.

Baskett, L. M. (1985). Understanding family interactions: Most probable reactions by parents and siblings. *Child and Family Behavior Therapy*, **7**, 41–50.

Bates, J. E., Marvinney, D., Bennet, D. S., Dodge, K. A., Kelly, T., & Pettit, G. S. (1991). *Children's daycare history and kindergarten adjustment*. Paper presented at the biennial meeting of the Society for Research in Child Development, Seattle, WA, April 1991.

Batten, M., & Girling-Butcher, S. (1981). *Perceptions of the quality of school life* (ACER Research Monograph no. 13). Hawthorn, Australia: Australian Council for Educational Research.

Baudonnière, P.-M. (1988). *L'évolution des compétences à communiquer*. Paris: Presses Universitaires de France.

Baumrind, D. (1967). Child care practices anteceding three patterns of preschool behavior. *Genetic Psychology Monographs*, **75**, 43–88.

Baumrind, D. (1968). Early socialization and adolescent competence. In S. E. Dragestin and G. H. Elder, Jr. (Eds.), *Adolescence in the life cycle* (pp. 117–143). New York: Halsted.

Baumrind, D. (1975). The contributions of the family to the development of competence in children. *Schizophrenia Bulletin*, **14**, 12–37.

Baumrind, D. (1989). Rearing competent children. In W. Damon (Ed.), *Child development today and tomorrow* (pp. 349–378). San Francisco, CA: Jossey Bass.

Beail, N. (1983). The psychology of fatherhood. *Bulletin of the British Psychological Society*, **36**, 312–314.

Bell, N. J., Avery, A. W., Jenkins, D., Feld, J., & Schoenrock, C. J. (1985). Family relations and social competence during late adolescence. *Journal of Youth and Adolescence*, **14**, 109–119.

Bell, R. Q. (1968). A reinterpretation of the direction of effects in studies of socialization. *Psychological Review*, **75**, 81–95.

Bell-Dolan, D. J., Foster, S. L., & Sikora, D. M. (1989). Effects of sociometric testing on children's behavior and loneliness in school. *Developmental Psychology*, **25**, 306–311.

Bellack, A. S., & Hersen, M. (Eds.). (1979). *Research and practice in social skills training*. New York: Plenum Press.

Belsky, J. (1984). The determinants of parenting: A process model. *Child Development*, **55**, 83–96.

Belsky, J., & Braungart, J. M. (1991). Are insecure-avoidant infants with extensive day-care experience less stressed by and more independent in the strange situation? *Child Development*, **62**, 567–571.

Belsky, J., & Rovine, M. (1988). Nonmaternal care in the first year of life and attachment security. *Child Development*, **59**, 157–167.

Belsky, J., Gilstrap, B., & Rovine, M. (1984). The Pennsylvania Infant and Family Development Project I: Stability and change in mother–infant and father–infant interaction in a family setting at 1- to 3- to -9 months. *Child Development*, **55**, 692–705.

Belsky, J., Robbins, E., & Gamble, W. (1984). The determinance of parental competence: Toward a contextual theory. In M. Lewis (Ed.), *Beyond the dyad* (pp. 251–279). New York: Plenum Press.

Bergmans, L. R. (1983). A developmental study of sex differences in some reactions to the school environment. *Reports from the Department of Psychology. University of Stockholm* (from *Psychological Abstracts*, 1984, **71**, Abstract No. 24435, p. 2592).

Bermann, S., & Hartup, W. W. (1991). Conflicts among children: Concordances between sibling and friendship relations in early and middle childhood. Paper presented to the International Society for the Study of Behavioral Development, Minneapolis, MN, July, 1991.

Berndt, T. J., & Bulleit, T. N. (1985). Effects of sibling relationships on preschoolers' behavior at home and school. *Developmental Psychology*, **21**, 761–767.

Bhavnagri, N. P., & Parke, R. D. (1991). Parents as direct facilitators of children's peer relationships: Effects of age of child and sex of parent. *Journal of Social and Personal Relationships*, **8**, 423–440.

Biesanz, R., Biesanz, K. Z., & Biesanz, M. H. (1982). *The Costa Ricans*. Englewood Cliffs, NJ: Prentice-Hall.

Bloom, B. S. (1977). Affective outcomes of school learning. *Phi Delta Kappan*, **59**, 193–198.

Bonino, S. (1989). *Cooperation and competition: The influence of two different training*. Paper presented at the biennial meeting of the International Society for the Study of Behavioral Development, Jyvaskyla, Finland, July 1989.

Bonino, S. (1991). Aggressività e capacità simbolica nella prima infanzia. In A. Fonzi (Ed.), *Cooperare e competere tra bambini* (pp. 42–49). Florence: Giunti.

Booth, C. L., Rose-Krasnor, L., & Rubin, K. H. (1991). Relating preschoolers' social competence and their mothers' parenting behaviors to early attachment security and high risk status. *Journal of Social and Personal Relationships*, **8**, 363–382.

Booth, C. L., Mitchell, S. K., Barnard, K. E., & Spieker, S. J. (1989). Development of maternal social skills in multiproblem families: Effects on the mother–child relationship. *Developmental Psychology*, **25**, 403–412.

Bossert, S. T. (1979). *Tasks and social relationships in the classroom*. New York: Cambridge University Press.

Bowlby, J. (1969). *Attachment and loss* volume 1: *Attachment*. Middlesex, England: Penguin Books.

Bowlby, J. (1988). *A secure base*. New York: Basic Books.

Brody, G. H., Stoneman, Z. & MacKinnon, C. E. (1982). Role asymmetries in interactions among school-aged children, their younger siblings, and their friends. *Child Development*, **53**, 1364–1370.

Bromet, E. J., & Cornely, P. J. (1984). Correlates of depression in mothers of young children. *Journal of the American Academy of Child Psychiatry*, **23**, 335–342.

Bronfenbrenner, U. (1963). Development theory in transition. In H. W. Stevenson (Ed.), *Child psychology. Sixty-second yearbook of the National Society for the Study of Education, part I*. Chicago: University of Chicago Press.

Bronfenbrenner, U. (1970). *Two worlds of childhood: U.S. and U.S.S.R.* New York: Russel Sage.

Bronfenbrenner, U. (1979). *The ecology of human development: Experiments by nature and design*. Cambridge, MA: Harvard University Press.

Bronfenbrenner, U. (1979). Contexts of child rearing: Problems and prospects. *American Psychologist*, **34**, 844–850.

Bronfenbrenner, U. (1986a). Ecology of the family as a context for human development: Research perspectives. *Developmental Psychology*, **22**, 723–742.

Bronfenbrenner, U. (1986b). Recent advances in research on the ecology of human development. In R. K. Silbereisen, K. Eyferth, & G. Rudinger (Eds.), *Development as action in context* (pp. 287–309). Berlin: Springer-Verlag.

Bronfenbrenner, U., & Crouter, A. C. (1983). The evolution of environmental models in developmental research. In W. Kessen (Ed.), *Handbook of child psychology, vol. 1. History, theory and methods* (pp. 357–414). New York: Wiley.

Brookover, W. B., Beady, C., Flood, P., Schweitzer, J., & Wisenbaker, J. (1979). *School social systems and student achievement*. New York: Praeger.

Brophy, J. E., & Good, T. L. (1974). *Teacher–student relationships: Causes and consequences*. New York: Holt, Rinehart & Winston.

Brown, J. (1989). *The relation between parenting styles and children's social cognitive skills*. Paper presented at the biennial meeting of the Society for Research in Child Development, Kansas, MO, April 1989.

Bryan, T. (1976). Peer popularity of learning disabled children. A replication. *Journal of Learning Disabilities*, **9**, 307–311.

Budd, K. S., & Itzkowitz, J. S. (1990). Parents as social skills trainers and evaluators of children. *Child and Family Behavior Therapy*, **12**, 13–29.

Burleson, B. R., Delia, J. G., & Applegate, J. L. (1989). *Effects of mothers' disciplinary comforting strategies on children's communication skills and acceptance by the peer group*. Paper presented at the International Communication Association convention, Dublin, Ireland, June 1989.

Buss, A. R. (1979). Dialectics, history, and development: The historical roots of the individual-society dialectic. In P. B. Baltes & O. G. Brim, Jr. (Eds.), *Life-span development and behavior* (pp. 313–333). New York: Academic Press.

Butkovsky, L. L. (1991). *Emotional expressiveness in the family: Connections to children's peer relations*. Paper presented at the biennial meeting of the Society for Research in Child Development, Seattle, WA, April 1991.

Butterworth, G., Rutkowska, J., & Scarfe, M. (Eds.) (1985). *Evolution and developmental psychology*. New York: St. Martin's.

Byrne, B., & Schneider, B. H. (1986). Student-teacher concordance on dimensions of student-social competence: A multi-trait, multi-method analysis. *Journal of Psychopathology and Behavioral Assessment*, **8**, 263–279.

Byrnes, D. A. (1985). Cipher in the classroom: The invisible child. *Childhood Education*, **62**, 91–97.

Cairns, R. B. (Ed.) (1979). *The analysis of social interaction: Methods issues and illustrations*. Hillsdale, NJ: Erlbaum.

Cairns, R. B., & Cairns, B. D. (1984). Predicting aggressive patterns in girls and boys: A developmental study. *Aggressive Behavior*, **10**, 227–242.

Camp, B. W. (1977). Verbal mediation in young aggressive boys. *Journal of Abnormal Psychology*, **86**, 145–153.

Campbell, D. T. (1963). Social attitudes and other acquired behavioral dispositions. In S. Koch (Ed.), *Psychology: A study of science* (pp. 94–172). New York: McGraw-Hill.

Caplan, M. Z., & Weissberg, R. P. (1989). Promoting social competence in early adolescence: Developmental considerations. In B. H. Schneider, G. Attili, J. Nadel, & R. P. Weissberg (Eds.), *Social competence in developmental perspective* (pp. 371–385). Dordrecht: Kluwer Academic Publishers.

Caplan, P. J., & Hall-McCorquodale, I. (1985). Mother-blaming in major clinical journals. *American Journal of Orthopsychiatry*, **55**, 345–353.

Carson, J. L. (1991). *In search of mediating processes: Emotional cues as links between family and peer systems*. Paper presented at the biennial meeting of the Society for Research in Child Development, Seattle, WA, April 1991.

Caspi, A., & Elder, G. H., Jr. (1988). Emergent family problems: The intergenerational construction of problem behavior and relationships. In R. A. Hinde & J. Stevenson-Hinde (Eds.), *Relationships within families: Mutual influences* (pp. 218–240). Oxford: Oxford University Press.

Caudill, W., & Plath, D. W. (1966). Who sleeps by whom? Parent–child involvement in urban Japanese families. *Psychiatry*, **29**, 344–366.

Caulfield, T. J. (1980). The successful ones. *Personnel and Guidance Journal*, **59**, 241–245.

Ceccarelli, F. (1983). Modelli di interazione fra biologia e cultura [Models of interaction between biology and culture]. *Rassegna Italiana di Sociologia*, **24**, 575–615.

Charlebois, P., Leblanc, M., Gagnon, C., Larivée, S., & Tremblay, R. (1992). *The effect of cumulative subtle coercion in the primary school classroom on juvenile delinquency*. Paper presented at the Society for Life History Research Conference in Philadelphia, April 1992.

Charlesworth, W. R., & Nakra, O. (1991). Cooperation and competition in Indian, Carribean and North American children. Paper presented at the XIth biennial meeting of the International Society for the Study of Behavioral Development, Minneapolis, MN, July 1991.

Christensen, A., & Margolin, G. (1988). Conflict and alliance in distressed and non-distressed families. In R. A. Hinde & J. Stevenson-Hinde (Eds.), *Relationships within families: Mutual influences* (pp. 263–282). Oxford: Oxford University Press.

Christensen, C. (1974). *Development and field testing of an interpersonal coping skills program*. Unpublished manuscript, Ontario Institute for Studies in Education, Toronto.

Christopher, J. S., Hansen, D. J. & MacMillan, V. M. (1991). Effectiveness of a peer–helper intervention to increase children's social interactions: Generalization, maintenance, and social validity. *Behavior Modification*, **15**, 22–50.

Christopoulus, C. (1991). *Childhood peer rejection and aggression as predictors of intimacy/involvement with the parent in adolescence*. Paper presented at the biennial meeting of the Society for Research in Child Development, Seattle, WA, April 1991.

Chu, L. (1979). The sensitivity of Chinese and American children to social influences. *The Journal of Social Psychology*, **109**, 175–186.

Clark, R. A., & Jones, J. (1990). *Parental reflection enhancing communication, children's person-centred communication skills, and children's success in peer relationships: An analysis with second- and seventh-graders and their mothers.* Paper presented at the Fifth International Conference on Personal Relationships, Oxford University, England, July 1990.

Clarke-Stewart, K. A. (1989). Infant day care: Maligned or malignant? *American Psychologist*, **44**, 266–273.

Clarke-Stewart, K. A. (1991). A home is not a school: The effects of environments on development. In M. Lewis, & S. Feinman (Eds.), *Social influences and socialization in infancy* (pp. 41–61). New York: Plenum Press.

Clements, M. (1991). *The impact of marital functioning on children's peer relations: An interactional study.* Paper presented at the biennial convention of the Society for Research in Child Development, Seattle, WA, April 1991.

Cohen, P. A., Kulik, J. A., & Kulic, C. L. C. (1982). Education outcomes of tutoring: A meta-analysis of findings. *American Educational Research Journal*, **19**, 237–248.

Cohn, D. A., Patterson, C. J. & Christopoulus, C. (1991). The family and children's peer relations. *Journal of Social and Personal Relationships*, **8**, 315–346.

Coie, J. D. (1985). Fitting social skills intervention to the target group. In B. H. Schneider, K. H. Rubin, & J. E. Ledingham (Eds.), *Children's peer relations: Issues in assessment and intervention* (pp. 141–156). New York: Springer-Verlag.

Coie, J. D., & Krehbiel, G. (1984). Effects of academic tutoring on the social status of low-achieving, socially rejected children. *Child Development*, **55**, 1465–1478.

Coie, J. D., & Kupersmidt, J. (1983). A behavioral analysis of emerging social status in boys' groups. *Child Development*, **54**, 1400–1416.

Coleman, J. S. (1961). *The adolescent society.* New York: Free Press of Glencoe.

Collett, P. (1971). On training Englishmen in the non-verbal behavior of Arabs: An experiment in intercultural communication. *International Journal of Psychology*, **6**, 209–215.

Cooper, C. R., & Ayers-Lopez, S. (1985). Family and peer systems in early adolescence: New models of the role of relationships in development. *Journal of Early Adolescence*, **5**, 9–21.

Cooper, C. R., Marquis, A., & Ayers-Lopez, S. (1982). Peer learning in the classroom: Tracing developmental patterns and consequences of children's spontaneous interactions. In L. Wilkinson (Ed.), *Communication in the classroom.* New York: Academic Press.

Corsaro, W. A. (1985). *Friendship and peer culture in the early years.* Norwood, NJ: Ablex.

Corsaro, W. A. (1988). Routines in the peer culture of American and Italian nursery school children. *Sociology of Education*, **61**, 1–14.

Coyne, J. C. (1976). Toward an interactional description of depression. *Psychiatry*, **39**, 28–40.

Cummings, E. M., Zahn-Waxler, C., & Radke-Yarrow, M. (1984). Developmental changes in children's reactions to anger in the home. *Journal of Child Psychology and Psychiatry and Allied Disciplines*, **25**, 63–74.

Daniels-Beirness, T. (1989). Measuring peer status in boys and girls: A problem of apples and oranges? In B. H. Schneider, G. Attili, J. Nadel, & R. P. Weissberg (Eds.), *Social competence in developmental perspective.* Dordrecht: Kluwer.

Daniels-Beirness, T. M., & LeShano, S. (1988). *Children's social relationships outside of school.* Paper presented at the NATO Advanced Study Institute: Social Competence in Developmental Perspective, Savoy, France, July 1988.

Datan, N., & Reese, H. W. (Eds.) (1977). *Life-span developmental psychology: Dialectical perspectives on experimental research.* New York: Academic Press.

Delia, J. G., & Applegate, J. L. (1990). *From cognition to communication to cognition to communication: Effects of mothers' cognition and communication on their children's social cognition and communication abilities.* Paper presented at the Fifth International Conference on Personal Relationships, Oxford, July 1990.

DellaPiana, G., & Gage, N. (1955). Pupils' values and the validity of the Minnesota Teacher Attitude Inventory. *Journal of Educational Psychology*, **46**, 167–178.

Denham, S. A., Renwick, S. M., & Holt, R. W. (1991). Working and playing together:

Prediction of preschool social-emotional competence from mother–child interaction. *Child Development*, **62**, 242–249.

DeRosier, M. (1989). *Costa Rican children's perceptions of their social networks*. Paper presented at the biennial meeting of the Society for Research in Child Development, Kansas, MO, April 1989.

Deutsch, F. (1983). Classroom social participation of preschoolers in single parent families. *Journal of Social Psychology*, **119**, 77–84.

Dishion, T. J., Patterson, G. R., Stoolmiller, M., & Skinner, M. L. (1991). Family, school, and behavior antecedents to early adolescent involvement with antisocial peers. *Developmental Psychology*, **27**, 172–180.

Dixon, R. A., & Lerner, R. M. (1988). A history of systems in developmental psychology. In M. H. Bornstein & M. E. Lamb (Eds.), *Developmental psychology: an advanced textbook* (pp. 3–50). Hillsdale, NJ: Erlbaum.

Dodge, K. A. (1985). Facets of social interaction and the assessment of social competence in children. In B. H. Schneider, K. H. Rubin, & J. E. Ledingham (Eds.), *Children's peer relations: Issues in assessment and intervention* (pp. 3–22). New York: Springer-Verlag.

Doise, W., & Mugny, G. (1984). *The social development of intellect*. Oxford: Pergamon Press.

Downey, G., & Coyne, J. C. (1990). Children of depressed parents: An integrative review. *Psychological Bulletin*, **108**, 50–76.

Draper, P. (1973). Crowding among hunter-gatherers: The Kung Bushmen. *Science*, **182**, 301–303.

Dreikurs, R., & Soltz, V. (1964). *Children: the challenge*. New York: Hawthorn.

Droege, K. L., & Howes, C. (1991). The influence of caregiver sensitivity on children's affective displays. Poster presented to the International Society for the Study of Behavioral Development, Minneapolis, MN, July, 1991.

Duck, S. (1989). Socially competent communication and relationship development. In B. H. Schneider, G. Attili, J. Nadel, & P. Weissberg (Eds.), *Social competence in developmental perspective* (pp. 91–106). Dordrecht: Kluwer Academic Publishers.

Dumas, J. E. (1986). Indirect influence of maternal social contacts on mother–child interactions: A setting event analysis. *Journal of Abnormal Psychology*, **14**, 205–216.

Dunn, J., & Plomin R., (1986). Determinants of maternal behavior toward three-year-old siblings. *British Journal of Developmental Psychology*, **4**, 127–137.

Dunn, J., & Plomin R. (1990). *Separate lives: Why siblings are so different*. New York: Basic Books.

Dunn, J., Plomin R., & Daniels, D. (1986). Consistency and change in mothers' behavior to two-year-old siblings. *Child Development*, **57**, 348–356.

Durlak, H. J. (1983). Social problem-solving as a primary prevention strategy. In R. Felner, L. Jason, J. Moritsugu, & S. Farber (Eds.), *Preventive psychology: Theory, research and practice* (pp. 31–48). New York: Pergamon Press.

Durlak, J. A. (1983). Social problem-solving as a primary prevention strategy. In R. D. Felner, L. A. Jason, J. N. Moritsugu, & S. S. Farber (Eds.), *Preventive psychology* (pp. 31–48). New York: Pergamon Press.

East, P. L. (1991). The parent–child relationships of withdrawn, aggressive and sociable children: Parent and child perspectives. *Merrill-Palmer Quarterly*, **37**, 425–444.

Easterbrooks, M. A., & Emde, R. N. (1988). Marital and parent–child relationships: The role of affect in the family system. In R. A. Hinde & J. Stevenson-Hinde (Eds.), *Relationships within families: Mutual influences* (pp. 83–103). Oxford: Oxford University Press.

Eaves, L. J., Eysenck, H. J., & Martin, N. G. (1989). *Genes, culture, and personality: An empirical approach*. London: Academic Press.

Edmonds, R. (1986). Characteristics of effective schools. In U. Neisser [Ed.), *The school achievement of minority children* (pp. 93–104). Hillsdale, NJ: Erlbaum.

Edwards, C. P. (1986). *Promoting social and moral development in young children: Creative approaches for the classroom*. New York: Teachers College Press.

Eiferman, R. (1970). Cooperativeness and egalitarianism in kibbutz children's games. *Human Relations*, **23**, 579–587.

Eisenberg, N., & Mussen, P. H. (1989). *The roots of prosocial behavior in children.* New York: Cambridge University Press.

Ekblad, S. (1984). Children's thoughts and attitudes in China and Sweden: Impacts of a restrictive versus a permissive environment. *Acta Psychiatrica Scandinavica,* **70,** 578–590.

Elder, G. H., Jr. (1979). Historical change in life patterns and personality. In P. B. Baltes & O. G. Brim, Jr. (Eds.), *Life-span development and behavior* (pp. 117–159). New York: Academic Press.

Elder, G. H., Jr., Caspi, A., & Nguyen, T. V. (in press). Resourceful and vulnerable children: Family influences in stressful times. In R. K. Silbereisen & K. Eyferth (Eds.), *Development in context: Integrative perspectives in youth development.* New York: Springer-Verlag.

Elder, G. H., Jr., Nguyen, T. V., & Caspi, A. (1985). Linking family hardship to children's lives. *Child Development,* **56,** 361–375.

Elicker, J. G. (1991), *Attachment history, interpersonal sensitivity, and peer competence in preadolescence.* Poster presented at the biennial meeting of the Society for Research in Child Development, Seattle, WA, April 1991.

Emery, R. E. (1982). Interparental conflict and the children of discord and divorce. *Psychological Bulletin,* **92,** 310–330.

Engfer, A., & Gödde, M. (1991). *The social networks of six-year-old children.* Paper presented at the XIth biennial meeting of the International Society for the Study of Behavioral Development, Minneapolis, MN, July 1991.

Epstein, J. L. (1983). Longitudinal effects of family–school-person interactions on student outcomes. In A. C. Kerckhoff (Ed.), *Research in sociology of education and socialization* (pp. 101–127). Greenwich, Conn.: JAI Press.

Epstein, J. L., & Karweit, N. (Eds.) (1983). *Friends in school: Patterns of selection and influence in secondary schools.* New York: Academic Press.

Erickson, F., & Shultz, J. (1981). When is a context? Some issues and methods in the analysis of social competence. In J. L. Green & C. Wallat (Eds.), *Ethnography and language in educational settings* (pp. 147–160). Norwood, NJ: Ablex.

Erikson, E. H. (1963). *Childhood and society.* New York: Norton.

Eron, L. D., & Huesmann, L. R. (1987). The stability of aggressive behavior in cross-national comparison. In C. Kagitcibasi (Ed.), *In growth and progress in cross-cultural psychology* (pp. 207–217). Lisse, Netherlands: Swets.

Fagot, B. I., & Kavanagh, K. (1990). The prediction of antisocial behavior from avoidant attachment classifications. *Child Development,* **61,** 864–873.

Falbo, R. (1987). Only children in the United States and China. *Applied Social Psychology Annual,* **7,** 159–183.

Fantuzzo, J. W., Polite, K., & Grayson, N. (1990). An evaluation of reciprocal peer tutoring across elementary school settings. *Journal of School Psychology,* **28,** 309–323.

Fantuzzo, J. W., DePaolo, L. M., Lambert, L., Anderson, G., & Sutton, S. (1991). Effects of interparental violence on the psychological adjustment of young children. *Journal of Consulting and Clinical Psychology,* **59,** 258–265.

Feinman, S., & Lewis, M. (1991). Influence lost, influence regained. In M. Lewis, & S. Feinman (Eds.), *Social influences and socialization in infancy* (pp. 1–19). New York: Plenum Press.

Feshbach, N. D. (1967). Effects of teachers' reinforcement style upon children's imitation and preferences. *Proceedings of the 75th annual convention of the American Psychological Association,* **2,** 281–282.

Feshbach, N. D. (1983). Learning to care: A positive approach to child training and discipline. *Journal of Clinical Child Psychology,* **12,** 266–271.

Feshbach, N. D., & Feshbach, S. (1982). Empathy training and the regulation of aggression: Potentialities and limitations. *Academic Psychological Bulletin,* **4,** 399–413.

Fischbein, S. (1987). Nature-nurture interaction in different types of school environments: A longitudinal study. *Acta Genet. Med. Gemellol.,* **36,** 155–163.

Flanders, N., & Havumaki, S. (1960). The effect of teacher–pupil contacts involving praise on sociometric choices of students. *Journal of Educational Psychology,* **51,** 65–68.

Floderus-Myrhed, B., Pedersen, N. L., & Rasmuson, I. (1980). Assessment of heritability for personality based on a short form of the Eysenck Personality Inventory. *Behavior Genetics*, **10**, 153–162.

Flourio-Ruane, S. (1989). Social organization of classes and schools. In M. Reynolds (Ed.), *Knowledge base for the beginning teacher: A handbook* (pp. 163–172). Oxford, U.K.: Pergamon Press.

Fonzi, A. (Ed.). (1991). *Cooperare e competere tra bambini* [Cooperation and competition among children]. Florence: Giunti.

Fonzi, A., & Tomada, G. (1991). *Conflict management and differing levels of competence in very young children.* Paper presented at the XIth biennial meeting of the International Society for the Study of Behavioral Development, Minneapolis, MN, July 1991.

Fonzi, A., Tomada, G., & De Domini, P. (1990). *Interpersonal conflict and acquisition of performance skills in children of 29 to 39 months.* Paper presented at the IVth European Conference on Developmental Psychology, Stirling, Scotland, August 1990.

Ford, M. (1982). Social cognition and social competence in adolescence. *Developmental Psychology*, **18**, 323–340.

Fox, N. A., Kimmerly, N. L., & Schafer, W. D. (1991). Attachment to mother/attachment to father: A mental-analysis. *Child Development*, **62**, 210–225.

Fromm, E. (1955). *The sane society*. New York: Rinehart.

Fromm, E. (1964). *The heart of man*. New York: Harper & Row.

Fry, D. P. (1988). Intercommunity differences in aggression among Zapotec children. *Child Development*, **59**, 1008–1019.

Furman, W., & Buhrmester, D. (1985). Children's perceptions of the personal relationships in their social networks. *Developmental Psychology*, **21**, 1016–1024.

Furman, W., & Robbins, P. (1985). What's the point? Issues in the selection of treatment objectives. In B. H. Schneider, K. H. Rubin, & J. E. Ledingham (Eds.), *Children's peer relations: Issues in assessment and intervention* (pp. 41–54). New York: Springer-Verlag.

Furman, W., & White, A. (1991). *The links between twins' relationships with each other and their friends.* Paper presented at the biennial meeting of the Society for Research in Child Development, Seattle, WA, April 1991.

Galambos, N. L., & Silbereisen, R. K. (1987). Influences of income change and parental acceptance on adolescent transgression proneness and peer relations. *European Journal of Psychology of Education*, **1**, 17–28.

Gallimore, R., Boggs, J. W., & Jordan. C. (1974). *Culture, behavior and education: A study of Hawaiian Americans.* Beverly Hills: Sage.

Garmezy, N. (1989). The role of competence in the study of children and adolescents under stress. In B. H. Schneider, G. Attili, J. Nadel, & R. P. Weissberg (Eds.), *Social competence in developmental perspective* (pp. 25–39). Dordrecht: Kluwer Academic Press.

Gauthier, D., Loranger, M., & Ladouceur, R. (1984). Le renforcement des comportements académiques: Une stratégie économique dans l'intervention en milieu scolaire. *Canadian Psychology*, **25**, 14–22.

George, C. & Main, M. (1979). Social interactions of young abused children: Approach, avoidance and aggression. *Child Development*, **50**, 306–318.

Getzels, J. W. (1975). Images of the classroom and visions of the learner. In T. G. David, & B. D. Wright (Eds.), *Learning environments* (pp. 1–14). Chicago: University of Chicago Press.

Giaconia, R. M., & Hedges, L. V. (1982). Identifying features of effective open education. *Review of Educational Research*, **52**, 579–602.

Gilmore, T. M. (1978). Locus of control as a mediator of adaptive behavior in children and adolescents. *Canadian Psychological Review*, **19**, 1–26.

Ginter, E. J., Lufi, D., Trotzky, A. S., & Richmond, B. O. (1989). Anxiety among children in Israel. *Psychological Reports*, **65**, 803–809.

Goldin, P. C. (1969). A review of children's reports of parent behaviors. *Psychological Bulletin*, **71**, 222–236.

Goldsmith, H. H., Buss, A. H., Plomin, R., Rothbart, M. K., Thomas, A., Chess, S., Hinde, R. A., & McCall, R. B. (1987). Roundtable: What is temperament? Four approaches. *Child Development*, **58**, 505–529.

Goldstein, A. P., & Glick, B. (1987). *Aggression replacement training.* Champaign, IL: Research Press.

Goldstein, A. P., & Segall, M. H. (Eds.). (1983). *Aggression in global perspective.* New York: Pergamon Press.

Good, T. L., & Brophy, J. F. (1986). School effects. In M. C. Wittrock (Ed.), *Handbook of research on teaching* (pp. 570–602). New York: Macmillan.

Goodland, S., & Hirst, B. (1989). *Peer tutoring.* London: Kogan-Page.

Goodnow, J. J. (1984). Parents' ideas about parenting and development: A review of issues and recent work. In M. E. Lamb, A. L. Brown, & B. Rogoff (Eds.), *Advances in developmental psychology* (pp. 193–242). Hillsdale, NJ: Erlbaum.

Gotlib, I. H., & Lee, C. M. (1990). Children of depressed parents: A review and directions for further research. In C. D. McCann & N. S. Endler (Eds.), *In depression: New directions in theory, research and practice.* Toronto: Wall/Emersen.

Gottman, J. M., & Katz, L. F. (1989). Effects of marital discord on younger children's peer interaction and health. *Developmental Psychology,* **25,** 373–381.

Gould, S. J. (1981). *The mismeasure of man.* New York: Norton.

Grabe, M. (1981). School size and the importance of school activities. *Adolescence,* **16,** 21–31.

Graves, N. B., & Graves, T. D. (1983). The cultural context of prosocial development: An ecological model. In D. L. Bridgeman (Ed.), *The nature of prosocial development* (pp. 243–264). New York: Academic Press.

Green, K. D., Forehand, R., Beck, J., & Vosk, B. (1980). An assessment of the relationship among measures of children's social competence and children's academic achievement. *Child Development,* **51,** 1149–1156.

Green, J. L., & Harker, J. (1982). Gaining access to learning: Communicative, contextual, and academic demands. In L. C. Wilkinson (Ed.), *Communicating in the classroom* (pp. 182–222). New York: Academic Press.

Greenberg, J. B. (1981) *Santiago's sword: Chatino peasant religion and economics.* Berkeley, CA: University of California Press.

Greenberg, M. T., Siegel, J. M., & Leitch, C. J. (1983). The nature and importance of attachment relationships to parents and peers during adolescence. *Journal of Youth and Adolescence,* **12,** 373–386.

Greenspan, S. I. (1981). *Psychopathology and adaptation in infancy and early childhood.* New York: International University Press.

Gresham, F. M. (1982). Misguided mainstreaming: The case for social skills training with handicapped children. *Exceptional Children,* **48,** 422–433.

Gresham, F. M. (1986). Conceptual issues in the assessment of social competence in children. In P. S. Strain, M. J., Guralnick and H. M. Walker (Eds.), *Children's social behavior: Development, assessment and modification* (pp. 143–180). Orlando: Academic Press.

Gresham, F. M., & Reschly, D. J. (1987). Dimensions of social competence: Method factors in the assessment of adaptive behavior, social skills, and peer acceptance. *Journal of School Psychology,* **25,** 367–381.

Gresham, F. M., Elliott, S. N., & Black, F. L. (1987). Factor structure replication and bias investigation of the teacher rating of social skills. *Journal of School Psychology,* **25,** 81–92.

Grossman, K. E., August, P., Scheurer-English, H., & Stefan, C. (1989). *Attachment research: Lasting effects on domains of validity.* Paper presented at the biennial meeting of the International Society for the Study of Behavioral Development, Jyvaskyla, Finland, July 1989.

Grossman, K. E., Grossman, K., Hubert, F., & Wartner, U. (1981). German children's behavior towards their mothers at 12 months and their fathers at 18 months in Ainsworth's strange situation. *International Journal of Behavioral Development,* **4,** 157–181.

Grotevant, H. D., & Cooper, C. R. (1986). Individuation in family relationships: A perspective on individual differences in the development of identity and role-taking skill in adolescence. *Human Development,* **29,** 82–100.

Grusec, J., & Lytton, H. (1988). *Social development.* New York: Springer-Verlag.

Grusec, J. E. (1972). Demand characteristics of the modeling experiment. *Journal of Personality and Social Psychology*, **22**, 139–148.

Gudykunst, W. B., & Ting-Toomey, S. (1988). *Culture and interpersonal communication*. Newbury Park: Sage.

Giudubaldi, J., & Perry, J. D. (1984). Divorce, sociometric status, and children's cognitive-social competence at school entry. *American Journal of Orthopsychiatry*, **54**, 459–468.

Haley, J. (1967). Towards a theory of pathological systems. In G. Zuk & I. Nagy (Eds.), *Family therapy and disturbed families*. Palo Alto, CA: Science and Behavior Books.

Hall, E. T. (1976). *Beyond culture*. New York: Doubleday.

Hallinan, M. T. (1976). Friendship patterns in open and traditional classrooms. *Sociology of Friendship*, **49**, 254–264.

Hansell, S., & Karweit, N. (1983). Curricular placement, friendship networks, and status attainment. In J. L. Epstein, & N. Karweit (Eds.), *Friends in school* (pp. 141–161). New York: Academic Press.

Hansen, D. A. (1986). Family–school articulations: The effects of interaction rule mismatch. *American Educational Research Journal*, **23**, 643–659.

Hargie, O. (1986). Communication as skilled behavior. In O. Hargie (Ed.), *A handbook of communication skills* (pp. 7–21). London: Croom Helm.

Harkness, S., & Super, M. (1985). The cultural context of gender segregation in children's peer groups. *Child Development*, **56**, 219–224.

Harris, M. B. (1972). *Classroom uses of behavior modification*. Columbus, OH: Merrill.

Hart, D., Lucca-Irizarry, N., & Damon, W. (1986). The development of self-understanding in Puerto Rico and the United States. *Journal of Early Adolescence*, **6**, 293–304.

Hartmann, E. (1991). *Long-term predictors of children's competence in school*. Paper presented at the XIth bienial meeting of the International Society for the Study of Behavioral Development, Minneapolis, MN, July 1991.

Hartmann, H. (1939). *Ego psychology and the problem of adaptation*. London: Imago.

Hartup, W. (1991). *Conflict in relationships*. Paper presented to the International Society for the Study of Behavioral Development, Minneapolis, MN, July 1991.

Hartup, W. W. (1983). Peer relations. In P. H. Mussen (Ed.), *Handbook of child psychology*, 4th edition (pp. 103–196). New York: Wiley.

Hawkins, J., & Berndt, T. J. (1985). *Adjustment following the transition to Junior High School*. Paper presented at the biennial meeting of the Society for Research in Child Development, Toronto, Canada.

Hayvren, M. & Hymel, S. (1984). Ethical issues in sociometric testing: The impact of sociometric measures on interaction behavior. *Developmental Psychology*, **20**, 844–849.

Hazel, J. S., Schumaker, J. B., Sherman, J. A., & Sheldon-Wildgen, J. (1985). *Asset: A social skills program for adolescents*. Champaign, IL: Research Press.

Heath, P. A., & Lynch, S. (1988). A reconceptualization of the time since parental separation variable as a predictor of children's outcomes following divorce. *Journal of Divorce*, **11**, 67–76.

Heath, P. A., & MacKinnon, C. (1988). Factors related to the social competence of children in single parent families. *Journal of Divorce*, **11**, 49–66.

Heath, S. B. (1983). *Ways with words: Ethnography of communication, communities and classrooms*. Cambridge: Cambridge University Press.

Hertz-Lazarowitz, R., Fuchs, I., Sharabany, R., & Eisenberg, N. (1989). Students' interactive and noninteractive behaviors in the classroom: A comparison between two types of classrooms in the city and the kibbutz in Israel. *Contemporary Educational Psychology*, **14**, 22–32.

Hetherington, E. M., Cox, M., & Cox, R. (1985). Long-term effects of divorce and remarriage on the adjustment of children. *Journal of the American Academy of Child Psychiatry*, **24**, 518–530.

Hewstone, M., Bond, M., & Wan, K. (1983). Social facts and social attributions: The explanation of intergroup differences in Hong Kong. *Social Cognition*, **2**, 142–157.

Heyneman, S., & Losley, W. (1983). The effect of primary school quality on academic achievement across twenty-nine high and low income countries. *American Journal of Sociology*, **88**, 1162–1194.

Hiester, M., & Sapp, J. (1991). *The relationship between maternal life stress and social support and quality of mother–infant attachment.* Paper presented at the biennial meeting of the Society for Research in Child Development, Seattle, WA, April 1991.

Hinde, R. A. (1989). On describing relationships. *Journal of Child Psychology and Psychiatry*, **17**, 1–19.

Hinde, R. A., Stevenson-Hinde, J., & Tamplin, A. (1985). Characteristics of 3- to 4-year-olds assessed at home and their interactions in preschool. *Developmental Psychology*, **21**, 130–140.

Hoffman, M. L. (1976). Empathy, role-taking, guilt, and development of altruistic motives. In T. Lickona (Ed.), *Moral development and behavior* (pp. 124–143). New York: Holt, Rinehart & Winston.

Hofman, T. (1985). Arabs and Jews, Blacks and Whites: Identity and group relations. *Journal of Multilingual and Multicultural Development*, **6**, 217–237.

Hofstede, G. (1979). Value systems in forty countries. In L. Eckensberger, W. Lonner, & Y. Poortinga (Eds.), *Cross-cultural contributions to psychology*. Lisse, The Netherlands: Swets & Zeitlinger.

Hofstede, G. (1980). *Culture's consequences: International differences in work-related values.* Beverly Hills, CA: Sage.

Hofstede, G. (1983). Dimensions of national cultures in fifty countries and three regions. In J. Deregowski, S. Dzuirawiec, & R. Annis (Eds.), *Explications in cross-cultural psychology*. Lisse, The Netherlands: Swets & Zeitlinger.

Hofstede, G. (1984). Hofstede's culture dimensions: An independent validation using Rokeach's value survey. *Journal of Cross-Cultural Psychology*, **15**, 417–433.

Hollos, M. (1974). *Growing up in Flathill.* Oslo: Universitets Forlaget.

Hollos, M. (1980). Collective education in Hungary: The development of competitive, cooperative and role-taking behaviors. *Ethos*, **8**, 3–23.

Holloway, S. D., & Reichart-Erickson, M. (1989). Child-care quality, family structure, and maternal expectations: Relationship to preschool children's peer relations. *Journal of Applied Developmental Psychology*, **10**, 281–298.

Homel, R., Burns, A., & Goodnow, J. (1987). Parental social networks and child development. *Journal of Personal and Social Relationships*, **4**, 159–177.

Hood, K. E., & McHale, S. M. (1987). Sources of stability and change in early childhood. *Advances in Applied Developmental Psychology*, **2**, 17–39.

Hops, H. (1983). Children's social competence and skill: Current research practices and future directions. *Behavior Therapy*, **4**, 3–18.

Hops, H., & Finch, M. (1985). Social competence and skill: A reassessment. In B. H. Schneider, K. H. Rubin, & J. E. Ledingham (Eds.), *Children's peer relations: Issues in assessment and intervention* (pp. 23–29). New York: Springer-Verlag.

Howe, H. (1992). *The influence of maternal behavior on early sibling relations.* Paper presented at the convention of the Canadian Psychological Association, Québec, QC, June 1992.

Howes, C. (1989). Friendships in very young children: Definition and functions (conversation summary). In B. H. Schneider, G. Attili, J. Nadel, & R. P. Weissberg (Eds.), *Social competence in developmental perspective* (pp. 127–129). Dordrecht: Kluwer Academic Press.

Howes, C. (1990). *A comparison of preschool behaviors with peers when children enroll in child care as infants or older children.* Paper present at the IVth European Conference on Developmental Psychology, Stirling, Scotland, July 1990.

Howes, C., & Eldredge, R. (1985). Responses of abuses, neglected and non-maltreated children to the behaviors of their peers. *Journal of Applied Developmental Psychology*, **6**, 261–270.

Howes, C., & Stewart, P. (1987). Child's play with adults, toys, and peers: An examination of family and child-care influences. *Developmental Psychology*, **23**, 324–430.

Howes, C., Phillips, D. A., & Whitebook, M. (1992). Thresholds of quality: Implications for the social development of children in center-based child care. *Child Development*, **63**, 449–460.

Howes, P., & Markman, H. J. (1989). Maternal quality and child functioning: A longitudinal investigation. *Child Development*, **60**, 1044–1051.

Humphrey, L. L. (1984). Children's self-control in relation to perceived social environment. *Journal of Personality and Social Psychology*, **46**, 178–188.

Hymel, S., & Asher, S. R. (1985). Children's peer relations: Assessing self-perceptions. In B. H. Schneider, K. H. Rubin, & J. E. Ledingham (Eds.), *Children's peer relations: Issues in Assessment and Intervention* (pp. 75–92). New York: Springer-Verlag.

Isherwood, G. I., & Ahola, J. A. (1981). School life: A conceptual model, or where you stand depends on where you sit. In J. K. Epstein (Ed.), *The quality of school life* (pp. 173–177). Lexington, MA: Lexington Books.

Ittelson, W. H., Rivlin, L. G., & Proshansky, M. (1970). The use of behavioral maps in environmental psychology. In M. Proshansky, W. H. Ittelson, & L. G. Rivkin (Eds.), *Environmental psychology: man and his physical setting* (pp. 658–668). New York: Holt, Rinehart & Winston.

Jacobson, J. L., Wille, D. E., Tianen, R. L., & Aytch, D. M. (1983). *The influences of infant–mother attachment on toddler sociability with peers.* Paper presented at the biennial meeting of the Society for Research in Child Development, Detroit, April 1983.

Janssens, J. (1990). *Parental locus of control, childbearing and the child's behavior style.* Paper presented at the IVth European Conference on Developmental Psychology, Stirling, Scotland, July 1990.

Jennings, W. S., & Kohlberg, L. (1983). Effects of a just community programme on the moral development of youthful offenders. *Journal of Moral Education*, **12**, 33–50.

Johnson, C., & Pelham, W. E., Jr. (1990). Maternal characteristics, ratings of child behavior, and mother–child interactions in families of children with externalizing disorders. *Journal of Abnormal Child Psychology*, **18**, 407–417.

Johnson, D. W., & Johnson, R. T. (1975). *Learning together and alone: Cooperation, competition and individualization.* Englewood Cliffs, NJ: Prentice-Hall.

Johnson, D. W., & Johnson, R. T. (1981). The integration of the handicapped into the regular classroom: Effects of cooperative and individualistic instruction. *Contemporary Educational Psychology*, **6**, 344–353.

Johnson, D. W., Maruyama, R., Johnson, R., Nelson, D., & Skon, L. (1981). Effects of cooperative, competitive and individualistic goal structures on achievement: A meta-analysis. *Psychological Bulletin*, **89**, 47–62.

Johnson, M. W. (1935). The effect on behavior of variation in the amount of play equipment. *Child Development*, **6**, 56–68.

Johnston, C. (1992). The influence of behavioral parent training on inattentive-overactive and aggressive-defiant behaviors in ADHD children. Paper presented to the Society for Research in Child and Adolescent Psychopathology, Orlando, FL, February 1992.

Jones, V. (1971). *The influence of teacher–student introversion, achievement and similarity on teacher–student dyadic classroom interactions.* Unpublished doctoral dissertation, University of Texas, Austin.

Jöreskog, K. G., & Sorbom, D. (1986). *LISREL: Analysis of linear structural relationships by the method of maximum likelihood (version VI).* Mooresville, IN: Scientific Software, Inc.

Jouriles, E. N., Pfiffner, L. J., & O'Leary, S. G. (1988). Marital conflict, parenting, and toddler conduct problems. *Journal of Abnormal Child Psychiatry*, **16**, 197–206.

Kagan, D. M. (1990). How schools alienate students at risk: A model for examining proximal classroom variables. *Educational Psychologist*, **25**, 105–125.

Kagan, J. (1989). *Unstable ideas: Temperament, cognition and self.* Cambridge: Harvard University Press.

Kalfus, G. R. (1984). Peer mediated intervention: A critical review. *Child and Family Behavior Therapy*, **6**, 17–43.

Kalfus, G. R., & Stokes, T. F. (1987). Generalization as a function of a preschool peer-tutor's presence: Facilitation or distraction? *Educational Research Quarterly*, **11**, 26–36.

Kalish, R. A., & Knudtson, F. W. (1976). Attachment versus disengagement: A life-span conceptualization. *Human Development*, **19**, 171–181.

Kasen, S., Johnson, J., & Cohen, P. (1990). The impact of school emotional climate on student psychopathology. *Journal of Abnormal Child Psychology*, **18**, 165–177.

Kaufman, J., Ciccheti, D. (1989). Effects of maltreatment on school-age children's socioemotional development: Assessments in a day-camp setting. *Developmental Psychology*, **25**, 516–524.

Kenny, D. A. (1975). Cross-lagged panel correlation: A test for spuriousness. *Psychological Bulletin*, **82**, 887–903.

Kerr, M. K. (1991). *Background factors predicting teacher ratings of children's school performance*. Paper presented at the biennial meeting of the International Society for the Study of Behavioral Development, Minneapolis, MN, July 1991.

Kleinfeld, J. (1972). *Instructional style and the intellectual performance of Indian and Eskimo students*. Final report, project no. 1-J-027, Office of Education, U.S. Department of Health, Education and Welfare.

Klimes-Dougan, B., & Kistner, J. (1990). Physically abused preschoolers' responses to peers' distress. *Developmental Psychology*, **26**, 599–602.

Klindová, L. (1985). Longitudinálne sledovanie niektorych ukazovateľov sociálnej aktivity y predskolson veku [Longitudinal investigation of some indicators of social activity in preschoolers]. *Psychológia a Patopsychológia Dietata*, **20**, 483–496.

Kohn, M. L. (1983). On the transmission of values in the family: A preliminary formulation. In A. C. Kerckhoff (Ed.), *Research in sociology of education and socialization* (pp. 1–12). Greenwich, CT: JAI Press.

Kontos, S. (1991). *Relationship of caregiver qualifications, stress, and working conditions to children's cognitive and social development*. Paper presented at the biennial meeting of the Society for Research in Child Development, Seattle, WA, April 1991.

Krantz, M., Webb, S. D., & Andrews, D. (1984). The relationship between child and parental social competence. *The Journal of Psychology*, **118**, 51–56.

Krappman, L., Oswald, H., & von Salisch, M. (1991). *Parents' support to their child's peer activities and relationships in middle childhood*. Paper presented at the XIth biennial meeting of the International Society for the Study of Behavioral Development, Minneapolis, MN, July 1991.

Kunze, J., & Brandt, L. (1991). *How peer relations help children coping with divorce*. Paper presented at the XIth biennial meeting of the International Society for the Study of Behavioral Development, Minneapolis, MN, July 1991.

Kupersmidt, J. B. & Trejos, L. (1987). *Behavioral correlates of sociometric status among Costa Rican children*. Paper presented at the biennial meeting of the Society for Research in Child Development, Baltimore, MD, April 1987.

Ladd, G. W. (1989). Children's social competence and social supports: Precursors of early school adjustment? In B. H. Schneider, G. Attili, J. Nadel, & R. P. Weissberg (Eds.), *Social competence in developmental perspective* (pp. 277–291). Dordrecht: Kluwer Academic Press.

Ladd, G. W. (1991). Family–peer relations during childhood: Pathways to competence and pathology? *Journal of Social and Personal Relationships*, **8**, 307–314.

Ladd, G. W., & Golter, B. S. (1988). Parents' management of preschooler's peer relations: Is it related to children's socal competence? *Developmental Psychology*, **24**, 109–117.

Ladd, G. W., & Price, J. M. (1986). Promoting children's cognitive and social competence. *Child Development*, **57**, 446–460.

LaFrenière, P. J. & Sroufe, L. A. (1985). Profiles of peer competence in the preschool: Interrelations between measures, influence of social ecology, and relation to attachment history. *Developmental Psychology*, **21**, 56–69.

Lamb, M. E., & Nash, A. (1989). Infant–mother attachment, sociability and peer competence. In T. J. Berndt & G. W. Ladd (Eds.), *Peer relationships in child development* (pp. 219–246). New York: Wiley.

Lamb, M. E., Hwang, C. P., Bookstein, F. L., Broberg, A., Hult, G., & Frodi, M. (1988). Determinants of social competence in Swedish preschoolers. *Developmental Psychology*, **24**, 58–70.

Lambert, W. E., Hamers, J. F., & Frasure-Smith, N. (1979). *Child rearing values*. New York: Praeger.

Land, J., & DiLorenzo, T. M. (1990). *Parental factors related to kindergartener's peer relations*. Paper presented at the meeting of the Association for the Advancement of Behavior Therapy, San Francisco, CA, November 1990.

Langer, J. (1969). *Theories of development*. New York: Holt, Rinehart & Winston.

Larson, R. W. (1983). Adolescents' daily experience with family and friends: Contrasting opportunity systems. *Journal of Marriage and the Family*, Nov. 1983, pp. 739–750.

Lazarus, R. S., & Launier, R. (1978). Stress related transactions between person and environment. In L. Pervin & M. Lewis (Eds.), *Perspectives in interactional psychology* (pp. 287–327). New York: Plenum Press.

Ledingham, J. E., & Younger, A. J. (1985). The influence of the evaluator on assessments of children's social skill. In B. H. Schneider, K. H. Rubin, & J. E. Ledingham (Eds.). *Children's peer relations: Issues in assessment and intervention*. New York: Springer-Verlag.

Lee, C. M. & Gotlib, I. H. (1989a). Clinical status and emotional adjustment of children of depressed mothers. *American Journal of Psychiatry*, **146**, 478–483.

Lee, C. M. & Gotlib, I. H. (1989b). Maternal depression and child adjustment: A longitudinal analysis. *Journal of Abnormal Psychology*, **98**, 78–85.

Legendre, A. (1987). Transformation de l'espace d'activités et échanges sociaux de jeunes enfants en crèche. *Psychologie Française*, **32**, 31–43.

Legendre, A. (1989). Young children's social competence and their use of space in day-care centers. In B. H. Schneider, G. Attili, J. Nadel, & R. P. Weissberg (Eds.), *Social competence in developmental perspective* (pp. 263–276). Dordrecht: Kluwer Academic Publishers.

Levy, R. I. (1978). Tahitian gentleness and redundant controls. In A. Montagu (Eds.), *Learning non-aggression* (pp. 222–235). New York: Oxford University Press.

Levy-Shiff, R., & Hoffman, M. A. (1985). Social behavior or urban and kibbutz preschool children in Israel. *Developmental Psychology*, **21**, 1204–1205.

Lewin, K. (1954). Behavior and development as a function of the total situation. In L. Carmichael (Ed.), *Manual of child psychology* (pp. 918–970). New York: Wiley.

Lewin, K., Lippitt, R., & White, R. (1939). Patterns of aggressive behavior in experimentally created social climates. *Journal of Social Psychology*, **10**, 271–299.

Lewis, M. (Ed.). (1984). *Beyond the dyad*. New York: Plenum Press.

Lewis, M. (1989). Commentary. *Human Development*, **32**, 216–222.

Lewis, M., & Feiring, C. (1989). Early predictors of children's friendships. In T. Berndt & G. Ladd (Eds.), *Peer relationships in child development* (pp. 246–274). Hillsdale, NJ: Erlbaum.

Libet, J. M., & Lewinsohn, P. M. (1973). Concept of social skill with special reference to the behaviour of depressed persons. *Journal of Consulting and Clinical Psychology*, **40**, 304–312.

Lieberman, A. F., Weston, D. R., & Pawl, J. H. (1991). Attachment to mother/attachment to father: A meta-analysis. *Child Development*, **62**, 199–209.

Light, P., & Pillemer, D. (1984). *Summung up: The science of reviewing research*. Cambridge, MA: Harvard University.

Lipsitz, J. (1984). *Successful schools for young adolescents*. New Brunswick, NJ: Transaction Books.

Liska, A. E. (1975). *The consistency controversy: Readings on the impact of attitude on behavior*. New York: Wiley.

Loehlin, J. C., Willerman, L., & Horn, J. M. (1987). Personality resemblance in adoptive families: A 10 year follow-up. *Journal of Personality and Social Psychology*, **53**, 961–969.

Lollis, S., & Ross, H. (1992). Children as creators of the context for their own socialization. Paper presented at the convention of the Canadian Psychological Association, Québec, QC, June 1992.

Loranger, M. (1984). *Social skills in the secondary school*. Paper presented at the Conference on Research Strategies in Children's Social Skills Training, Ottawa, Ontario, June 1984.

Loranger, M., Tremblay, L., & Parent, A. (1986). Rendement scolarie et tutorat en mathématiques au secondaire III. *Canadian Psychology*, **27**, 75–82.

Lytton, H. (1980). *Parent–child interaction*. New York: Plenum Press.

Lytton, H., & Romney, D. M. (1991). Parents' differential socialization of boys and girls: A meta-analysis. *Psychological Bulletin*, **109**, 267–296.

Lytton, H., Watts, D., & Dun, B. E. (1988). Continuity and change in child characteristics and maternal practices between ages 2 and 9: An analysis of interview responses. *Child Study Journal*, **18**, 1–15.

Maccoby, E., & Martin, J. A. (1983). Socialization in the context of the family: Parent–child interaction. In P. H. Mussen (Ed.), *Handbook of child psychology* (pp. 1–101). New York: Wiley.

MacDonald, K. (1987). Parent–child physical play with rejected, neglected and popular boys. *Developmental Psychology*, **23**, 705–711.

MacDonald, K., & Parke, R. D., (1984). Bridging the gap: Parent–child play interaction and peer interactive competence. *Child Development*, **55**, 1265–1277.

MacKinnon, C. E., Curtner, M. E., & Baradaran, L. P. (1991). *The relation between social cognition and aggressive behavior: A cross-contextual analysis.* Paper presented at the biennial meeting of the Society for Research in Child Development, Seattle, WA, April 1991.

Madsen, M. C. (1971). Developmental and cross-cultural differences in the cooperative and competitive behavior of young children. *Journal of Cross-Cultural Psychology*, **2**, 365–371.

Madsen, M. C., & Shapira, A. (1970). Cooperative behavior of urban Afro-American, Anglo-American and Mexican village children. *Developmental Psychology*, **3**, 16–20.

Manetti, M., & Campart, M. (1987). Spazio e interazione in gruppo pre-scolare: Struttura della communicazione [Space and interaction in the preschool group: Communication structure]. In L. Camaioni (Ed.), *Origine e sviluppo della competenza sociale infantile* (pp. 155–180). Milan: Angeli.

Manetti, M., & Campart, M. (1989). The structure of communication: space and interaction in a pre-school group. In B. H. Scheider, G. Attili, J. Nadel, & R. Weissberg (Eds). *Social Competence in Developmental Perspective* (pp. 405–406). Dordrecht, Netherlands: Kluwer.

Margalit, M., & Weisel, A. (1990). Computer-assisted social skills learning for adolescents with mild retardation and social difficulties. *Educational Psychology*, **10**, 343–354.

Mash, E. J., & Terdal, L. G. (1988). Behavioral assessment of child and family disturbance. In E. J. Mash & L. G. Terdal (Eds.), *Behavioral assessment of childhood disorders* (pp. 3–65). New York: Guilford.

Matarazzo, J. D. (1983). Computerized psychological testing. *Science*, **221**, 323.

McClelland, D. C., Atkinson, J. W., Clarke, R. A., & Lowell, E. L. (1958). A scoring manual for the achievement motive. In J. W. Atkinson (Ed.), *Motives in fantasy action and society*. Princeton, NJ: Van Nostrand.

McCombs, A., Forehand, R., & Brody, G. H. (1987). Early adolescent functioning following divorce: The relationship to parenting and non-parenting ex-spousal interactions. *Child Study Journal*, **17**, 301–310.

McCord, J. (1990). Long-term perspectives on parental absence. In L. N. Robins & M. Rutter (Eds.), *Straight and devious pathways from childhood to adulthood* (pp. 116–134). Cambridge: Cambridge University Press.

McDill, E. L., & Rigsby, L. C. (1973). *Structure and process in secondary schools: The academic impact of educational climates*. Baltimore, MD: Johns Hopkins University Press.

McFall, R. M. (1982). A review and reformulation of the concept of social skills. *Behavioral Assessment*, **4**, 1–35.

McGuire, W., McGuire, C., Child, P., & Fujioka, P. (1978). Salience of ethnicity in the spontaneous self-concept as a function of one's ethnic distinctiveness in the social environment. *Journal of Personality and Social Psychology*, **36**, 511–520.

McMichael, P. (1980). Reading difficulties, behavior, and social status. *Journal of Educational Psychology*, **72**, 76–86.

McNally, S., Eisenberg, N., & Harris, J. D. (1991). Preventive intervention and outcome with anxiously attached dyads. *Child Development*, **62**, 190–198.

Medinnus, G. (1962). An examination of several correlates of sociometric status in a first-grade group. *Journal of Genetic Psychology*, **101**, 3–13.

Mehan, H. (1980). The competent student. *Anthropol. Educ. Q.*, **11**, 131–152.

Meichenbaum, D., Butler, L., & Gruson, L. (1981). Toward a conceptual model of social competence. In J. Wine & H. Smye (Eds.), *Social competence* (pp. 36–60). New York: Guilford Press.

Michelson, L., & Mannarino, A. T. (1986). Social skills training with children: Research and clinical application. In P. S. Strain, J. M. Guralnick, & H. Walker (Eds.), *Children's social behavior: Development, assessment and modification.* New York: Academic Press.

Miller, A. G., & Thomas, R. (1972). Cooperation and competition among Blackfoot Indian and Urban Canadian children. *Child Development, 43,* 1104–1110.

Miller, J. (1984). Culture and the development of everyday social explanation. *Journal of Personality and Social Psychology, 46,* 961–978.

Miller, J. G. (1986). Early cross-cultural commonalities on social explanation. *Developmental Psychology, 22,* 514–520.

Miller, N., & Maruyama, G. (1976). Ordinal position and peer popularity. *Journal of Personality and Social Psychology, 33,* 123–131.

Mills, R. S. L., & Rubin, K. H. (1990). Parental beliefs about problematic social behaviors in early childhood. *Child Development, 61,* 138–151.

Montagu, A. (Ed.). (1978). *Learning non-aggression.* New York: Oxford University Press.

Moore, H. A., & Porter, N. K. (1988). Leadership and nonverbal behaviors of Hispanic females across school equity environments. *Psychology of Women Quarterly, 12,* 147–163.

Moos, R. (1979). *Evaluating educational environments: Methods, procedures, findings, and policy implications.* San Francisco: Jossey Bass.

Moreno, J. L. (1978). *Who shall survive?* New York: Beacon House.

Moreno, M. C. (1990). *Parents' ideas, organization and richness of stimulation in children's daily life.* Paper presented at the IVth European Conference on Developmental Psychology, Stirling, Scotland, August 1990.

Moreno, M. C., & Palacios, J. (1991). *Continuity and change in parents' ideas about child development and education: A longitudinal study.* Paper presented at the XIth biennial meeting of the International Society for the Study of Behavioral Development, Minneapolis, MN, July 1991.

Morrison, H. L. (Ed.) (1983). *Children of depressed parents: Risk, identification, and intervention.* New York: Grune & Stratton.

Nadel, J., & Fontaine, A.-M. (1989). Communicating by imitation: A developmental and comparative approach to transitory social competence. In B. H. Schneider, G. Attili, J. Nadel, & R. P. Weissberg (Eds.), *Social competence in developmental perspective* (pp. 131–144). Dordrecht: Kluwer.

Neill, R. S. St. J. (1982). Experimental alterations in playroom layout and their effect on staff and child behavior. *Educational Psychology, 2,* 103–119.

Noack, P. (1991). *Adolescents' friendship relations and friends' attitudes as a function of family relations and parental attitudes.* Poster presented at the biennial meeting of the Society for Research in Child Development, Seattle, WA.

Northway, M. L. (1952). *A primer of sociometry.* Toronto: University of Toronto Press.

Ogbu, J. U. (1981). Origins of human competence: A cultural-ecological perspective. *Child Development, 52,* 413–429.

Oh, S. Y., Bronstein, P., D'Ari, A., Peniadz, J., Abrams, C., Hunt, O., Duncan, P., & Frankowski, B. (1989). *Parental overprotection: Effects on self-concept and social and school functioning.* Paper presented to the American Psychological Association, Los Angeles, CA, August 1989.

Ollendick, T. H., Oswald, D. P., & Francis, G. (1989). Validity of teacher nominations in identifying aggressive, withdrawn, and popular children. *Journal of Clinical Child Psychology, 18,* 221–229.

Olweus, D. (1980). Familial and temperamental determinants of aggressive behavior in adolescent boys: A causal analysis. *Developmental Psychology, 6,* 644–660.

Olweus, D. (1991). Bully/victim problems among schoolchildren: Basic facts and effects of a school based intervention program. In K. Rubin & D. Pepler (Eds.), *The development and treatment of childhood aggression* (pp. 411–448). Hillsdale, NJ: Erlbaum.

Olweus, D. (in press). Victimization by peers: Antecedents and long-term outcomes. In K. H. Rubin and J. B. Asendorpf (Eds.), *Social withdrawal, inhibition, and shyness in childhood.* New York: Lawrence Erlbaum Associates.

Oppenheim, D., Sagi, A., & Lamb, M. E. (1988). Infant–adult attachments on the kibbutz and their relation to socioemotional development four years later. *Developmental Psychology*, **24**, 427–433.

Oppenheimer, L. (1989). The nature of social action: Social competence versus social conformism. In B. H. Schneider, G. Attili, J. Nadel, & R. P. Weissberg (Eds.), *Social competence in developmental perspective* (pp. 41–49). Dordrecht: Kluwer Academic Publishers.

O'Reilly, J. P., Tokuno, K. A., & Ebata, A. T. (1986). Cultural differences between Americans of Japanese and European ancestry in parental valuing of social competence. *Journal of Comparative Family Studies*, **17**, 87–97.

Paddock, J. (1975). Studies on antiviolent and normal communities. *Aggressive Behavior*, **1**, 217–233.

Palacios, J. (1991). *Parents' ideas about their children and parent–child interaction*. Paper presented at the biennial meeting of the International Society for the Study of Behavioral Development, Minneapolis, MN, July 1991.

Palkovitz, R. (1987). Consistency and stability in the family microsystem environment. *Advances in Applied Developmental Psychology*, **2**, 41–67.

Parke, R. D., MacDonald, K. B., Beitel, A., & Bhavnagri, N. (1988). The role of the family in the development of peer relationships. In R. D. Peters & R. J. McMahon (Eds.), *Social learning and systems approaches to marriage and the family* (pp. 17–44). New York: Brunner/Mazel.

Parker, J. G., & Asher, S. R. (1987). Peer relations and later personal adjustment: Are low-accepted children at risk? *Psychological Bulletin*, **102**, 357–389.

Parkhurst, J. T., & Asher, S. R. (1987). *The social concerns of aggressive-rejected children*. Symposium conducted at the biennial meeting of the Society for Research in Child Development, Baltimore, MD, April 1987.

Parks, M. R. (1985). Interpersonal communication and the quest for personal competence. In M. L. Knapp & G. R. Miller (Eds.), *Handbook of interpersonal communication* (pp. 171–201). Beverly Hills, CA: Sage.

Parsons, T. (1951). *The social system*. Glencoe, IL: Free Press.

Parsons, T., & Bales, R. F. (1955). Family, socialization and interaction process. Glencoe, IL: Free Press.

Pastor, D. L. (1980). *The quality of mother–infant attachment and its relationship with toddlers' initial sociability with peers*. Paper presented at the International Conference on Infant Studies, New Haven, CT, April 1980.

Patterson, C. J., Vaden, N. A., & Kupersmidt, J. B. (1991). Family background, recent life events and peer rejection during childhood. *Journal of Social and Personal Relationships*, **8**, 347–362.

Patterson, G. R. (1982). *Coercive family process*. Eugene, OR: Castalia.

Patterson, G. R. (1983). Stress: A change agent for family process. In N. Garmezy & M. Rutter (Eds.), *Stress, coping, and development in children* (pp. 235–264). New York: McGraw-Hill.

Patterson, G. R. (1985). A microsocial analysis of anger and irritable behavior. In M. A. Chesney & R. H. Rosenman (Eds.), *Anger and hostility in behavioral and cardiovascular disorders* (pp. 83–100). Washington, D.C.: Hemisphere.

Patterson, G. R. (1986). Performance models for antisocial boys. *American Psychologist*, **41**, 432–444.

Patterson, G. R. (1986). The contribution of siblings to training for fighting: A microsocial analysis. In D. Olweus, J. Block, & M. Radke-Yarrow (Eds.), *Development of antisocial and prosocial behavior: Research theories and issues* (pp. 235–261). New York: Academic Press.

Pederson, N. L., Plomin, R., McClearn, G. E., & Friberg, L. (1988). Neuroticism, extra-version and related traits in adult twins reared apart and reared together. *Journal of Personality and Social Psychology*, **55**, 950–957.

Pellegrini, A. D., & Perlmutter, J. C. (1989). Classroom contextual effects on children's play. *Developmental Psychology*, **25**, 289–296.

Pellegrini, D., & Urbain, E. S. (1985). An evaluation of interpersonal cognitive problem-solving training efforts with children. *Journal of Child Psychology and Psychiatry*, **26**, 17–41.

Peres, Y., & Pasternack, R. (1991). To what extent can the school reduce the gaps between children raised by divorced and intact families? *Journal of Divorce and Remarriage*, **15**, 143–158.

Peters, D. L., & Kontos, S. (Eds.). (1987). *Continuity and discontinuity of experience in child care: Advances in applied development psychology* (vol. 2). Norwood, NJ: Ablex.

Petschaver, P. (1989). The childrearing modes in flux: An historian's reflections. *The Journal of Psychohistory*, **17**, 1–41.

Pettit, G. S., & Bates, J. E. (1989). Family interaction patterns and children's behavior problems from infancy to 4 year. *Developmental Psychology*, **25**, 413–420.

Pettit, G. S., & Sinclair, J. J. (1991). *Synchronous and asynchronous family interaction patterns in early childhood: Contexts for the social transmission of interpersonal style.* Paper presented at the biennial meeting of the International Society for the Study of Behavioral Development, Minneapolis, MN, July 1991.

Pettit, G. S., Dodge, K. A., & Brown, M. M. (1988). Early family experience, social problem solving patterns, and children's social competence. *Child Development*, **59**, 107–120.

Pettit, G. S., Harrist, A. W., Bates, J. E., & Dodge, K. A. (1991). Family interaction, social cognition and children's subsequent relations with peers at kindergarten. *Journal of Social and Personal Relationships*, **8**, 383–402.

Phelps, R. E., & Huntley, D. K. (1985). *Social networks and child adjustment in single-parent families.* Paper presented at the annual convention of the American Psychological Association, Los Angeles, CA, August 1985.

Philips, S. V. (1972). Participant structures and communicative competence: Warm Springs children in community and classroom. In C. B. Cazden, V. P. John, & D. Hymes (Eds.), *Functions of language in the classroom* (pp. 370–394). New York: Teachers College Press.

Phillips, E. L. (1978). The social skills basis of psychopathology. New York: Grune & Stratton.

Pierrehumbert, B., Iannotti, R. J., Cummings, E. M., & Zahn-Waxler, C. (1986). *Social functioning with mother and peer at 2 and 5 years of age: The influence of attachment.* Unpublished manuscript. Laboratory of Developmental Psychology, National Institute of Mental Health, Bethesda, MD.

Pigott, H. E., Fantuzzo, J. W., & Clement, P. W. (1986). The effect of reciprocal tutoring and group contingencies on the academic performance and peer rankings of elementary school students in three regular classrooms. *Journal of Applied Behavior Analysis*, **19**, 93–98.

Pisterman, S., McGrath, P., Firestone, P., Goodman, J. T., Webster, I. & Mallory, R. (1989). Outcome of parent-mediated treatment of preschoolers with attention deficit disorders with hyperactivity. *Journal of Consulting and Clinical Psychology*, **57**, 628–635.

Plattner, S., & Minturn, L. (1975). A comparative longitudinal study of the behavior of communally raised children. *Ethos*, **3**, 469–480.

Plomin, R. (1990). *Nature and nurture: An introduction to human behavioral genetics.* Pacific Grove, CA: Brooks/Cole.

Plomin, R., & Daniels, D. (1987). Children in the same family are very different, but why? *Behavioral and Brain Sciences*, **10**, 44–59.

Portuges, S. H., & Feshbach, N. D. (1972). The influence of sex and socioethnic factors upon imitation of teachers by elementary school children. *Child Development*, **43**, 981–989.

Posada, G. (1990). *Predictive relationships between marital discord and child behavior problems: Contributions of attachment and temperament.* Paper presented at the International Conference on Personal Relationships, Oxford University, England.

Priel, B., Assor, A., & Orr, E. (1990). Self-evaluations of kindergarten children: Inaccurate and undifferentiated? *Journal of Genetic Psychology*, **151**, 377–394.

Prohansky, H. M., (1974). Theoretical issues in environmental psychology. In T. G. David & B. D. Wright (Eds.), *Learning environments* (pp. 91–94). Chicago: University of Chicago Press.

Putallaz, M. (1987). Maternal behavior and children's sociometric status. *Child Development*, **58**, 324–340.

Putallaz, M. (1991). *Models of family and peer influence: Conflict management and the growth of social competence*. Paper presented at the biennial meeting of the International Society for the Study of Behavioral Development, Minneapolis, MN, July 1991.

Putallaz, M., & Gottman, J. M. (1981). Social skills and group acceptance. In S. R. Asher & J. M. Gottman (Eds.), *The development of children's friendships* (pp. 116–149). Cambridge, U.K.: Cambridge University Press.

Putallaz, M., & Heflin, H. (1986). Towards a model of peer acceptance. In J. M. Gottman and J. G. Parker (Eds.), *Conversation of friends* (pp. 315–345). Cambridge, U.K.: Cambridge University Press.

Putallaz, M. & Heflin, A. H. (1990). Parent-child interaction. In S. R. Asher & J. D. Coie (Eds.), *Peer rejection in childhood* (pp. 189–216). New York: Cambridge University Press.

Putallaz, M., Costanzo, P. R., & Smith, R. B. (1991). Maternal recollections of childhood peer relationships: Implications for their children's social competence. *Journal of Social and Personal Relationships*, **8**, 403–422.

Quadrio, A., Saita, A. G., & Iezzi, V. M. (1991). *Pregiudzi e atteggiamenti educativi: Il Caso con figili con genitori divorziati*. Paper presented at the XXIInd Congresso Degli Psicologi Italiani, Republic of San Marino, May 1991.

Radin, N., & Russell, G. (1983). Increased father participation and child development outcomes. In M. E. Lamb and A. Sagi (Eds.), *Fatherhood and family policy* (pp. 191–218).

Radke-Yarrow, M. (1989). Developmental and contextual analysis of continuity. *Human Development*, **32**, 204–209.

Radke-Yarrow, M., Cummings, E. M., Kuczynski, L., & Chapman, M. (1985). Patterns of attachment in two- and three-year-olds in normal families and families with parental depression. *Child Development*, **56**, 884–893.

Rapoport, R., Rapoport, R. N., Strelitz, Z., & Kew, S. (1977). *Fathers, mothers and others*. London: Routledge & Kegan Paul.

Reinhold, D. P., & Lochman, J. E. (1991). *Atttibutional and affect labeling biases in mothers and aggressive sons*. Paper presented at the biennial meeting of the Society for Research in Child Development, Seattle, WA, April 1991.

Renshaw, P. D. (1981). The roots of peer interaction research: A historical analysis of the 1930's. In S. R. Asher & J. M. Gottman (Eds.), *The development of children's friendships* (pp. 1–25). Cambridge: Cambridge University Press.

Riegel, K. T. (1976). The dialectics of human development. *American Psychologist*, **31**, 689–700.

Roberts, G. C., Block, J. H., & Block, J. (1984). Continuity and change in parents' child-rearing practices. *Child Development*, **55**, 586–597.

Rogoff, B. (1981). Adults and peers as agents of socialization: A Highland Guatemalan profile. *Ethos*, **9**, 18–36.

Rogoff, B. M., Sellers, M. J., Pirrotta, S., Fox, N., & White, S. H. (1975). Age of assignment of roles and responsibilities to children: A cross-cultural survey. *Human Development*, **18**, 353–369.

Rogosa, D. (1988). *Casual models do not support scientific conclusions*. Paper presented at the annual meeting of the American Educational Research Association, New Orleans, LA, April 1988.

Roseby, V., & Deutsch, R. (1985). Children of separation and divorce: Effects of a social role-taking group intervention on fourth and fifth graders. Special issue: Childhood vulnerabilty: Families and life stress: I. *Journal of Clinical Child Psychology*, **14**, 55–60.

Roth, D. (1991). *Linking the family and the world of peers: Parenting style and sociocognitive competence in adolescence*. Paper presented at the biennial meeting of the Society for Research in Child Development, Seattle, WA, April 1991.

Rothbaum, F. (1988). Maternal acceptance and child functioning. *Merrill-Palmer Quarterly*, **34**, 163–184.

Rotter, J. B. (1966). Generalized expectancies for internal versus external control of reinforcement. *Psychological Monographs*, **80**, 1–28.

Rowe, D. C. (1989). Families and peers: Another look at the nature-nurture question. In T. J. Berndt, & G. W. Ladd (Eds.), *Peer relationships in child development* (pp. 274–299). New York: Wiley.

Rubenstein, J. L. (1985). The effect of maternal employment on young children. In F. J. Morrison, C. Lord, & D. P. Keating (Eds.), *Applied developmental psychology* (pp. 99–128). Orlando, FL: Academic Press.

Rubin, K. H., Fein, C. G., & Vandenberg, B. (1983). Play. In E. M. Hetherington (Ed.), *Handbook of Child Psychology*, Vol. IV (pp. 693–774). New York: Wiley.

Rubin, K. H., & Mills, R. (1988). The many faces of isolation. *Journal of Consulting and Clinical Psychology*, **6**, 916–924.

Rubin, K. H., & Mills, R. S. L. (1990). Maternal beliefs about adaptive and maladaptive social behaviors in normal, aggressive, and withdrawn preschoolers. *Journal of Abnormal Child Psychology*, **18**, 419–435.

Rubin, K. H., LaMare, L. J., & Lollis, S. (1990). Social withdrawal in childhood: Developmental pathways to peer rejection. In S. R. Asher & J. D. Coie (Eds.), *Peer rejection in childhood* (pp. 217–249). New York: Cambridge University Press.

Rubin, K. H., Mills, R. S. L., & Rose-Krasnor, L. (1989). Maternal beliefs and children's competence. In B. H. Schneider, G. Attili, J. Nadel, & R. P. Weissberg (Eds.), *Social competence in developmental perspective* (pp. 313–331). Dordrecht: Kluwer.

Rubin, K. H., Booth, L., Zahn-Waxler, C., Cummings, M., & Wilkinson, M. (in press). The dyadic play behaviors of children of well and depressed mothers. *Development and Psychopathology*.

Rubin, L. (1971). *A study on teaching style*. Paper presented at the annual meeting of the American Educational Research Association.

Rubin, Z. & Sloman, J. (1984). How parents influence their children's friendships. In M. Lewis (Ed.), *Beyond the dyad* (pp. 223–250). New York: Plenum Press.

Russell, A. & Finnie, V. (1990). Preschool children's social status and maternal instructions to assist group entry. *Developmental Psychology*, **26**, 603–611.

Rutter, M. (1979). Protective factors in children's responses to stress and disadvantage. In M. W. Kent & J. F. Rolf (Eds.), *Primary prevention of Psychopathology: vol. III. Social competence in children* (pp. 49–74). Hanover, NH: University Press of New England.

Rutter, M. (1985). Family and school influences on behavioural development. *Journal of Child Psychology and Psychiatry*, **26**, 349–368.

Rutter, M., Maughan, B., Mortimore, P., Ouston, J., & Smith, A. (1979). *Fifteen thousand hours*. Cambridge: Harvard University Press.

Saal, C. D. (1982). A historical and present-day view of the position of the child in family and society. *Journal of Comparative Family Studies*, **13**, 119–132.

Sagi, A., & Sharon, N. (1983). Costs and benefits of increased paternal involvement in childrearing: The societal perspective. In M. E. Lamb & A. Sagi (Eds.), *Fatherhood and family policy* (pp. 219–233). Hillsdale, NJ: Erlbaum.

Salzinger, S., Feldman, R. S., Hammer, M., & Rosario, M. (1991). *The effects of physical abuse on children's social relationships*. Paper presented at the biennial meeting of the Society for Research in Child Development, Seattle, WA, April 1991.

Santrock, J. W., & Warshak, R. A. (1979). Father custody and social development in boys and girls. *Journal of Social Issues*, **35**, 112–135.

Sarason, S. B. (1974). *The psychological sense of community*. San Francisco: Jossey-Bass.

Scarr, S. (1987). Distinctive environments depend on genotypes. *Behavioral and Brain Sciences*, **10**, 38–39.

Scarr, S., Webber, P. L., Weinberg, R. A., & Wittig, M. A. (1981). Personality resemblance among adolescents and their parents in biologically related and adoptive families. *Journal of Personality and Social Psychology*, **40**, 885–898.

Schaefer, E. S. (1965). A configural analysis of children's reports of parent behavior. *Journal of Consulting Psychology*, **29**, 552–557.

Schaffer, H. R., & Emerson, P. (1964). The development of social attachments in infancy. *Monographs of the Society for Research in Child Development*, **29**.

Schmuck, R. (1963). Some relationships of peer liking patterns in the classroom to pupil attitudes and achievements. *School Review*, **71**, 337–359.

Schneider, B. H. (1977). *An elaboration of the relationship between parental behaviour and children's moral development*. Unpublished manuscript.

Schneider, B. H. (1987). *The gifted child in peer group perspective*. New York: Springer-Verlag.

Schneider, B. H. (1989). Between developmental wisdom and children's social skills training. In B. H. Schneider, G. Attili, J. Nadel, & R. P. Weissberg (Eds.), *Social competence in developmental perspective* (pp. 339–353). Dordrecht: Kluwer Academic Press.

Schneider, B. H. (1991). Reviewing previous research by meta-analysis. In B. M. Montgomery & S. Duck (Eds.), *Studying interpersonal interaction* (pp. 303–320). New York: Guilford.

Schneider, B. H. (1992). Didactic methods for enhancing children's social competence: A quantitative review. *Clinical Psychology Review*, **12**, 363–382.

Schneider, B. H., & Byrne, B. M. (1985). Children's social skills training: A meta-analysis. In B. H. Schneider, K. H. Rubin, & J. E. Ledingham (Eds.), *Children's peer relations: Issues in assessment and intervention* (pp. 175–192). New York: Springer-Verlag.

Schneider, B. H., & Byrne, B. (1987). Individualizing social skills training for behavior-disordered children. *Journal of Consulting and Clinical Psychology*, **55**, 444–445.

Schneider, B. H., & Byrne, B. M. (1989). Parents rating children's social behavior: How focused the lens? *Journal of Clinical Child Psychology*, **18**, 237–241.

Schneider, B. H., & Murphy, K. (1990). *Making the transition from popularity based on social skills interventions to friendship-oriented training program*. Paper presented at the International Conference on Personal Relationships, Oxford, England, July 1990.

Schneider, B. H., Kerridge, A., & Katz, J. (in press). Teacher acceptance of psychological interventions of varying theoretical orientation. *School Psychology International*.

Sears, R. R. (1957). Identification as a form of behavior development. In D. B. Harris (Ed.), *The concept of development* (pp. 149–161). Minneapolis: University of Minnesota Press.

Segall, M. H. (1979). *Cross-cultural psychology: Human behavior in global perspective*. Monterey, CA: Brooks/Cole.

Segall, M. H. (1983). Aggression in global perspective: A research strategy. In A. P. Goldstein, & M. H. Segall (Eds.), *Aggression in global perspective* (pp. 1–43). New York: Pergamon Press.

Selman, R. L. (1980). *The growth of interpersonal understanding: Developmental and clinical analyses*. New York: Academic Press.

Serow, R., & Solomon, D. (1979). Classroom climates and students' intergroup behavior. *Journal of Educational Psychology*, **71**, 669–676.

Shapira, A., & Madsen, M. C. (1974). Between and within group cooperation and competition among kibbutz and non-kibbutz children. *Developmental Psychology*, **10**, 1–12.

Sharabany, R. (1982). Comradeship: Peer group relations among preadolescents in kibbutz versus city. *Personality and Social Psychology Bulletin*, **8**, 302–309.

Sherman, H., & Farina, A. (1974). Social adequacy of parents and children. *Journal of Abnormal Psychology*, **83**, 327–330.

Shweder, R. A. (1979). Rethinking culture and personality theory. Part I. *Ethos*, **7**, 255–278.

Siegler, R. S. (1991). *Children's thinking*. Englewood Cliffs, NJ: Prentice-Hall.

Silbereisen, R. K., & Eyferth, K. (1986). Development as action in context. In R. K. Silbereisen, K. Eyferth, & G. Rudinger (Eds.), *Development as action in context* (pp. 3–16). Berlin: Springer-Verlag.

Simmons, R. G. (1987). Social transition and adolescent development. In C. E. Irwin, Jr. (Ed.), *Adolescent social behavior and health*. San Francisco: Jossey-Bass.

Skinner, B. F. (1962). *Walden Two*. New York: Macmillan.

Slavin, R. E. (1987). *Cooperative learning*. Washington, DC: National Education Association.

Smetana, J. G. (1989). Commentary. *Human Development*, **32**, 210–215.

Smith, P. K. (1989). The role of rough and tumble play in the development of social competence: Theoretical perspectives and empirical evidence. In B. H. Schneider, G. Attili, J. Nadel, & R. P. Weissberg (Eds.), *Social competence in developmental perspective* (pp. 239–255). Dordrecht: Kluwer.

Smorti, A., & Tani, F. (1991). Il rapporto genitori-figli e l'interazione sociale tra bambini. In A. Fonzi (Ed.), *Cooperare e competere tra bambini* (pp. 93–103). Florence: Giunti.

Snyder, D. K., Klein, M. A., Gdowski, C. L., Faulstich, C., & La Combe, J. (1988). Generalized dysfunction in clinic and nonclinic families: A comparative analysis. *Journal of Abnormal Child Psychology*, **16**, 97–109.

Snyder, J., Dishion, T. J., & Patterson, G. R. (1986). Determinants and consequences of associating with deviant peers during preadolescence and adolescence. *Journal of Early Adolescence*, **6**, 29–43.

Sommer, D., & Langsted, O. (1990). *Peer interaction of Nordic children in day care.* Paper presented at the IVth European Conference on Developmental Psychology, Stirling, Scotland. August, 1990.

Spain, D. H. (1988). Taboo or not taboo: Is that the question? *Ethos*, **16**, 285–301.

Spiro, M. E. (1958). *Children of the kibbutz.* Cambridge, MA: Harvard University Press.

Spitzberg, B. H. & Cupach, W. R. (1989). *Handbook of interpersonal competence research.* New York: Springer-Verlag.

Spivack, G., & Shure, M. B. (1982). The cognition of social adjustment: Interpersonal cognitive problem-solving thinking. In B. B. Lahey & A. E. Kazdin (Eds.), *Advances in child clinical psychology* (pp. 323–372). New York: Plenum Press.

Sroufe, L. A. (1983). Infant–caregiver attachment and patterns of adaption in preschool: The roots of maladaption and competence. In M. Perlmutter (Ed.), *Minnesota Symposia on Child Psychology* (vol. 16, pp. 41–81). Hillsdale, NJ: Lawrence Erlbaum.

Sroufe, L. A. (1985). Attachment classification from the perspective of infant–caregiver relationships and infant temperament. *Child Development*, **56**, 1–14.

Sroufe, L. A., & Fleeson, J. (1986). Attachment and the construction of relationships. In W. Hartup & Z. Rubin (Eds.), *Relationships and development* (pp. 51–71). Hillsdale, NJ: Erlbaum.

Sroufe, L. A., & Jacobvitz, D. (1989). Diverging pathways, developmental transformations, multiple etiologies and the problem of continuity in development. *Human Development*, **32**, 196–203.

St. John, N. (1971). Thirty-six teachers: Their characteristics, and outcomes for black and white pupils. *American Educational Research Journal*, **8**, 635–648.

Steinberg, L. (1987). Single parents, step-parents and the susceptibility of adolescents to antisocial peer pressure. *Child Development*, **58**, 269–275.

Stephens, T. M. (1976). *Directive teaching of children with learning and behavioral handicaps.* Columbus, OH: Merrill.

Stephens, T. M. (1981). *Social behavior assessment: Technical information.* Unpublished manuscript.

Stewart, R. B., Jr. (1983). Sibling interaction: The role of the older child as teacher for the younger. *Merrill-Palmer Quarterly*, **29**, 47–68.

Strain, P. S. (1985). Programmatic research on peers as intervention agents for socially isolated classmates. In B. H. Schneider, K. H. Rubin, & J. E. Ledingham (Eds.), *Children's peer relations: Issues in assessment and intervention* (pp. 193–205). New York: Springer-Verlag.

Strassburg, Z., & Dodge, K. A. (1990). *Parental conflict strategies and children's social preference in kindergarten.* Paper presented at the annual meeting of the American Psychological Association, Boston, MA, May 1990.

Strayer, F. F. (1989). Co-adaptation within the early peer group: A psychobiological study of social competence. In B. H. Schneider, G. Attili, J. Nadel, & P. Weissberg (Eds.), *Social competence in developmental perspective* (pp. 145–174). Dordrecht: Kluwer Academic Press.

Stryker, S., & Serpe, R. T. (1983). Toward a theory of family influence in the socialization of children. In A. C. Kerckhoff (Ed.), *Research in sociology of education and socialization* (pp. 47–71). Greenwich, CT: JAI Press.

Sullivan, H. S. (1953). *The interpersonal theory of psychiatry.* New York: Norton.

Super, C. M., & Harkness, S. (1986). The developmental niche: A conceptualization at the interface of child and culture. Special issue: Cross-cultural human development. *International Journal of Behavioral Development*, **9**, 545–569.

Szalay, L. B., & Maday, B. C. (1983). Research reports: Implicit culture and psychocultural distance. *American Anthropologist*, **85**, 110–118.

Tagiuri, R. (1968). The concept of organizational climate. In R. Tagiuri & G. H. Litwin (Eds.), *Organizational climate: Exploration of a concept*. Boston: Harvard University, Division of Research, Graduate School of Business Administration.

Tajfel, H. (1978). Social categorization, social identity, and social comparison. In H. Tajfel (Ed.), *Differentiation between social groups* (pp. 61–76). London: Academic Press.

Tauber, M. A. (1979). Sex differences in parent–child interaction styles during a free-play session. *Child Development*, **50**, 981–988.

Taylor, V., Hurley, E. C., & Riley, M. T. (1986). The influence of acculturation upon the adjustment of preschool Mexican-American single-parent families. *Family Therapy*, **13**, 249–256.

The *Shorter Oxford English Dictionary*. (1973). Oxford: Clarendon Press.

Thelen, H. A. (1981). *The classroom society: The construction of educational experience*. London: Croom Helm.

Thomas, A., & Chess, S. (1977). *Temperament and development*. New York: Brunner/Mazel.

Thomas, W. B. (1984). Competition and cooperation as contradictory norms in urban schools: A sociological perspective. *Journal of Negro Education*, **53**, 147–160.

Thompson, L. (1950). *Culture in crisis*. New York: Russell & Russell.

Tietjen, A. (1986). Prosocial reasoning among children and adults in a Papua New Guinea society. *Developmental Psychology*, **22**, 861–868.

Tinsley, B. R., & Parke, R. D. (1984). Grandparents as support and socialization agents. In M. Lewis (Ed.), *Beyond the diad: vol. 4. Genesis of behavior* (pp. 182–185). New York: Plenum Press.

Tishelman, A., Engler, L., D'amico, P., Gyato, K., & Stein, L. (1990). *Differential predictions of social popularity by parents, teachers and peers using a rating scale or nomination approach*. Poster presented at the Association for the Advancement of Behavior Therapy, San Francisco, U.S.A., November 1990.

Toro, P. A., Cowen, E. L., Gesten, E. L., Weissberg, R. P., Rapkin, B. D., & Davidson, E. (1985). Social environmental predictors of children's adjustment in elementary school classrooms. *American Journal of Community Psychology*, **13**, 353–363.

Triandis, H. (1986). Collectivism vs. individualism: A reconceptualization of a basic concept in cross-cultural psychology. In C. Bagley, & G. Verma (Eds.), *Personality, cognition, and values: Cross-cultural perspectives of childhood and adolescence*. London: Macmillan.

Triandis, H., & Berry, J. (Eds.), (1980). *Handbook of cross-cultural psychology: vol. 2: Methodology*. Boston, MA: Allyn & Bacon.

Trower, P. (1982). Towards a generative model of social skills: A critique and synthesis. In J. P. Curran & P. M. Monti (Eds.), *Social skills training: A practical handbook for assessment and treatment*. New York: Guilford Press.

Trower, P., Bryant, B., & Argyle, M. (1978). *Social skills and mental health*. Pittsburg, PA: University of Pittsburg Press.

Tryon, A. S., & Keane, S. P. (1991). Popular and aggressive boys' initial social interaction patterns in cooperative and competitive settings. *Journal of Abnormal Child Psychology*, **19**, 395–406.

Tudge, J. (1981). Lack of control and the development of incompetence. *Cornell Journal of Social Relations*, **16**, 84–97.

Tulkin, S. R., & Cohler, B. J. (1973). Child rearing attitudes and mother–child interaction in the first year of life. *Merrill-Palmer Quarterly*, **19**, 95–106.

Turner, P. J. (1991). *Links between attachment, gender and peer relationships at age 4 years*. Paper presented at the biennial meeting of the International Society for the Study of Behavioral Development, Minneapolis, MN, July 1991.

Urbain, E. S., & Kendall, P. C. (1980). Review of social-cognitive problem-solving interventions with children. *Psychological Bulletin*, **8**, 109–143.

Van Aken, M. A. G., Riksen-Walraven, J. M., & Van Lieshout, C. F. M. (1991). *Parental sensitivity and children's peer competence*. Paper presented at the XIth biennial meeting of the International Society for the Study of Behavioral Development, Minneapolis, MN, July 1991.

Van Buren, T. (1990). *Family life and the emergence of adolescent social competence.* Unpublished manuscript.

Van Dam, M., & Van IJsendoorn, M. H. (1991). *Working mothers and their infants: Insecure attachment relationships.* Paper presented at the biennial meeting of the International Society for the Study of Behavioral Development, Minneapolis, MN, July 1991.

Van der Kooij, R., & Neukäter, H. (1989). Elterliches erzieherverhalten und spiel im internationalen vergleich. *Zeitschrift für Pädagogische Psychologie, 3,* 259–263.

Van IJsendoorn, M. H., Van der Veer, R. & Van Vliet-Visser, S. (1987). Attachment three years later: Relationships between quality of mother–infant attachment and emotional/cognitive development in kindergarten. In L. W. C. Tavecchio, & M. H. Van Ijsendoorn (Eds.), *Attachment in social networks* (pp. 185–224). Amsterdam: North Holland.

Vandell, D. L. (1985). *Relations between infant–peer and infant–mother interactions: What we have learned.* Paper presented at the biennial meeting of the Society for Research in Child Development, Toronto, April 1985.

Vandell, D. L., & Wilson, K. S. (1987). Infants' interactions with mother, sibling, and peer: Contrasts and relations between interaction systems. *Child Development, 58,* 176–186.

Vedder, P. (1985). *Cooperative learning: A study on process and effects of cooperation between primary school children.* Groningen: Rijksunwerscheit Groningen.

Vernberg, E. M. (1990). Experiences with peers following relocation during early adolescence. *Amer. J. Orthopsychiatry, 60,* 466–472.

Volling, B. L., Youngblade, L. M., & Belsky, J. (1991). *Children's social relationships: Interactive and subjective links between siblings, peers, and friends.* Paper presented at the biennial meeting of the International Society for the Study of Behavioral Development, Minneapolis, MN, July 1991.

Vygotsky, L. S. (1978). *Mind in society: The development of higher psychological processes.* Cambridge: Harvard University Press.

Walker, H. M., & Lamon, W. E. (1987). Social behavior standards and expectations of Australian and U.S. teacher groups. *The Journal of Special Education, 21,* 56–82.

Waters, F., & Sroufe, L. A. (1983). Social competence as a developmental construct. *Developmental Review, 3,* 79–97.

Weade, R., & Green, J. L. (1985). Talking to learn: Social and academic requirements for classroom participation. *Peabody Journal of Education, 62,* 6–19.

Weber, G. (1971). *Inner city children can be taught to read: Four successful schools* (Occasional paper 18). Washington: D.C.: Council for Basic Education, October 1971.

Webster-Stratton, C. (1990). Stress: A potential disruptor of parent perceptions and family interactions. *Journal of Clinical Child Psychology, 19,* 302–312.

Weinraub, M., & Ansul, S. (1985). *Children's responses to strangers: Effects of family status, stress, and mother–child interaction.* Paper presented at the meeting of the Society for Research in Child Development, Toronto, April 1985.

Weinstein, C. S. (1991). The classroom as a social context for learning. *Annual Review Psychology, 42,* 493–525.

Weinstein, C. S., & Pinciotti, P. (1988). Changing a schoolyard: Intentions, design decisions, and behavioral outcomes. *Environment and Behavior, 20,* 345–371.

Weisfeld, G. E., Weisfeld, C. C., & Callaghan, J. W. (1984). Peer and self-perceptions in Hopi and Afro-American third and sixth graders. *Ethos, 12,* 64–84.

Weissberg, R. P. (1985). Developing effective social problem-solving programs for the classroom. In B. Schneider, K. H. Rubin, & J. Ledingham (Eds.), *Peer relationships and social skills in childhood* (pp. 225–242). New York: Springer-Verlag.

Weissberg, R. P., & Allen, J. P. (1986). Promoting children's social skills and adaptive interpersonal behavior. In B. A. Edelstein & L. Michelson (Eds.), *Handbook of prevention* (pp. 153–175). New York: Plenum Press.

Weisz, J. R., Suwanlert, S., Chaiyasit, W., Weiss, B., Walter, B. R., & Anderson, W. W. (1988). Thai and American perspectives on over- and undercontrolled child behavior problems: Exploring the threshold model among parents, teachers, and psychologists. *Journal of Consulting and Clinical Psychology, 56,* 601–609.

Werner, E. E. (1979). *Cross-cultural child development: A view from the planet Earth* (pp. 307–326). Belmont, CA: Wadsworth.

Wertsch, J. V. (1985). *Vygotsky and the social formation of mind*. Cambridge, MA: Harvard University Press.

White, K. J., Smith, S. G., & Kuzma, B. (1991). *The influence of teacher feedback on children's peer preferences and perceptions: Replication and test of order effects*. Paper presented at the biennial meeting of the Society for Research in Child Development, Seattle, WA, 1991.

Whiting, B. B. (1977). Changing lifestyles in Kenya. *Daedalus*, **106**, 211–225.

Whiting, B. B. (1986). The effect of experience on peer relationships. In E. C. Mueller & C. R. Cooper (Eds.), *Process and outcome in peer relationships* (pp. 79–99). Orlando: Academic Press.

Whiting, B. B., & Edwards, C. P. (1988). *Children of different worlds: The formation of social behavior*. Cambridge, MA: Harvard University Press.

Whiting, B. B., & Whiting, J. W. M. (1975). *Children of six cultures: A psychocultural analysis*. Cambridge, MA.: Harvard University Press.

Wiener, J. (1987). Peer status of learning disabled children and adolescents: A review of the literature. *Learning Disabilities Research*, **2**, 62–79.

Witt, J. C. (1986). Teachers resistance to the use of school-based interventions. *Journal of School Psychology*, **24**, 37–44.

Wright, S., & Cowen, E. L. (1982). Student perception of school environment and its relationship to mood, achievement, popularity, and adjustment. *American Journal of Community Psychology*, **10**, 687–703.

Wright, S., & Cowen, E. L. (1985). The effects of peer-teaching on student perceptions of class environment, adjustment, and academic performance. Special issue: Children's environments. *American Journal of Community Psychology*, **13**, 417–431.

Yando, R. M., Seitz, V., & Zigler, E. F. (1978). *Imitation: A developmental perspective*. Hillsdale, NJ: Erlbaum.

Young, H. B., & Ferguson, L. R. (1981). *Puberty to manhood in Italy and America*. New York: Academic Press.

Youniss, J. (1980). *Parents and peers in social development: A Sullivan-Piaget perspective*. Chicago: University of Chicago Press.

Zahn-Waxler, C., Radke-Yarrow, M., & King, R. A. (1979). Child rearing and children's prosocial initiations toward victims of distress. *Child Development*, **49**, 319–330.

Zigler, M. E. (1983). *The time parents and children spend together*. Paper presented at the American Psychological Association, Los Angeles, CA, August 1983.

Zigler, E., & Trickett, P. K. (1978). IQ, social competence, and evaluation of early childhood intervention programs. *American Psychologist*, **33**, 789–798.

Zigler, E. F., Lamb, M. E., & Child, I. L. (1982). *Socialization and personality development* (2nd ed.). New York: Oxford University Press.

Ziv, A. (1979). The teacher's sense of humour and the atmosphere in the classroom. *School Psychology International*, **1**, 21–23.

Author Index

Abramovich, R., Pepler, D. and Corter, C., on influence of siblings 7
Abramovitch, R., Corter, C., Pepler, D. and Stanhope, L., on peer relationships of twins 39
Abroms, K. I., on socially gifted children 78
Adalbjarnardottir, S., on social skills training 111
Adler, Alfred,
  on family composition and birth order 37, 38
  "individual psychology" 1–2
Ahern, F. M., Johnson, R. C., Wilson, J. R., McClearn, G. and Vandenberg, S., on environment 34
Ahola, J. A. and Isherwood, G. B., on communication in school 89
Aiello, J. R. and Jones, S. E., on non-verbal behaviours 154
Ainsworth, M., on attachment 42
Ainsworth, M., Bell, S. M. and Stayton, D. J., Strange Situation task 42–3
Albersheim, L. M. and Carter, T. N., on attachment 42
Allen, J. and West, L., on communes 143
Amato, P. R. and Ochiltree, G., on effect of marital conflict on adolescents 66
Amidon, E. and Flanders, N., on teacher warmth and enthusiasm 100
Anderson, B. E., on effects of daycare 86
Anderson, Brewer and Read (in Brophy, J. E. & Good, T. L.), on teachers' interpersonal styles 100
Anderson, C. S., "The search for school climate: A review of the research" 90, 91, 113
Anderson, S. and Messick, S., "bag of virtues" approach to social competence 13
Ansbacher, H. L. and Ansbacher, R. R., on Adlerr 1, 37
Argyle, M.,
  on common pastimes and friendship 20
  on learning social competence 120
  on non-verbal behaviours 153
  on social information processing 26
  on social rules 13, 123
Argyle, M. and Furnham, A., on common pastimes and friendship 20
Argyle, M., Furnham, A. and Graham, J. A., on interpreting social situations 122
Argyle, M., Henderson, M., Bond, M., Contarello, A. and Iizuka, Y., cultural difference 123
Armentrout, J. A., on parental control and aggression 58
Aronson, E., Blaney, N., Stephan, C., Sikes, J. and Snapp, M., on "jigsaw classroom" 105
Asher, S. R.,
  on coaching behaviour 112
  on sociometric rating scales 23, 24
Asher, S. R., Markell, R. S. and Hymel, S., on social competence 25
Asher, S. R., Oden, S. L. and Gottman, J. M., on academic achievement and peer acceptance 104
Asher, S. R., on peer relations 15, 23
Attili, G., on social skills and developmental levels 18, 20
Austin, A. M. B. and Lindauer, S. L. K., on parental structuring of play 50, 51

Bachtold, L. M., on attitudes to co-operation 132, 138–9
Bakeman, R. and Gottman, J. M., on social exchanges 25
Baltes, P. B., Reese, H. and Lipsett, L., on life-span development 8
Bandura, A., on reciprocal determinism in development 4
Bandura, A. and Walters, R. H., on reciprocal determinism in development 4
Bar-Tal, D., on attribution 116

187

Subject Index